A VOICE OUT OF NOWHERE

A VOICE OUT OF NOWHERE

Inside the mind of a mass murderer.

Janice Holly Booth

A Voice out of Nowhere

A non-fiction novel

© 2013 Janice Holly Booth

This book is based on a true story. No material facts of the criminal case have been altered. The names of the victims, the accused, court personnel and named doctors giving testimony have not been changed. All other characters, conversations, opinions and identifying features have been fictionalized. Any resemblance to persons living or dead is purely coincidental. Where a conversation is presented verbatim, that is noted.

Printed in the United States of America

ISBN-13: 978-1492235583
ISBN-10: 149223558X

Cover design and artwork by Joel Dinkel
Author photo by Image Gallery igstudio.biz

First Edition

10 9 8 7 6 5 4 3 2 1

Also by Janice Holly Booth

Only Pack What You Can Carry

i

ACKNOWLEDGMENTS

I WROTE THE most difficult parts of this book between November and March, a dreary time even in North Carolina. I am grateful to my friends for hauling me away from the laptop for a lunch, or a drink, or a walk in the park. Without their intervention, I never would have sought the light. They are too numerous to mention, but they know who they are. And I can't imagine having endured this journey without the loving support of TJ Solomon II, BBE.

My sincere thanks to Dr. Eugene Maloney and his wife Judy for their insights into this project and for the friendship which grew out of our time together.

I cannot thank enough my early readers whose honest feedback and unique perspectives have made this a far better book for you: Arcangela Mazzariello; the Honorable Timothy S. Hillman; Mary Layton; Laurel Hicks; Jean-Marie Torrence, TJ and the Maloneys. Thank you to Carole Bugge and my Gotham Writers classmates for their excellent critiques when this book was in draft form.

Thank you also to Joel Dinkel for his powerful and scarily intuitive cover design; to US Navy AD1 Michael Daley for sharing his stories; and to Andrea Gordon at the Canadian Press for her outstanding efforts in helping me locate and acquire archival photographs. She is the epitome of exceptional customer service.

And finally, my gratitude to the Blumenthal family and Kathryn and Mike House for the time and space at Wildacres Retreat in Little Switzerland, NC to complete this dark project surrounded by peace, beauty and light.

GENESIS

ON A DRIZZLY, frigid night in December, 1980, an emaciated young woman clung to the upper railings of the Lion's Gate Bridge[1], threatening to jump into the black, shiny water flowing like molasses below. In the crowd that gathered underneath her, one voice — from a psychiatrist who'd happened to be driving by — was able to talk her down. As she made her breathless way to the pavement, nearly falling twice, she called out, *"Don't lie to me!"*

Safely at the bottom, she placed her hand inside the psychiatrist's, grateful for the warmth. At the same time, an RCMP[2] officer slapped handcuffs around her wrists. He sent her for observation to a mental hospital known as Riverview.

A week later I was working at my job as a court recorder when this woman was brought into the courtroom. I hadn't seen her in years, but recognized her right away as someone who'd been in one of my undergraduate writing classes. She didn't recognize me, though. According to the court testimony, her suicide attempt came on the heels of social services abducting her son, and she was despondent. She was also — according to the social worker giving evidence — a paranoid schizophrenic with delusions of grandeur. "Ms. Mitchell believes she is a writer," said the social worker, "and says that she has written a novel. This is just one example of her delusional world, Your Honour."

But she *was* a writer, and a good one, too. Later, I spoke to the judge and told him I could vouch for that. I remembered her writing —

---

[1] An iconic bridge in Vancouver, British Columbia, Canada, linking Stanley Park with the North Shore
[2] Royal Canadian Mounted Police

how she was somehow able to imbue dark subjects with a humour that was both delightful and sobering. "I'm afraid that's not really the issue now," the judge told me, "but I'll keep your words in mind." Over the course of the next few months I followed her tortuous path and watched with dismay as my former friend was literally railroaded into failure. She committed suicide in Riverview while under suicide watch. In my outrage, I blamed "the system" for her death, and really have never gotten over it. To channel my anger into something positive, I began to study psychology with a particular focus on schizophrenia. I thought that was the least I could do for her.

One year later, another of my fellow writing students — a paranoid schizophrenic taking anti-psychotic medication and trying to make a life for himself — was murdered by his roommate at the half-way house where they lived. His roommate, also a paranoid schizophrenic but with a violent past, had stopped taking his medication when he believed he was no longer ill. They'd both been incarcerated and released from Riverview mental hospital at the same time. Neither had family or other support, so they decided to room together. My friend's death barely even made the newspaper. The system had failed yet again. It incited me to another level of outrage.

And then, in January of 1983, a case came before the court that was — at the time — one of Canada's worst mass murders, committed by a young man only a year younger than I. The central question in the trial was whether or not he was insane at the time of the murders. For a writer with a fascination for abnormal psychology and a hefty block on her shoulder against the system, this case was the Holy Grail. Yet, despite the sensationalism of the case, there was something eerily familiar about it, as if this particular tragedy could be visited upon anyone, any family, anytime, anywhere, even to people who had never had a violent thought in their lives.

I followed the trial closely, interviewed witnesses, law enforcement officials, doctors, and lawyers. I researched everything I could get my hands on and compiled extensive notes, knowing that someday I would share this disturbing yet instructive story. Then, in 1985 — with my box of writings about the case in tow — I moved to the United States of America. Over the years, I've performed many ritual purgings of all things unused and unread…but I could never bring myself to part with those papers.

For 30 years, this story has lived in a cocoon inside me, incubating in all its raw, tragic detail. I knew that it would eventually transform into something ready to be released into the world, and that I would somehow know when to let it have its wings.

In 2012, amidst an epidemic of violent, psychotic crimes in the U.S., I decided it was time.

Come with me on a journey inside the mind of a mass murderer. You may be very surprised — as I was — to discover how this act of violence could come out of love, and equally as important – how this awful tragedy could have been prevented.

—Janice Holly Booth
August, 2013
North Carolina

This story is based on true events as described in court transcripts, eye witness statements and interviews. No material facts of the criminal case have been altered. The names of the victims, the accused, the attorneys and named doctors giving testimony have not been changed.

All other names, conversations and identifying details of persons depicted in this story have been fictionalized; they are not meant to identify a specific person or place, and any resemblance to persons living or dead is purely coincidental. Where a conversation, interview or testimony is verbatim, that is noted. This story is written using Canadian English, out of respect for the country in which the tragedy occurred.

For Irene

"In this darkness,

we are coming closer to you.

In this darkness,

we will take the place of everything."

- *the voices*

Based on a true story

A VOICE OUT OF NOWHERE

YOU LIGHT YOUR tenth cigarette of the day. It's only nine a.m., but you've been pacing since dawn. You can't remember sleeping, but you must have because there's a chunk of time that's missing, as if you've set it down somewhere and now can't find it.

"Shit!"

You know better than to fall asleep. Sleeping is dangerous. That's when the voices come. That's when you see those apocalyptic visions of the world ending, blowing up into smithereens. That's when the white woman with eyes of fire insists you are God.

Yesterday's brew sits cold and black in the coffee maker. You pour the remains into a mug and place it in the microwave, noticing the red spackle of pizza explosions covering the inside. "I should clean this place up," you mutter, looking around at the crumpled clothes strewn about your shabby apartment. Hundreds of "The Watchtower" and "Awake!" pamphlets cover every surface like giant snowflakes. While the microwave hums, you sniff your armpits. It's been two weeks since you washed and now you stink like a wet dog. One more long drag off

1

the cigarette: You tilt your head back and blow smoke all the way to the ceiling.

There is no fighting it any longer. You need a shower.

Reflected in the bathroom mirror is some version of you that no longer fits. Your eyes seem wrong. They're all one color – dark and glittering. The hair you were once so proud of hangs off your head like a black, greasy mop; your shiny bangs flutter every time you blink your eyes. And your *skin – God!* Have you ever been this *pale* before? You rub the sides of your face with balled-up fists, feeling rough stubble that's about to cross over into a beard. You hate beards. Even though Jesus had one, and God did too, you find them creepy, as if the person sporting one is trying to conceal something.

You reach for another cigarette but stop. "It's just a shower," you say, "for Christ's sake." While the water runs from cold to hot, you remove your clothes. It's getting harder and harder to manage the buttons on your shirt. *Too much caffeine, too many cigarettes,* you tell yourself, but that's a lie. The real reason why your hands shake all the time? You're terrified.

"Don't close your eyes," you say aloud as you step into the hard, hot spray. Oh, it feels good. It feels *so* good. You smile, a gesture that feels more and more foreign to you with each passing day. The steamy scent of pine soap travels deep into your lungs as you rub the bar all over your body. You feel ribs protruding. *I've got to eat something*, you think, but you know you won't. Food, even though it beckons, is revolting.

You stand in the stream of cleansing water for a long time before you lather up your hands to wash your face. *Only close your eyes for a second*, you warn yourself. But a second is already too long. As soon as you shut your eyes against the bite of the soap, you hear the voice as clear as day, right there in the shower with you. It's the Devil.

"I've got you now. I'm going to eat you alive."

WITNESS

Coquitlam, British Columbia
January 18, 1983   05:30

WILLIAM LOOKED OUT the window at blackness so deep it defied any hope of morning. This was the pause between nighttime and daylight when anything was possible. These moments in the pre-dawn were moments so open to potential, the stillness outside literally *beckoning* a declaration of action.

William wanted something new; this early morning rendezvous with a hot cup of tea was boring. It was another predictable part of his retirement routine: bed at 10, sleep 'til 4:30, toss and turn, then get out of bed before his thrashings woke his wife and her ire.

While waiting for the water to boil, William brought his face as close to the window pane as he could without touching it. He felt winter on the other side, trying to make its way in. His steady breathing formed little circles of fog on the inside of the glass. By adjusting his outward breath, he could make tiny circles, then huge ones. That didn't hold his attention for long. Two more months of this Canadian west coast winter

4

and he could finally look forward to dogwood blooms and daffodils. Colour, finally, and an end to dismal black and white.

The whistling kettle snapped him out of his reverie. He bolted to the stove before Iris woke up and started yelling bloody murder. By the time he reached it, the kettle was screaming. Simultaneously, William turned off the gas and snatched the kettle off the burner.

But the screaming didn't stop.

It was coming from outside; a piercing, primal scream that made William's gut tighten as if he'd been punched. Squinting through the window he scanned the dark landscape. Two human shapes — outlined by pale yellow light from an open garage — moved through his neighbour's yard. One shape pushed the other from behind.

And then the voices:

"Help! *Help!*"

"Get in the house. *Get in there now!*"

The bigger one stumbled to his knees. The other one pushed and kicked. *"Get in the house!"* he commanded. Lurching and stumbling, the other one complied, and the two shapes disappeared inside the garage.

William held his breath. Was this just a family squabble? Two men drinking and fighting? He didn't recognize either of the men, but it would be hard to recognize anyone in this darkness. He knew his neighbours had a big, extended family, but why would they be visiting and running around at 5:30 in the morning? Should he call the police? What if it turned out to be nothing?

William returned to the kettle and poured steaming water into a mug. He noticed that his hands were shaking a little, and that surprised him. *Calm down*, he told himself. Steam rose from the mug, the warmth of the water and the aroma of the teabag bringing him back to his comfortable routine. A family squabble, that's all that was going on next door. Holding his mug in both hands, William went back to the window. He saw the man who'd been chasing the other appear in the garage and take something from a bench. The man paused for a moment, grasping the thing in his hand. Then he strode back into the house — forceful, with purpose.

Within minutes, another scream made William drop his mug. It smashed into seven pieces and hot water sprayed across his pajama bottoms. Two more shapes ran through his neighbour's yard. William couldn't tell if they were men or women; both had longish hair, but both had boyish frames. "No, *no!* Not me! *Not me!*" It was the desperate, pleading voice of a woman. Two firecracker pops and one of the shapes — the one being pursued — fell to the ground.

There was a moment, just a moment, when everything froze. Then William watched one shape drag the other by its arms into the garage. A cold progression of goose bumps prickled at William's scalp and crawled all the way down to his groin. He watched as the garage door slowly closed, sealing away whatever was about to happen next.

6

Had he just seen this? William looked at the clock. It was 05:48. He looked back at the neighbour's house. Lights shone from every window. It was the only house on the block lit up like a bonfire. He blinked twice then ran to the phone.

"What is your emergency?" asked the measured voice on the other end.

William spewed out breathless words:

"Oh my God. I'm not sure what I just saw, but I think there's been gunfire."

"Sir, what is your location?"

"I don't know the address next door," William fumbled. He gave the operator his address instead. "I can go and wait for the police outside. To show them where it is."

"Is anyone hurt?" asked the operator.

"I'm not sure. I think so. It's dark. "

"Sir, stay on the line while I dispatch a car."

William's heart was pounding now. He answered the operator's questions about name and contact information, more details. "We'll have an officer there soon," she said, thanked him for his call, and hung up.

He went back to the window. Nothing stirred as he stared at the house next door, which — after all that commotion — had become deathly quiet. Just as his heart began to beat in a normal rhythm, he saw a spotlight turn on over the garage and a young man walk out into the cone of light illuminating the wet driveway. He wore a leather jacket, and there was something wrapped around his head.

He walked as if he had somewhere to go and in three strides disappeared into darkness.

SCENE

Coquitlam, British Columbia
January 18, 1983   05:55

ROYAL CANADIAN MOUNTED Police officers Sergeant Brent Watts and Corporal Dave Bogan were on patrol, driving on Lougheed Highway just west of the Port Coquitlam/Coquitlam line. This was a depressing area even in the daylight: rows of dilapidated apartments and rental houses covered in mold and algae fed by the persistent rain and cloud cover of the Pacific Northwest. In a way, darkness made the scene more palatable, its ugliness less harsh when shadowed by night.

Their radio crackled: a report of shots fired on Spuraway Avenue, a residential area close by. Watts and Bogan responded, with Constables Nichols and Darden acting as backup a short distance behind.

The homes on Spuraway were newer, more modern and fashionable than the gloomy neighbourhoods surrounding them. Watts and Bogan parked their marked police cruiser three houses away from the address provided by the caller. The residence in question supposedly had lights on in every room. They quickly located the house, exited the car, and proceeded on foot.

Silently, out of the rainy darkness, a young male appeared. He was backlit by a streetlight. Bogan noted that he was "wandering in various directions" close to the residence in question. The man looked to be in his early twenties and wore a leather jacket, blue jeans, and black boots. A brown, woven leather band encircled his forehead. As Watts and Bogan approached him, the young man dug both hands into his jacket pockets.

"Hands out of your pockets!" Watts ordered. The young man complied, raising his hands in the air. Watts searched the jacket by patting and pressing the pockets. He found no weapons.

"Where are you coming from?" Watts asked.

"From the school."

There was an elementary school approximately two blocks away, but it was in the direction he was walking *to*, not from.

The young man's scowl was intense, but his skin was pale as plaster. His straight, brown hair ended in severe bangs that brushed against thick, furrowed brows. Below them, his dark eyes looked as black and flat as asphalt. He was shaking.

"We received a call about gunshots," Watts said.

"I don't know anything about that," the man said, his voice trembling. Watts squinted. The man's chin quivered, as if he were about to cry and was trying hard not to.

Watts looked past the young man to the house up ahead with lights ablaze. He had to get there. If shots had been fired, he needed to get there now. He began to walk, leaving Bogan behind as another police car approached. Constables Darden and Nichols parked, then exited their police cruiser and joined Bogan as he questioned the suspect.

The young man made a sudden motion toward the rear pocket of his jeans and Bogan grabbed his arm.

"Just my wallet," said the man. He handed it to Darden. Bogan, a tall, wiry, black-haired man of Russian descent, stared at the suspect with an intensity meant to intimidate.

"What do you know about this report we have of shots fired?" Bogan pressed.

"Nothing."

"I know you're lying. Your face says you're lying."

The young man continued to protest his innocence.

"Dave!" Watts shouted from up ahead. Watts needed his backup. He was already 15 feet away from the other officers when he turned and ordered Darden to take the man to the police car.

"Darden, you need help?" Bogan asked before he left.

Darden shook his head. "Go on."

Bogan quickly caught up to Watts, taking Nichols with him.

The three officers approached the well-kept Spanish-style house from the east side. A light from downstairs, below grade, illuminated raindrops on the wet grass in the front yard. The view inside was partially blocked by a curtain, but Watts could see a pool table.

Suddenly, a man burst out of the house across the street and ran toward the officers. Watts and Nichols prepared to draw their weapons; Bogan drew his and aimed.

"I'm William Turnbridge," the man sputtered . "I'm the one who called." Despite the man's obvious agitation, Bogan lowered his weapon. William wore blue pajamas that were wet at the cuffs. Over them, a red, tattered robe was cinched tightly but unevenly, and he wore green rubber boots on his feet. Watts noted he'd forgotten to put in his teeth.

"I saw someone walk out of this house just seconds ago," said William.

"Where did he go?" asked Watts.

William pointed in the direction of the school.

"Who was it?" Bogan asked.

"I can't say for sure," said William. "A man. Young. I couldn't really see in the dark. But he's the one talking to the officer over there."

"Was there anyone else?" Watts asked.

William slowly shook his head, signaling no. "Oh, wait, yes. There were two other men. They were each fighting with this guy at different times, but I didn't see them come out of the house. They must still be inside."

Watts looked at Bogan and jerked his head in the direction of the house. "Thank you sir," said Watts to William. "Now, go back into your house and stay there."

William paused. "What do you think happened?" he asked. Bogan took a step toward him and stared with such force that William stepped back.

"Dave," said Watts. "Easy."

"Sir," said Bogan, glaring at William, "Go ... back ...into ...your ...*home*."

"You'll be safer there," added Watts.

"Well," William said finally, "I'll be across the street if you need any more information."

William turned and jogged back to his house, his bare feet inside the green rubber boots making a squishing sound. Watts and Bogan crossed the yard of the house in question, revolvers drawn. Nichols followed. They stopped in front of the garage door, and listened.

Silence.

Watts walked to the side of the garage to peer through a window. He saw blue clothing heaped in a doorway that connected the garage to the house. He called Bogan, who was taller.

"Dave, come look at this."

Bogan looked. The blue clothing was a pair of jeans attached to a female body lying face first in the garage.

"Shit," said Bogan. "We better call for backup." As the two officers quickly discussed the situation, their radio crackled. It was Darden.

"Suspect has just admitted he is the Antichrist and the world is going to end on the thirty-first."

"We're going in," said Watts. "Nichols, call for backup. Guard the front door." With all three service revolvers drawn, the officers prepared for what might be waiting inside.

Watts opened the unlocked storm door and froze.

He heard his measured breathing and the thudding sound of his heart.

Otherwise: utter silence.

Now he was at the main front door. It, too, was unlocked. He pushed it in then waited, listening. Hearing nothing, Watts and Bogan entered.

Immediately inside to the right was a raised living room fenced in by a decorative railing. Watts and Bogan quickly made their way through the short hallway and stopped at a huge pool of wet blood at the base of three stairs that led from a family room to a raised kitchen.

Watts' jaw tightened. Bloody drag marks and footprints were all over the carpet. Both officers stepped around them as they made their swift but cautious way through the house.

Fifteen feet inside, down the main hallway and to their left, was the body of a male on his side, his upper torso extended into a laundry room. A gallon jug of fabric softener sat near his head, which was surrounded by a thick halo of blood. His facial features were almost indecipherable, as if covered by clear gelatin.

Watts heard it first: gurgling, labored breathing. Despite the obvious trauma to his face and head, the man was still alive. Watts called for the paramedics at 06:10, his heart thudding in his ears as he crouched next to the man. Could he administer mouth-to-mouth? "Sir," he whispered, "*Hang on*. Help is coming." The injured man wheezed and Watts saw tiny bubbles forming as air forced its way out of the place where his mouth had once been. It was the most nightmarish thing he would ever see in his life.

Meanwhile, Bogan saw blood sprayed all over the kitchen, but no bodies. He followed the drag marks down a set of basement stairs to a games room where two males lay side by side, next to a pool table. One was middle aged and lying on his back. The other was a teenager, face down. They were so close together that their heads and shoulders touched. Blood had pooled and begun to cake around both of them. Bogan stood quietly for a moment, staring, listening for any signs of life. Both bodies were completely still, even as blood continued to seep from under the older man's shoulders. Bogan felt a familiar rage begin to rise inside him.

He returned to the main floor and saw a .22 calibre rifle leaning on the three stairs between the family room and the kitchen, muzzle pointing upward. It sat there, posed, in a sopping pool of darkening blood. It looked to Bogan as if it had been placed there deliberately, with great care, as if to signify something.

"Two DB's downstairs," Bogan said to Watts.

"Living room and bathroom clear," Watts responded. They proceeded up the main stairs to the darkened upper floor. The only light came from a doorway at the end of the hall to the right. Weapons drawn, they walked sideways toward it. The door was partially closed. Watts pushed it open with his foot as Darden covered him. There in the master bedroom lay the body of a middle-aged woman on her back with both arms up, one of them across her face. She was nude, except for a pair of white panties and white tennis socks. Around her, the cream-coloured, blood-soaked carpet had begun to turn brown.

Watts stepped toward her to look for signs of life. The woman's eyes were open, but unblinking. Watts turned to Bogan and shook his head, signifying no, then checked the ensuite bathroom.

"Clear," he said. Bogan finally lowered his weapon.

They checked two smaller bedrooms on the upper floor. Both were empty, but all the beds, Watts noted, were "mussed."

After making a radio call for the Identification unit to attend, Bogan checked the condition of the man in the hallway. Incredibly, despite the ferocious trauma to his face, he was still breathing, though with great difficulty. Bogan shouted at Nichols, *"Where the fuck is that ambulance?"*

Three steps into the garage, Bogan discovered two more bodies. One was the body he'd seen from the outside window. The victim had an obvious gunshot wound to her head and appeared to have fallen where she'd been shot. Another body lay between two cars with arms upraised and a blue jacket covering its face. Its shoes were wet and muddy. Because the size and shape of the body were somewhat androgynous, Bogan couldn't be sure if it was a woman or man. On a workbench in the garage, Bogan spied a hammer covered in blood.

At 06:20, the Coquitlam Fire Department arrived.

"In here!" Nichols motioned them through the front door and directed them to the injured male who was still struggling to breathe. The three paramedics were a blur of ripping paper, jerking elbows and quick hand movements as they supplied oxygen to the victim, but he stopped breathing three or four minutes later.

"You!" barked Watts, focusing his attention on the paramedic in charge. "Check the rest." The sandy-haired, doe-eyed young man looked at Watts as if to say, *"What do I do?"*

Bogan said, "Come on," and accompanied the paramedic to check every body, careful to preserve the crime scene by not stepping in

17

blood or moving any physical evidence. Reporting back, the ashen-faced paramedic confirmed, "They're all dead, sir."

Watts looked at his officers, then at the medical team. "Thank you for your work here," said Watts to the ambulance crew. "You can all leave."

As the emergency personnel departed, the three officers gathered at the front door.

"Jesus," said Bogan.

"Jesus had nothing to do with this," said Watts, looking at his corporal. "Dave, you strong?" Watts had worked with Bogan long enough to know that he responded to violent crime with a violence of his own — a temper that was purely dangerous.

"I'm *p e r f e c t i o n*," Bogan answered, his clipped tone telling Watts Bogan was using every molecule of restraint to hold himself back from punching a wall...or a suspect.

"What about you, Nichols?" asked Watts.

"Sir..." he answered, then stopped.

Watts nodded. "This may be as bad as it ever gets, Nichols." Watts paused. "If you're lucky."

None of them had ever seen — nor would ever see again — such carnage all in one place. Even Watts — the most senior of the three by far — was rattled. He kept clearing his throat. It was 06:29, and there was nothing to say. The silence was eerie.

They all jumped when an alarm radio blasted on at 06:30. The Bee Gees' "Night Fever" rocked the house. Nichols chuckled grimly: Here they were, three trained police officers surrounded by six dead bodies, and a little radio music practically gave them all a seizure? It was funny in a sick way. They waited for their hearts to calm down.

Moments later, a second alarm shrieked, jolting them back into the moment.

The radios were left untouched for the benefit of the Identification Unit.

"All right," said Watts. "Let's check outside while we wait for Ident. Nichols, you stand guard at the front here."

"Yes, sir," answered Nichols. As he watched the drizzling rain dance through the cone of light beaming down from the front of the garage, he heard the bedroom radio. The upbeat music seemed particularly obscene in contrast to the bloodbath below. He tried his best to block it out.

Outside, in the rain, Watts and Bogan checked the front and back yards and the two vehicles parked in the driveway. They found a brown, semi-automatic rifle on the lawn between the victims' house and the neighbour's house to the east. There were drag marks in the grass. They left the rifle for Ident to photograph.

As night gave way to day, in the weak light of morning, Watts noted a pair of eyeglasses lying on the cement driveway in front of the closed garage door. One lens lay on the ground beside the frames and there was some blood splatter on the driveway next to the garage door. A spent .22 calibre rifle shell lay a few feet away from the glasses. Watts left them untouched.

At 07:15, others began to arrive. Two officers from the Identification unit set about their work of photographing and recording physical evidence. Coroner Brenda Bolin, along with a pathologist and the regional coroner, were escorted into the house. Newspaper and television reporters began to converge. Neighbours came. School age teens gathered, ignoring the school bus that waited on the corner. One girl — later identified as someone who had dated the young man who lived in the house — howled. "Please," she cried, *"Please,* turn out the light in his bedroom!"

Watts remained at the house until 09:30, continuing to secure the scene, manage the change of shift of members[3] for security and deal with the press. He conducted his work proficiently, professionally, and without emotion, but he couldn't shake the images of what he'd just seen. He wondered if he'd ever be able to forget them.

Meanwhile, Constable Darden listened to the suspect, the self-professed "Antichrist," tell what had happened in the early morning hours of January 18, in the Spanish-style house on Spuraway Avenue.

---

[3] The term "members" refers to officers of the Royal Canadian Mounted Police

DESCENT

AT NORTH VANCOUVER'S Argyle Secondary School, nestled at the base of a spectacular mountain range, a teenage Bruce Blackman went mostly unnoticed but not unliked. Grade 8 was a disaster for the dark-haired, handsome young man whose high cheekbones and long-bridged nose hinted that he might have a little Native blood coursing through his veins. His academic catastrophe was an unfortunate and utterly unanticipated consequence of too much "taking things easy" and too little academic focus. Adding to his profound embarrassment about this failure was the fact that his identical twin brother, Todd, had sailed through school with good grades and an ease of accomplishment that Bruce just couldn't replicate.

Bruce's mother, Irene, worried. A petite woman with long-lashed, light brown eyes that sparkled like ginger ale, she reminded Bruce of Donna Reed with her perfectly coiffed hair, pretty smile, and willingness to endure the never-ending demands of her husband and six kids. She'd passed on her tiny build and elegant bone structure to all of her five children, save for one girl. Everyone loved Irene, including

21

Bruce, but she could drive a monk crazy with her incessant talking and hand-wringing.

"Bruce," she told him when his mid-year report card spelled disaster, "you've got to work harder at school. I know you can do better. If Todd can do it, you should be able to do it, too." That was another thing. Just because they were twins, Bruce and Todd were supposed to be identical in every way, but they weren't: Even though they'd always dressed alike until Grade 7, their differences were becoming apparent. Todd was organized and logical; Bruce was erratic and impulsive. Todd dressed well and kept his hair short; Bruce grew his hair long and would sometimes wear the same clothes for a week.

"I'm going to take you to a doctor," Irene said.

"What kind of doctor?" Bruce asked, scowling beneath long, black bangs.

"The kind of doctor who can see if you have some kind of learning disability."

"What are you saying, Mom, that I'm *retarded?*"

"Of course you're not retarded, Bruce, but if you say you're doing your best and you're getting F's in everything, well…maybe there's something wrong and maybe a doctor can figure out a way to help you."

"I got an A in shop, Mom, did you forget about that?"

At the psychologist's office, Bruce sat with arms and legs tightly crossed, sullen, staring at the floor. The doctor — a tall, needle-nosed man with a ramrod straight back and a British accent — had already interviewed him for an hour, asking what Bruce thought were stupid questions: did he get dizzy or nauseous when he tried to read (sometimes); did words on the page seem to move (sometimes); was he good at mechanics (yes). Then the doctor asked Bruce to fill out some papers that were like tests but not really. Bruce complied while his mother and the doctor waited in another room. Now they were all back together in the doctor's office. The doctor wore a plaid jacket with suede elbow patches. Bruce thought it was the ugliest coat he had ever seen.

"Bruce is a mirror[4] twin," the doctor announced, startling both Bruce and Irene. She instinctively grabbed for Bruce's hand. He let her hold it, just for a moment.

"This is quite rare among twins," he continued, "but it could account for some of Bruce's problems." Mirror twins, the doctor explained, was a phenomenon where one twin "mirrors" the traits or afflictions of the other. "For example," he explained, "one twin might be right-handed, while the other will be left-handed. One twin might have dental issues on one side of the mouth; the mirror twin will have the same problems on the other side of the mouth. In Bruce's case," he continued, "his twin brother Todd sees words as they are meant to be seen. Bruce sees them reversed, or opposite."

---

[4] A controversial diagnosis.

When the doctor said the word "opposite," Bruce heard an echo. *"Opposite, opposite, opposite…"* The word careened around the doctor's office, bouncing off the walls, until it faded away. When it did, Bruce once again focused on what the doctor was saying. "I can make a recommendation to the school to provide some extra help, if it's available," he said. Irene nodded like a bobble-head toy on the dashboard of a car. She crumpled a tissue in her hand and pulled at it until it was nothing more than a pile of confetti in her lap.

On the drive home, Irene talked and Bruce looked out the window, tuning her out so he could think about what the doctor had just said. *Mirror twins. Rare. Opposite.* It was the notion of opposites that really intrigued him.

"We'll figure out a way to get you some help," his mother said when he turned to look at her. He could tell by the way she bit down on her lower lip that she was about to cry or become hysterical — or both.

"Mom," said Bruce, "tell me about the time I was born." He knew how much she loved to tell the story. So often when he was growing up, Irene would sit with Bruce on one side of her, Todd on the other, hug both of them to her body and describe their entrance into the world. The act of telling the story always calmed her down and made her happy. It made Bruce happy, too. He'd lean into her ribcage, feel the vibration of her voice, smell her rose-scented perfume, hear her heart beat steady. But early on, he heard something else, too: his twin brother's heartbeat, all the way on the other side of his mother's body. It came to him as if on a wire, something that cut completely and purely

24

through all the other noise. Sometimes, Todd and Bruce would sneak a peek at each other while she was talking. They never had to say a word. They knew exactly what the other one was thinking. In second grade, Irene and Senior and the schoolteachers had conspired to separate Bruce and Todd and didn't allow them to attend class together. But it didn't matter. They were joined in a way no entity could sever.

Whenever she'd finish telling the story, Irene would loudly kiss them both on their heads; first Todd, then Bruce. "My angels," she would say.

"Not right now, Bruce," she said.

"Please?"

Irene braked for a red light and flicked down the left turn signal. Amidst the *click-click, click-click, click-click*, she began.

"Well, it was at St. Joseph's Hospital in Victoria[5]," she said, "and *oh my,* did those nuns mean business!" She chuckled at the memory, then shook her head and got back to the story. "Well, Todd was born first. He was big — nine pounds, six ounces. You came a little later. You were six pounds, nine ounces and they put you in an incubator, just like a little chick." This was usually the point in the story when Irene would run her hand through Bruce's hair. "You were my first boys, after three girls. And to get two of you at once. I didn't know whether to laugh or cry."

---

[5] Capital of British Columbia, situated on southern Vancouver Island.

"Todd was nine pounds six ounces and I was six pounds nine ounces," Bruce said.

"That's right."

"Think about it, Mom."

The traffic light turned green and Irene made the left hand turn. She was silent for a moment, then shook her head and said, "Think about what?"

"We were exactly the opposite, just like the doctor said."

Irene looked over her left shoulder before changing lanes, then accelerated so fast it knocked Bruce's head back against the headrest. She'd never win any prizes for her driving ability.

"Well, isn't that something…" she trailed off. "I never thought about that before. You know the other thing that's odd?"

"What?"

"There's no history of twins on either side of the family. And then I go on to have not just one, but two sets of twins. I think that's strange. Don't you think that's strange?"

"Strange *and* rare."

Irene reached over and patted Bruce on the thigh. "Special."

So he wasn't stupid and he wasn't a loser. He was born to mirror Todd. That meant everything in his life would mean the opposite from now on. For some reason, this new knowledge filled him with a kind of peace. It meant he could stop trying.

Within days of the revelation, Bruce tried marijuana. He liked the way it made him feel, the way it numbed the humiliation of being labeled a failure, and it made him forget his mother's disappointment in his grades. Soon, Bruce began to smoke marijuana every day, along with cigarettes. He liked his new persona of laid back, easy-going, and loving the world.

"I'm the last of the hippies," he joked, "We're a dying breed."

1982
Four years later

IN 1978, ALTHOUGH it was difficult for him, Bruce made it all the way to Grade 12, but couldn't finish. By now, his marijuana habit was an addiction. At family dinners, where his siblings and his parents gathered, he'd smoke up before he had to endure the loud talking and constant interrupting. The sideways looks from his two older sisters made him feel itchy. His younger brother Ricky — who was also a twin (the brother, Raymond, was stillborn) — didn't really care whether Bruce did well or not. Ricky was busy building his own teenage resume of rebellion; truancy, drug abuse. He tried to stay under his parents' radar and get away with as much as he could while they were busy focusing on Bruce. Bruce's sisters were a different story. Roberta — whom everyone called Bobi — was six years older than Bruce and was just like their mother. Petite and pretty with Cleopatra eyes and long black hair parted on the side, she worried about everything to the point where she lost weight over it. Bobi — although she had the classic Blackman native-looking features — was straight and thin, with angular edges a lot like Bruce's. From the back, you couldn't tell whether she was male or female. Bobi had made Bruce her "special project." She was always trying to find ways to help him.

Karon, three years older than Bruce and considered to be the "beauty" of the family, was more womanly, with soft, round contours also like their mother, but without the obsessive worrying. And Angela was different from all of them, as if she'd come from a different gene pool, but she lived away, as did his twin brother Todd. They weren't there to help Bruce endure the glances and the whispers. Or maybe they would have contributed to them. It didn't matter. Some good, deep tokes made it all go away.

In 1980, Bruce walked into a party where the Rolling Stones "Start Me Up" was blasting. Bruce could feel the music vibrating in his chest. All around him black light posters glowed while people flashed unnaturally white smiles.

From behind him he heard, "*Hey, man!*"

Bruce turned and saw Jerry Walters, a classmate from way back in '78 at Argyle. Jerry held up a joint and beckoned. Bruce didn't need a second invitation.

Jerry took a long toke then handed the joint to Bruce, who did the same. They both held their breath, then released the smoke at the same time, aiming it at the ceiling. Jerry smacked Bruce on the back twice, took another toke, held his breath, squinted his eyes, nodded four times, coughed once, then took his joint and walked away. Later, they bumped into each other outside where Bruce had gone to pee.

"Bruce, right?" said Jerry.

"Yeah. It's been awhile."

Although they'd never socialized in school, they now found no shortage of things to talk about. The asshole math teacher. The gorgeous assistant principal who wore wraparound dresses that left nothing to a teenage boy's imagination. Now, after discovering their mutual love of weed and parties, they were about to become best friends.

By the time Jerry and Bruce decided to live together in May of 1982, they'd spent a lot of time enjoying each others' easy-going ways. Jerry — even by 1980's standards (a decade known for appalling fashion trends) — was a bit of a geek. His curly red hair wouldn't quite tighten itself into the afro-look that was popular at the time: Even as he attempted to coax his hair into a cool, copper-colored 'fro, he always appeared a little startled and wind-blown. His over-sized, thick-lensed aviator glasses didn't help either. Jerry squinted a lot. He'd constantly flare his nostrils to try and coax the heavy eye-glasses back up onto the bridge of his nose. He was a mouth breather. Yet he had a kind of deluded self-confidence that served him well. As far as Jerry was concerned, he was the spitting image of the movie actor William Katt. After the 1976 film *Carrie* was released, a few girls told Jerry he looked like the handsome actor who played Tommy Ross. That was the only morsel Jerry needed to feed his over-generous self-image. While Bruce was possessed of authentically attractive features, it was Jerry who initially lured the females. Nevertheless, shy and polite Bruce indirectly benefitted from Jerry's odd bravado, meeting far more girls than if he had to take the initiative to woo them himself.

Bruce and Jerry, together with a group of other friends — Don, Phil and Gail — attended parties, watched movies, went out weekly for pizza, and — as the Pacific Northwest spring gave way to summer — played Frisbee in the park nearby. They'd see each other four to five times a week and considered themselves to be a close-knit group. Bruce hated being left out of any social excursion with his four close friends, but sometimes his father Richard, (Senior they called him, to minimize confusion when talking about all the Blackman males), visited from Coquitlam and they'd work on cars together. Bruce owned two vehicles: a Corvair (the car declared by Ralph Nader as "unsafe at any speed"); and a Datsun[6] 240Z. In addition to suffering from a terminal case of rust, there seemed to always be something wrong with the sports car. Fixing the mechanical *failure du jour* was a way for Bruce and his dad to bond. Sometimes, they'd fix whatever was ailing Jerry's car, too. It was a good arrangement. Everyone seemed happy, though Senior wished Bruce would aspire to more in his life than working dead-end jobs and fixing cars on the side.

---

[6] The precursor to Nissan.

Bruce and Jerry's apartment on Lonsdale Avenue in North Vancouver wasn't fancy. Lonsdale was a busy commercial street, lined on either side by ethnic restaurants, dry-cleaners and 1-hour photo mats[7]. It hosted non-stop traffic — loud at all hours, but particularly during the busy parts of the day. The apartment building rose above the retail stores that were at street level and stuck out like the proverbial sore thumb. Bruce and Jerry entered through a green door next to the bookshop. A narrow, cramped staircase led to four units in two floors above. The hallways always stunk of other people's cooking. "Old people food," Jerry called it.

"Shit on a shingle," Bruce added, referring to a dish his father used to eat in the Navy. But for two young men in their early twenties, the apartment represented freedom and maturity. Never mind that it was furnished with cast-offs from Jerry's and Bruce's parents: an old TV; a kitchen dining set from the '50's; mismatched plates and cooking utensils; mattresses on the floor. Decorative art took the form of posters: the Rolling Stones, the Who, motorcycles, Farrah Fawcett. The only really nice thing Jerry and Bruce owned was their stereo system. It held a place of honour in the living room. Jerry and Bruce kept their record albums in milk crates set atop makeshift shelves of planks and cinderblocks. It was the quintessential, stereotypical, broke, twenty-something's bachelor pad.

---

[7] A photo mat was where one took photos for processing, back in the days of film.

Bruce's twin, Todd, had joined the Canadian Armed Forces two years earlier in 1980, and was away from home all the time, except for visits now and then. At his father's urging, Bruce had applied to serve in the Armed Forces too, but an arrest for possession of a narcotic knocked Bruce out of contention. Now he worked for the District of North Vancouver as a swamper on a garbage truck. He neither liked nor hated the job — it paid the bills and gave him just enough money to support his marijuana habit. Best of all, the supervisors turned a blind eye to the men when they'd smoke the occasional joint or drink a beer while hanging off the sides of the trucks as they made their loud, smelly way through the streets of North Van[8]. There were worse jobs for someone whose future wasn't particularly promising. And being a garbage man was pretty straightforward, too. Bruce liked the repetition. Jump off the truck, toss the trash, jump back on. There were no manuals to read, no reports to write. He liked the structure. Here, he could succeed. Bruce was often surprised by what people threw away: perfectly good chairs, vacuum cleaners, beds. Even clothes: Bruce found a brown leather jacket in someone's discarded belongings. It was much nicer than what he could afford, so he took it home and wore it all the time. Once, he found a Bible in the trash. For some reason, this really bothered him, though he couldn't say why. He'd never been interested in religion, except for occasionally reading the "The Watchtower," or "Awake!" and even then, only when a visiting Jehovah's Witness left pamphlets at the entrance to the apartment. He read these alone, never sharing his interest in them with anyone.

---

[8] Local slang for "North Vancouver."

SUMMER CAME AND went. Autumn arrived, a particularly beautiful time in southwestern British Columbia, especially when the sun set fire to the bright blazes of yellow and red leaved trees nestled amidst mountainsides of dark evergreens. Jerry loved fall, but it made him feel a little depressed. It meant the true end of summer and the beginning of a long, dreary winter. Bruce, on the other hand, welcomed fall because it meant hunting with his brothers and his Dad. Bruce even prayed – for the first time in his life – that they'd get a moose on their next trip, just a few weeks away.

"*Bruce!*" shouted Jerry from the kitchen as he rooted around in the fridge. "Are you going to eat these leftovers?"

"No," yelled Bruce, who was balled up in a corner of the couch, chewing his nails, watching TV. "You can have them."

Jerry retrieved the 3-day-old pizza remnants. He took a bite of the cold pepperoni and cheese and walked into the living room.

"Bruce," he said. There was no response. "Bruce," he said again.

Jerry waited. "*Bruce!*"

Without taking his eyes off the TV, Bruce answered, "What?"

"Have you eaten anything today?" Bruce shook his head, signaling no.

"Why not?" asked Jerry.

No answer. "When was the last time you ate?" Jerry pressed.

"I'm not sure," Bruce answered. "Maybe Wednesday?" It was now Friday.

"Are you hungry?"

"Yeah," Bruce said. "I guess so."

Jerry stared hard at his friend. Something wasn't right. Bruce's eyes were more bloodshot than usual, even though the familiar scent of marijuana had been absent in the apartment for the last few days.

"I can't sleep," Bruce said abruptly, then leaned toward the TV, completely engrossed. He was watching a commercial for corn flakes.

"How 'bout I make dinner? Will you eat something if I make it?" Jerry asked.

Bruce looked at Jerry as if just noticing him for the first time. "Oh, hi," Bruce answered. "Yeah, I'll eat something if you're going to make it. I'm hungry. I'm *really* hungry. I don't remember the last time I ate."

Something fast, Jerry thought as he finished off the cold pizza. Kraft Dinner was a favorite staple — quick, easy, hot, and could satisfy the munchies any time.

"You want me to help?" Bruce called.

"No man, I've got it," Jerry answered.

Fifteen minutes later, Jerry called Bruce to the kitchen. *"It's ready,"* he shouted.

When a minute passed and Bruce did not appear Jerry peeked in the living room. His friend sat expressionless on the sofa.

"Bruce," Jerry said, "did you hear me?" Bruce seemed deaf. Jerry walked over and waved his hand in front of his friend's face.

"No thanks," Bruce said, "I'm not hungry." As he stared at the TV, Bruce gasped and said, "Do you see that?"

"See what?" Jerry answered. An episode of *All in the Family* was playing.

Bruce shook his head slowly, his face deeply solemn even as the laugh track roared. "Oh, man, that's bad."

"What's bad?" asked Jerry.

Bruce looked up at his friend. Jerry saw something like fear flickering in Bruce's dark eyes. "Can't you see it?"

Jerry noticed, with alarm, that Bruce was shaking.

"See what?" Edith Bunker was talking to Archie; Archie was telling Edith to "stifle." It wasn't ominous and it certainly wasn't frightening.

Jerry brought Bruce's dinner to him in the living room, but it would remain uneaten.

This, according to Jerry, is when it all began.

October 1982

IN THE WEEKS before the annual moose hunting trip, Bruce didn't sleep much. He'd been reading the Bible and believed there was some special message in it for him, but he had yet to figure out what that was. He'd mentioned it to his father who was surprised since the family had never been overly religious.

"Dad," said Bruce, "There's something in here I'm supposed to understand." He held the Bible open and pointed to the Book of Revelation.

"Well, Son," said Senior. "I think there's something in there we're *all* supposed to try and understand." He ran his hands over his belly, feeling the one big round curve that had overtaken his former military physique. "As far as I'm concerned," he joked, "I'd like to understand how *this* happened." He slapped his gut with both palms.

"Dad, listen. Armageddon is coming. The big bang is coming. The end of the world is coming, and there's something in this Bible I'm supposed to figure out."

There was no diffusing Bruce's distress. He was convinced that something was at hand.

"Dad, listen: *'Another angel came out of the temple and called to him who was sitting on the cloud, 'Take your sickle and reap, because the time to reap has come, for the harvest of the earth is ripe.'"*

Senior sighed. "Try to take it easy, Bruce," he said, putting a hand on his son's small shoulder. "It'll be OK."

Every day before the hunting trip, Bruce called his father, several times, to read another passage from the Bible and to insist that Armageddon loomed on the horizon.

Senior could do little more than listen. Every conversation ended the same way, "Bruce, try to relax. It's not that bad, I promise."

Whenever Bruce closed his eyes, he heard a woman's voice urging him to know God, telling him that an end was coming. *An end to what?* Bruce wondered. *And what did it mean to know God?* Bruce suddenly remembered what he'd read in one edition of "The Watchtower": That God would only allow a few people into heaven; that it was important to see God; and that the end of the world was coming. *Was this the end to which the woman referred? The end of the world?*

The night before the hunting trip, the woman's voice spoke: "Time goes forward and backward, Bruce. It begins and ends with you."

"What are you telling me?" he asked aloud. "*Why* are you telling me?"

"You are the key, Bruce. You are about to become Time."

When she'd first appeared to him, it was only while Bruce slept. But now he could hear her as he went about his day. She was becoming more insistent that something was going to happen, and that Bruce was going to be a part of it. He couldn't escape her, especially if he dared to close his eyes and try to rest. If he went to sleep, he was sure the woman would kill him.

In late October, the long-awaited trip to hunt moose began. Bruce joined his brother Todd, his father, and three of his dad's Navy buddies and headed to the Blackwater region of Quesnel in central British Columbia. Getting there meant enduring an eight to nine-hour drive straight up the middle of the province, through miles and miles of wild and undisturbed panorama. Bruce enjoyed these trips: he was a good shot and knew how to handle guns. He'd taken a hunter safety program in 1977 and hunted with his father on a regular basis. Bruce viewed firearms as tools, not weapons, and he helped his father keep those tools clean, well-oiled, and operating efficiently. If the hunting party didn't bag a moose, it wouldn't be because of a jammed rifle.

On the long drive to the hunting grounds, Bruce was unusually quiet. He stared out the camper van window at the snow-dusted mountains as they whizzed by in the distance. *What does it mean to know God?* How would he know God if he saw Him? Suddenly, Bruce remembered all those years ago when the doctor explained about being a mirror twin. *That's it!* he thought. *I'm supposed to see everything as an opposite. Does that mean the woman is God?* The idea that he might have deciphered a little clue gave Bruce a brief surge of excitement. In the great, wide sky over the vast landscape of mountaintops and rolling meadows, Bruce watched clouds form and re-form as they moved from west to east, casting running shadows on the land. It was mesmerizing, this ever-changing palette of light and dark. Calming.

A bank of clouds suddenly approached from the opposite direction. A huge, planet-shaped cloud rolled west toward the big bank of clouds moving east. *How could this be? How could the wind be blowing in opposite directions at the same time?* The two opposing cloud shapes collided, and when they did Bruce gasped in wonder at what they formed: an almost perfect star shape. "Look at *that*," he whispered.

"Look at what?" Todd asked, pulling himself out of an animated conversation with his father and his father's long-time Navy buddy, John.

Bruce pointed, never taking his eyes off the star-shaped cloud.

"What is it, a bald eagle?" asked Todd.

"No," said Bruce, "Can't you see it? It's a seven-pointed star."

Todd looked. Bruce watched his brother's eyes search the sky. "I don't see it buddy," Todd said, then returned to his conversation.

OK, Bruce thought. Todd hadn't seen this cloud star that took up half the sky. That could only mean one thing: It was meant for Bruce's eyes only. It was a sign.

At the campsite, Bruce pitched in as he always did, helping with whatever needed to be done. While Bruce organized the rifles and ammunition, Todd pulled their father aside.

"Dad," he said, "what's wrong with Bruce?"

Senior shook his head. "I don't know," he answered. "Too much pot for sure. Now he's on this tear about the Bible and Armageddon. I hear he's been late for work a lot. I wish we could get him into some kind of training program so he can get focused on his future."

"How long has he been like this?" Todd asked.

Bruce was far out of earshot but suddenly stared at both of them with such intensity it made them both flinch.

"About a month, maybe?" Blackman Senior whispered, turning his back to Bruce. "Try talking to him. You know how much he looks up to you. See if you can find out what's going on."

Todd took stock of his father who suddenly looked old; old, tired, sick and something Todd had never seen before: frightened.

That night, Bruce lay in his sleeping bag listening to nature's evening orchestra. There were still a few hardy crickets chirping the swan song of summer. Raccoons foraging around in the dried leaves sounded as big as bears. The wheezes and snorts of five snoring men were both comforting and irritating. Bruce listened to the wind as it wound an invisible path through the trees, proof that things which cannot be seen nevertheless exist. The groaning tree limbs, the squeaking of one branch as it rubbed on the other, was evidence that a force of nature was at hand. Sometimes the branches moaned as if they were in agony. Amidst all this, he heard the voice again, but now he saw her, too — a white woman in a diaphanous gown. "The end is the beginning," she said. "You are God."

"I'm not God," he answered, "I'm Bruce Blackman."

THE NEXT DAY, the men shot and killed a moose. There was high-fiving and back slapping as Senior gutted the enormous creature. He'd done this countless times over the years, but Senior had let his once muscular and fit frame soften into a pudgy outline of middle age. Bruce heard Senior wheeze and cough as he reached inside the moose's body to pull out piles and piles of guts and organs. "I think I'm getting too old for this," Senior said, grunting as he leaned in to yank out the heart.

John, Senior's Navy buddy — a thin and meticulous man whose hair and moustache were always perfect no matter what the circumstances — said, "I think you were too old for this ten years ago."

Senior pulled back from the moose and slammed the knife down into the dirt. "It wouldn't hurt if you'd spend a little more time helping and a little less time foaming at the mouth."

The other men laughed, but Bruce frowned. John was his father's best friend. He'd never heard him talk to John like this.

That night, Bruce was both ecstatic and scared: He'd prayed that they would kill a moose and God had delivered. It was another sign, a sign that more was coming, a sign that Bruce needed to figure things out, and fast. It was overwhelming, though — these thoughts, the voices, all colliding into a jumble inside his head. And, he noted with some dread, he was now hearing not just the white woman, but other voices as well, more malevolent ones, whispering in the background. Bruce felt his skin vibrating: To distract himself, he smoked one cigarette after another until he'd gone through a whole pack in two hours.

Around the campfire that evening, the men drank beer and wove a tapestry of stories, telling and re-telling favorite memories of their time in the Navy. Bruce sat on a stump, away from the group — within earshot and eyesight — but separate.

"Remember when we ran into those hookers in the Philippines?" Senior asked John, who shifted in his camp chair. "We were walking down this alley which just stunk of piss and shit, and this hooker comes up to John and says, 'you buy me drink, you take me home.' And she starts grabbing at his arms while another hooker comes up behind him and starts tugging on his shirt. Well, John kind of liked the look of the one who was fondling his arm, and you could — uh — sort of see the evidence of that."

John twirled the end of his moustache and turned red.

Senior continued, "So, we're all standing there drunk as hell and watching this and Brian realizes that the one on John's arm is actually

42

undoing his watch. He also sees that John has a hard-on which was obviously affecting his ability to think. Then Brian shouts, 'John, she's ripping you off!' John doesn't know what to do, and these two hookers get kind of menacing and you know, those women all have knives and they'll cut you faster than you can blink. So Brian hauls off and punches this hooker in the face. She goes down, Bam! And we're all just kind of standing there thinking, 'oh shit, now what?' and then all these hookers come out from the alleyways. It was like *Night of the Living Dead!* John's still trying to figure out what's happening when Brian looks at the hooker lying on the ground and sees that her wig has come off and it's not a woman, *it's a guy!* We found out later that they were *all* guys, all of them transvestites in hooker gear."

"How'd you get away?" asked Todd.

"We ran," said John, clearing his throat and sitting ever taller. "We were outnumbered but they were all wearing high heels and they couldn't run as fast as we could stagger. And for the record, I did not have a hard-on. I had to take a piss."

"That tranny was pretty cute, John, but you would have gotten a little more than you'd bargained for. I'd pay anything to have heard you scream when she showed you the merchandise."

The men roared and threw insults at each other. After an hour and a half of listening quietly to their belly-laughs, Bruce exploded in a fury.

"You are all goddamned war mongers!" he screamed, propelling himself off the stump then pacing frantically back and forth behind the flames of the campfire. Todd and Senior were speechless. The other men watched in disbelief as Bruce ranted and shouted, flailing his arms and kicking at logs, sending bright orange sparks upward into the black night air. With flames both lighting and shadowing his face, Bruce looked positively, utterly possessed.

"You've fallen for a lie!" he shouted. "Our government created war to make you *kill, kill, kill.* You can't kill and know God. You can't kill and be pure. *You're all fucking hypocrites!"*

Several times Todd tried to intervene, then Senior, but it only incited Bruce to another level of outrage. The diatribe persisted for twenty minutes until he abruptly stopped and went to bed. The night was silent now, except for the crackling of wood and hissing of sparks from the fire. The men looked at each other, incredulous and embarrassed. "I'm sorry, Blackie," John said to Senior, using the nickname he'd assigned him 30 years ago in the Navy. "Maybe he's just going through a bad time."

The next morning, Bruce acted as if nothing had happened. He cooked breakfast for everyone, and asked Senior, "Fred's coming, right?"

Fred was his brother-in-law, married to his sister Angela, who lived nearby in Quesnel.

"Fred's coming," answered Senior.

"Dad," asked Bruce, "why are you so down?"

"I'm not down," he said, "I'm tired."

Fred arrived later that day. As his truck bounced into the campsite, dust flying out like a fan behind it, Bruce smiled. He liked Fred. Handsome and tall, he always knew the right thing to do in an emergency. Bruce felt calmer already.

The morning that Fred and Bruce went out to hunt, Bruce was nagged by a premonition that something was about to happen. While sitting quietly in the grass, in the middle of their silence, a huge cow moose ambled into an algae covered pond and started to graze on submerged grass. Neither man leveled their weapon. The female was out of season, and it was fairly rare to see one. Bruce watched enraptured at what he took to be another sign from God. He looked over at Fred, who was smiling as he gazed at the moose and the water that streamed off her muzzle. *"I love it out here,"* he whispered.

At the conclusion of the week-long hunt, as they were packing up to leave, Bruce said to his father, "You weren't very nice to John. I think you should apologize."

Senior looked at his son in disbelief. Who was the one going crazy here? Bruce may have ranted and raved, but it was Senior who'd lashed out at a dear friend. It reminded Senior of what a good heart his son had. Bruce had always been one to try and make peace in the family.

"You're right, son," said Senior, "You're right."

As for Bruce's explosion earlier in the trip, neither he nor anyone else in the group would ever speak of it to each other again.

November 1982

GOD NEEDED BRUCE for some important task; the signs from the hunting trip convinced him of that. After the moose had been delivered unto them, the white woman began speaking more frequently and with greater intensity. She told Bruce that he was God, the Devil and Revelation 12 and 13. She told him the world was going to end and that he could stop it. *But how?* Bruce shouted aloud after one particularly vivid encounter. *How can I stop the world from ending?*

The woman teased Bruce with the concept of opposites. This "white woman" was God, so as a "black man," Bruce must be the Antichrist. If the world was going to end, then didn't that mean the world was going to begin? And how did the world begin anyway? With the big bang. She kept talking about time. Time goes forward. The opposite is that it goes backward.

Bruce gave up on sleep: He replaced it with a fanatical focus on two chapters in the Book of Revelation, 10 and 11. The Four Horsemen of the Apocalypse. Armageddon. The big bang. The End. It was November, and Bruce believed something was going to happen very soon. Sickened by the prospect of doom, he couldn't eat. One verse kept repeating: "Let the seven thunders utter their voices." Seven. Seven. It meant something.

46

Twenty-four; that meant something, too.

One afternoon in mid-November, Bruce pulled three coffee cups from the cupboard and two from the sink full of dirty dishes. He washed and dried them thoroughly, arranging them on the kitchen table so that they were exactly the same distance apart. Satisfied they were in the right place, he placed a pot of coffee on the stove to brew. At about five p.m., Jerry walked into the apartment. With him was their friend Phil, who, as always, had to duck to avoid hitting his head on the doorframe. The two men were laughing.

"Have some coffee," Bruce offered, pouring coffee into all five cups.

"Thanks Bruce," said Jerry, surprised. Then he looked at the table. "What gives? Who are the other two for?"

"For Don and Gail," Bruce answered, "We have to be together."

"Why?" asked Phil, slurping from his mug.

"Because the world is going to end at 8:00 tonight."

"Well what are we waiting for?" said Phil, throwing one arm up into the air. "Let's go out and spend all our money!"

"I'm serious," said Bruce, his former happy expression now suddenly grave. "We have to be together. Look." Bruce turned on the television. The local news was playing. They all watched: Phil and

Jerry for news of the world ending; Bruce for the hidden sign only he could interpret.

"There it is!" Bruce practically shrieked.

Phil and Jerry looked at each other then at Bruce. "There's what?" they asked in unison.

Bruce grabbed his head with both hands. *"Didn't you see it?"* he demanded, incredulous. *"You've got to believe me,"* Bruce pleaded. "I've been seeing the signs for weeks. Call Don and Gail. Get them over here now!"

Phil and Jerry finished their coffee. "Cool down, Bruce," Jerry said, but picked up the phone and called Don. After a brief, muttered conversation, Jerry hung up.

"Don doesn't want to come over," he reported, "and Gail's home in bed sick."

Bruce shook his head. "No," he said, "this won't do."

Phil sat in the kitchen finishing his coffee while Jerry shoveled cold leftovers from the fridge into his mouth. "God, I'm so hungry!" he exclaimed, rolling his eyes as he swallowed the questionable-looking remnants of a bologna sandwich.

From the living room they could hear Bruce laughing wildly, then, in an instant, declaring that all hell was about to break loose. "It's

Armageddon, I'm telling you!" Bruce shouted from the couch. "Stick with me. You'll see!"

Jerry finished his sandwich. "You know," he whispered to Phil, "I'm really getting tired of this bullshit. Let's go over to Don's for awhile. Maybe wing nut will calm down while we're gone."

"No, no!" Bruce shouted. "We've got to be together," he said, running into the kitchen and blocking the door. Jerry thought, *there's no way he could have heard us.*

"Get out of the way," Phil said, placing his huge, open hand on Bruce's chest and pushing him aside as if he were a gauze curtain. Phil and Jerry proceeded to the front door. Bruce positively hovered around them both, wringing his hands and pleading.

"You guys, *come back,"* he shouted as he watched them leave the apartment.

Bruce paced back and forth in the living room, thinking about what he should do. He alternated between chewing his nails, taking long, deep drags off a cigarette, and staring intently at the television screen. There it was, again — the world was going to end at 8:00 p.m. *that night.*

Outside, a cold, soft rain dripped out of the evening sky, but at 7:30 p.m. Bruce tore down the stairs of the apartment building and onto Lonsdale Avenue, coatless. Don's place was six blocks away. Bruce ran as fast as he could, dodging cars on the busy street, impervious to the honks and gestures of startled drivers.

When Bruce burst into Don's apartment, Phil and Jerry were already there. All three men jumped.

"*Jesus Christ*, Bruce," yelled Don, "are you fucking trying to scare us to death?"

"Where's Gail?" Bruce demanded, "Is she here?"

"No," answered Don, "She's home sick in bed."

"Will you call her, please?" asked Bruce. "It's very important that we're all together by eight p.m."

"I'm not calling her," said Don. "Gail's got the flu, and the world isn't going to end. Why are you acting so crazy?"

Bruce's whole body was quaking. Sweat and rain poured down his forehead into his eyes. He wiped at them with his forearms.

"*Don,*" Bruce pleaded. "You've *got to call Gail*. Here," he said, digging into his pockets, pulling out his keys, wallet and some spare change. He shoved them into Don's unenthusiastic hands. "Take all my possessions. They won't matter soon, *but we've all got to be together by eight tonight*."

"Look, Bruce, you need to calm down. I'm not calling Gail, and that's all there is to it. Here," he said, handing Bruce back his belongings, "take your stuff and stay or go. I don't care, but quit the crazy talk. You're pissing me off."

Bruce's face turned stormy. He furrowed his brows and his eyes flashed with a fury Jerry had never seen before. *"You guys don't believe me!"* Bruce shouted, then stomped out of the living room, through the kitchen and pulled open the door to leave.

A bayonet of fear stabbed him right through the heart.

"The Beast!" he shouted, breathless. *"The Beast. Oh!"* It was hideous and huge, with yellow eyes and fangs dripping blood. It had come for them. Bruce slammed the door before it could get inside.

The three men, mouths agape, stared at Bruce as he fell to his knees and begged Don to call Gail. *"Please, please Don, please call her!"*

Jerry felt something small and sharp flip in his stomach. "Come on Bruce," he said, putting his hand on his friend's shoulder, "It's just the neighbour's dog. The world is not going to end. Come on, get up." Jerry helped Bruce into a standing position and could now feel the totality with which Bruce was shaking. He was surprised his friend could even stay upright. "Sit down for a minute," Jerry said.

Instead, Bruce bolted from the apartment and disappeared into the night.

December 3, 1982

TODD BLACKMAN — STATIONED 2,000 miles away in Ottawa, Ontario — woke with a sense that something was wrong with his twin brother. He was in a time zone three hours ahead and didn't want to call too early, so he waited. At 09:00 EST, he called Bruce.

Bruce Blackman's phone rang at 06:00 in North Vancouver, BC. He grabbed the receiver immediately.

"Bruce," said Todd, surprised he'd picked up the phone so quickly. "Where are you?"

"Todd," said Bruce in a tone Todd had never heard before. "I haven't eaten for two days. I can't sleep. I'm hearing strange things all the time and I'm getting messages from the TV."

"What kind of messages?"

"That the end of the world is coming. The white woman tells me I am Chapter 11 of the Book of Revelations."

"What white woman? Bruce, where is all this coming from?"

"From her, Todd, from the white woman. She is talking to me all the time. I feel like if I go to sleep, she'll kill me."

Todd hadn't anticipated this. He'd never heard his twin brother so distraught. Todd's work shift was about to start. "Bruce, I've got to get to work. Listen, talk to Dad. Tell him how you're feeling. Maybe you could go stay with one of our sisters. I really don't think you should be by yourself."

"It doesn't matter where I am, Todd. She follows me wherever I go. I can't run away."

"Bruce, call Dad. Let him know what's going on. I'll be home in a couple of weeks, and we can talk more then." Todd paused. "Try to stay calm, Bruce. Everything will be OK."

Bruce made his way to work that day, but kept to himself. The other men were more quiet than usual, *probably because they're afraid of me,* Bruce thought. The truck bumped its way along the route toward Deep Cove, a picturesque little ocean inlet on the easternmost point of North Vancouver.

"Look at that, Bruce," one of his coworkers said, gazing out across the water. "The Cove has frozen over. I didn't think salt water could freeze."

"It can't," said Bruce.

This was another sign from God.

That evening, Bruce lay on his couch watching *The Magic Christian* featuring Ringo Starr and Peter Sellers. In the background, behind the soundtrack, Bruce heard a man's voice, dogs barking, and the white woman. Every single scene in the movie spoke to him. He saw the heavens collide. He saw the Devil. He saw the white woman: There she was on the screen; a great, white whore with eyes of fire. "You are God, the Devil and the Antichrist," she said. "You are Zeus."

It was all coming together now: the sounds, the visions, the words. They all whirled around him like a tornado. Bruce pressed his hands against his ears and shut his eyes tight against the spirits that were overtaking him. He heard the Devil say, "I'm going to eat you up, eat you whole."

"No, no," Bruce whimpered. The voices shrieked with delight. Bruce felt the Devil enter his body and snatch his breath away.

When he opened his eyes, he felt nothing. Everything was quiet, except for the television. He knew then what he had to do. The fear was gone.

And so was the Bruce he'd been trying to hang on to for so long.

Two weeks later

JERRY WALKED IN at 11 p.m. to find Bruce on the sofa, pale, damp and tousled. Bruce's red plaid shirt was only partially buttoned, and even those were wrong. The hem of the shirt was three inches longer on one side.

"What would you think if I was God?" Bruce asked.

Jerry laughed, "A pot-smoking God, yeah, I can see that."

"I'm God, Jerry. Believe me. The problem is I'm not sure if I'm supposed to die or the people around me."

Jerry pushed his glasses up on the bridge of his nose and stared at his friend.

"I can't sleep," Bruce complained. "I'm possessed by a female spirit, and if I go to sleep, she'll kill me."

It was stifling hot in the apartment, but Bruce was soaking in a cold sweat, shaking so hard his teeth chattered. Jerry felt that strange sensation in his stomach again, a recognition that something was awfully wrong.

"The Bible," Bruce said, "Jerry, the Bible is telling me that I'm God and the Antichrist. Can you understand that?"

"Bruce," Jerry answered, "I've never been to church in my life."

"In the Book of Revelations, Chapter 10..."

Jerry put a hand on Bruce's arm.

"Bruce," he said, sitting next to his friend on the sofa. "I can't help you with the Bible stuff. Look, you have to talk to someone about this. Do you want me to phone your parents? Who do you want to talk to?"

"There's this Jehovah's Witness guy I talked to once. Can I talk to him?"

Jerry pulled out the telephone book and looked up the number for the crisis hotline. He thought it was a long shot to ask for an emergency number for the Jehovah's Witness hall, but the operator gave it to him, and it led, indeed, to the person to whom Bruce wanted to speak. Jerry called and asked if he would come over. At around midnight, Zoltan LaBrosse arrived at the apartment and knocked on the door. As soon as the short haired, crisply dressed young man entered the apartment, Bruce exhaled noisily, and shot Jerry a smile of relief. Bruce rose and approached Zoltan with crossed arms. "We have to go to a Kingdom Hall right now," Bruce demanded.

Zoltan paused for a moment then stated calmly, "Given the hour, Bruce, I don't think that's a good idea."

Bruce: "I can't stay here."

Zoltan: "OK, we can go to my place if you want."

Jerry handed Bruce a coat and watched as he and Zoltan left the apartment. Jerry shook his head. What in the world was happening to his friend?

It was freezing cold outside. "Thanks for seeing me," Bruce said to Zoltan as they shivered their way to Zoltan's apartment just a few blocks away. Every word out of Bruce's mouth created a perfect, little white cloud.

"It's OK, Bruce," said Zoltan. "It's good to see you again, but I'm sorry you're having a hard time." Bruce took two deep breaths, wiped his nose, then announced, "Zoltan, I'm possessed."

Once inside his apartment, Zoltan made a quick call to another Witness, Bob Kothe, and asked him to come over. While they waited, Bruce told Zoltan about how he'd begun to hear voices recently and how another personality was speaking to him.

"It's talking to me about opposites," Bruce began. "Starting with my name. My name is Black-man, but I'm actually a white man. I'm a Black-man, but the voice I hear is a white-woman. Time goes forward, so therefore it must go backward." Bob Kothe arrived, also meticulously dressed in a white shirt and tie, with close-cropped hair. Zoltan made the introductions, and Bruce continued. "The woman tells me I am God, so I must be the Antichrist."

"Bruce, hang on a sec," said Bob. "Are you doing any drugs?"

"Yeah, I smoked a joint earlier, but that's all. I don't drink."

"Well," said Zoltan, "let's talk about what the Bible says about drugs. Without going into it too deeply, Bruce, as a Jehovah's Witness you must strive to remain separate from the world that is morally contaminated and under the control of Satan."

"That's right, that's right," Bruce said, becoming animated at the mention of Satan. Maybe these guys could help him after all.

Zoltan and Bob took turns explaining the expected behavior of a Jehovah's Witness but Bruce kept arguing that whatever they told him, Bruce needed to convert into an opposite.

"The only part of the Bible that matters," Bruce said, "is Chapter 10 of Revelations. I am Chapter 10. The rest of the Bible is meaningless. Do you know what the Tree of Knowledge is? Catholics think it's an apple. Jehovah's Witnesses think it's a pear, but what is the real Tree of Knowledge?"

Zoltan and Bob waited for Bruce to answer his rhetorical question, but he trailed off.

"Bruce," said Zoltan, "Regarding Revelations…you can't just focus on one part of a whole. You'll lack context. You'll fail to see the full meaning. That makes sense, doesn't it?"

"It does," said Bruce. "You know I'm a born-again Christian."

"Have you accepted the Bible as truth?"

"Some of it."

"Have you been baptized?"

"No. What do you guys think about Buddhism?"

"The only religious teaching we accept is the truth and reject all others that are false."

"Hmmm," said Bruce, scratching his head. "I think that you're wrong. I think you need to be open to *all* religions. I am."

Zoltan and Bob listened patiently while Bruce talked in circles about God, the Devil, and the end of the world. He barely paused for breath.

It was now 1:30 a.m. and Zoltan was tired, exhausted by Bruce's incessant and mostly incoherent babbling. "Bruce," he said, "Can we feed you before you leave? Your stomach's been growling the whole time. You must be hungry."

"Yeah, I'm hungry."

Bruce ate the sandwich hand-made by Zoltan, then stood up to leave. In the doorway, he shook both men's hands and told them he felt better.

"Sorry I kept you up 'til two a.m. Maybe we can finish this another time. Can I call you?"

"Sure," said Zoltan, "you can call us any time for any reason."

"Good luck, Bruce," said Bob as he closed the door.

They never heard from him again.

REVELATION

BY MID-DECEMBER, Bruce knew that the world was going to end, and that it would probably end on the thirty-first. He also knew that this end of the world really meant the beginning and that it fell to him to save the universe. Other than dragging himself to work, Bruce spent all his time studying the Bible, reading mythology and any numerology text he could get his hands on. Each day brought a new insight. The great white whore kept insisting he must see God. Over and over he read Chapter 10 in the Book of Revelation, focusing on verses eight, nine, and 10 and the "little book." The idea of the "little book" became an obsession, as did eating it. Bruce had read something about how the rituals of communion — eating the flesh and the blood — also included the collection of semen and menstrual blood. If this was true, then "eating the little book" meant men and women had to eat their own secretions. Bruce began to masturbate and eat his ejaculate. This simple act brought him closer and closer to God. He could feel it.

Everywhere in the Book of Revelation there were signs. In 6:1, the Lamb opened the first four of seven seals. The Lamb was Jesus Christ. Jesus Christ was Bruce's brother Raymond, twin to Ricky, who had died at birth. Bruce believed that The Four Horsemen of the

Apocalypse were the two sets of Blackman twins. And — he reasoned — if Randy were Jesus Christ, then all the Blackmans were part of the family of God. It made sense, then, that they must all strive to see God, because every one of the Blackman clan had a role to play in helping to keep the world from blowing up.

Bruce neither ate nor slept for days on end. On the fifteenth, Jerry was fed up with Bruce's late night rants and his endless pacing around the apartment. Jerry was also deeply worried about his friend who was no longer anything like the Bruce he'd known since high school. "Bruce," said Jerry, "I think you should go stay with your sister Karon and her husband, at least for a couple of days. Someone needs to watch you."

"I'm already being watched," Bruce said, "The great white whore sees everything I do."

"No, I just mean someone should be watching out for you – you know, cooking for you, doing your laundry, making sure you get some sleep."

"I'm OK here."

"No, really Bruce, I think you need to be with your family now."

Bruce stared at his friend. *Of course!* Bruce thought. *Get next to the family.* Things would be easier to figure out with them close by. Plus, he needed to convince all of them to eat their "book" and he could only do that in person. "I'm going," he said.

"Good," Jerry nodded.

Later that day while driving to his sister Karon's house, the voices announced, "You are the Angel of Revelations." The number seven kept invading his thoughts. In the Book of Revelation there were the seven stars, and the seven candlesticks, and in Revelation 10:3 "The seven thunders uttered their voices." *It must mean my siblings,* Bruce thought. But there were only six of them, excluding the deceased Raymond. That could only mean one thing: One of his sisters must be pregnant.

Bruce recalled the hunting trip when he'd seen that sign from God in the sky; two planet shaped clouds colliding to form a star. The Star of David. It represented the new universe. But there was another star — the Satanic Star — that was moving toward the Star of David. When the two collided, the world would end. That was his job then, to keep the two stars from colliding, and to keep the Star of David intact.

When he arrived at his sister's house on Secret Court in Coquitlam, her husband Robert was home. He'd booked off sick from his work as a heavy duty mechanic for the District of North Vancouver. Even though Robert was only in his mid-thirties, his sandy brown hair was already beginning to gray at the temples. He was not exactly handsome, but his plain features formed a pleasant enough collaboration. Bruce thought there wasn't a thing that could bring a scowl to Robert's face.

"I want to stay with you a few days, can I?" asked Bruce, when Robert looked surprised to see him. "I've got some things I need to figure out." Bruce clutched a Bible in his right hand.

"You can stay," Robert answered. "Is everything OK?"

"No, not really."

"All right. Stay as long as you want, and I can drive you to work." Robert had married Karon six years earlier, and had become a beloved member of the family. Bruce liked Robert and the feeling was mutual. In fact, Robert had helped Bruce get his job with the sanitation department. There wasn't a single thing Robert wouldn't do for Karon or her family. He adored her.

Bruce strode to the couch and sat down. "Robert, come here," demanded Bruce, smacking the spot on the sofa next to him. Robert sat. This close, he recoiled a bit from the stink of cigarette smoke and sour, days-old sweat emanating from Bruce.

"Is Karon pregnant?" Bruce asked.

"No," Robert answered, "Why?"

Bruce proceeded to read all of Chapter 12 of the Book of Revelation, and some of Chapter 11. Robert listened patiently, waiting for a moment when he could cram a word in between the vehemently spoken verses. Then suddenly, Bruce veered off.

"Robert," Bruce asked, "do you know about the Tree of Knowledge? Every man and woman has their own book, and they must eat from it in order to see God. Your book is your semen, and Karon's book is her menstrual blood. Is she on her period?"

"Yes, Bruce, but you shouldn't be talking about these things."

"I've already eaten my book and you need to eat yours." Bruce stared at Robert, who could not form a single word. The two stared at each other for what felt like minutes, when Robert suddenly remembered he needed to fetch his wife from work.

"I'll only be gone 30 minutes or so," he said, "Are you OK by yourself?"

Bruce waved him away, like shooing a fly.

While Robert was off to get Karon, Bruce thought through the problem of convincing his family members that eating their book would bring them closer to God. This was going to be a lot harder than he had anticipated. But in the half hour it took for Robert to leave and return with Karon, Bruce had hatched a plan.

"I'm the Antichrist," Bruce announced when they walked in the house. Karon and Robert looked at each other.

"I'm going to go change my clothes," said Karon, removing her woolen winter coat and hanging it up in the hallway closet. Robert unzipped his blue down jacket and handed it to Karon. After she'd hung it in the closet, she left Robert and Bruce alone in the living room.

"What do you want for dinner?" Robert asked, when Bruce suddenly shouted, "Karon!" He bolted out of the living room, running in search of his sister. When Bruce reappeared, Karon was with him, blushing, and scolding him. *"I don't want to ever hear any of that nonsense again."* She wagged a finger at her brother. Bruce dug his hands deep in his jean pockets and hopped from one foot to the next as if he were on hot coals. Karon glared at her husband and threw her hands up in exasperation.

In bed that night, Bruce thought about all the numbers that seemed to have special meaning. There were six points on the Star of David. His parents represented the total star, and he, Todd, Ricky, Angela, Karon and Bobi each represented one point of the star. He couldn't shake the feeling that one of his sisters was pregnant. That would change the numbers and the "seven" would make sense. Tomorrow, he'd call Bobi and Angela and ask their status.

Next on his mind was the number twelve. Jesus had 12 disciples. Counting all the Blackmans and the in-laws, there were 12. That part of the puzzle was solved.

But the number seven was still bothering him. Seven. December 25. Two plus five equals seven. Was that going to be the end of the world? Bruce and Todd were born on October 24. Angela was born on October thirty-first, seven days apart. Angela was the second born, Bruce was the fifth. Two plus five equals seven. Angela and Todd were an important part of the solution. If Bruce was an Antichrist, they must be Antichrists, too.

The next day, Bruce stayed home from work while Karon and Robert went off to their jobs. If Karon wasn't going to eat her book on her own, he'd have to help her. Searching the house, he found a wastebasket in the master bathroom and dumped it in the center of Karon and Robert's bed. He found what he was looking for: a discarded menstrual pad. Bruce tore out the center and squeezed what he could into a Dixie cup. It was only a couple of drops, but that's all he needed. Down in the kitchen, he pulled half a quart of orange juice out of the refrigerator and poured it into a blender. To that he added his sister's blood, two pages torn from his Bible, and two packets of chicken soup. He turned on the blender and watched the ingredients whirl round and round until they transformed into a thick, orange-colored pulp. Bruce poured the lumpy concoction into a wine carafe and stuck it in the refrigerator.

He telephoned his sister Bobi. "Are you pregnant?" he asked. "No," she answered, "Why?" "Then it must be Angela," he said and hung up the phone.

He telephoned Angela in Quesnel. Fred answered the phone. "Is my sister pregnant?" Bruce asked, dispensing with niceties.

"We haven't told anyone," answered Fred. "How did you know?"

WHILE BRUCE WAS busy making drinks and placing calls, there had been a flurry of telephone activity between Karon and Bobi. One of the sisters checked in with Bruce's roommate Jerry who confirmed that Bruce was "wacked out." Bobi spoke with Senior and Irene who expressed utter frustration.

"Honestly, Honey," Irene sighed, "I don't know how to help my son."

What happened next would propel them to action.

When Karon came home from work that day, Bruce was waiting. Impatient, he wouldn't let her even take off her coat or put down her purse.

"I made something special for you," Bruce announced. Karon sighed and rolled her eyes. She plopped herself down at the table and watched Bruce pull the carafe out of the fridge. The contents had settled and looked revolting. He quickly stirred them with a wooden spoon, poured some into a wine glass and handed it to her. He sat across from her, staring. She sniffed the beverage and made a face. "I'm not drinking this. It smells bad. What is it?"

"Drink it Karon. I made it for you. It's very, *very* important that you *drink this now*."

Karon shook her head. "No, I won't."

Bruce slammed both hands down on the table, making her gasp. "*Drink it,* Karon. I'm not going to tell you again."

She had never seen her brother so intense, so hateful, so not himself. Well, what would it hurt to drink a little? It would calm him down, hopefully. She put the wine glass to her mouth and tilted it so a little of the concoction ran into her mouth.

Bruce raised his eyebrows and smiled.

Karon worked the liquid around in her mouth then made a noise like she was going to vomit. She ran to the sink and spat it out.

"God, Bruce, that's *disgusting!*" She poured the contents of the wine glass into the sink.

Robert walked in from work. "What's going on?" he asked. Karon shook her head and left the room.

"I made her eat her book," said Bruce, smiling, relieved.

"What?" Robert felt his face grow hot. "Bruce, *what did you do?"*

Bruce explained what was in the concoction. Robert himself wanted to vomit.

"I've left the rest in the refrigerator," Bruce said, "in case she wants some later."

Robert found his wife. "Bruce needs help," is all he would say. He couldn't — and never would — bring himself to tell her what she'd just had in her mouth.

"Something has changed," Karon told Robert. "I'm afraid of him. I won't stay here while he's here."

"Well, how's *that* going to work? He's got to stay somewhere."

"I'm going to stay with the neighbours."

"Don't you think you're over-reacting?"

"No, I don't. This is not the Bruce I know. He's scaring me. I'll come back once he's gone."

Karon called Bobi. Bobi called a psychiatrist and asked him to come see her brother. In the meantime, Robert dumped the contents of the wine carafe into the sink and ran the garbage disposal for a very long time.

ON DECEMBER 16, at 11:00 in the morning, Bruce called his brother Todd in Ottawa, 2,000 miles and three time zones away. Todd was working in the military pay office, and things were busy on his end.

"Todd," said Bruce, "I really have to talk to you. Do you have a minute?"

Todd had never heard his brother sound so anxious or agitated. "Bruce, I'm working right now and there are people waiting in line. Look, I'll have to call you back, OK?"

As Todd went about his administrative chores — making small talk with the other military personnel who'd come to collect their pay — he couldn't help but feel rattled by this change in his brother's demeanor. Never once — even as kids — had he ever seen Bruce lose his composure as completely as he had during the hunting trip. Nor had Todd ever noticed the edge in his brother's voice that seemed to get more ragged every time he heard it. As Todd prepared to finish up with his last customers, the phone rang again.

"Todd," Bruce said, his voice quaking as if holding back tears, "Do you love me?"

On Todd's end of the phone, he looked across the counter at the three people waiting for their paycheques.

"Bruce," he said, "Look, just wait a minute and I'll call you back."

"No!" shouted Bruce. "Todd, *you've got to tell me you love me. I'm really, really scared.* Please, *please* tell me you love me."

Todd began to speak, but Bruce cut him off, his voice suddenly — eerily — calm: "Todd, do you know what the Tree of Knowledge is? It's your 'book.' Do you know what your book is?"

"No."

"It's your semen. You must eat from the Tree of Knowledge in order to understand. You must eat your semen to know God."

70

"Stop talking nonsense."

"No, really, you have to do it," he said. "Promise me you'll do it. Go do it now and call me back."

At 4:00 p.m., after Todd had finished work, he called his brother. Their mostly rambling conversation lasted an hour. Bruce was convinced the world was going to end and that Todd would play a big role in helping to stop it. "Todd," asked Bruce, "when can I see you? When can we be together?"

"Bruce, I was just there for the hunting trip. I can't come back until Christmas. Can you hang on until then?"

"I don't know. I guess if the world doesn't end first." Silence. "Todd," Bruce paused, his voice breaking, "Do you love me?"

"Of course I love you, Bruce. You're my brother. Just hang in there. Everything will be OK. We'll talk more when I come home in a few weeks, OK?" Todd paused. "Promise me you won't do anything stupid."

Phone records show that on this day Bruce called eight numbers across the country, including the Canadian Department of National Defence. He also attempted to call the Pope in Rome and Poland.

Thirty-two miles away in Vancouver — as Bruce was talking to his brother and making other calls — psychiatrist Dr. Jeff Jefson received a telephone call from Bobi who stated that her brother Bruce was in a highly confused state and babbling all sorts of religious nonsense. Could Dr. Jefson please come to the house in Coquitlam to examine her brother? After a brief discussion, Jefson agreed.

It was later in the day when Jefson arrived with a psychiatric nurse in tow. The address on Secret Court was a little too secret. They got lost while trying to find the place.

When Jefson entered, Bruce was thumbing through a Bible, mumbling with intense focus passages from the Book of Revelation. Bobi and Senior both watched Bruce, their faces rigid and unsmiling. Robert had left to go for a walk. He'd had enough of Bruce's ramblings. And Karon had made it clear she wasn't coming home until "that nut" was out of their house for good.

"Hello, Bruce," said Jefson, extending his hand. Bruce looked up from the Bible and blinked at the doctor through the greasy bangs that partially obscured his eyes, then gazed back down at his Bible. Even though Bruce had only looked at him for a moment, Jefson noticed right away that he was distracted and haggard, probably from too little sleep.

Bruce looked up again. *"Someone contact the Zionist Church right now,"* he demanded. "Find out how many candles they use on their candelabra." Under his breath, Bruce mumbled words unintelligible except for the numbers six and seven. "Someone *call them!"* he insisted. He paused. "I know they use seven."

Bobi wrung her hands while she looked first at Bruce, then the doctor, and back again. Jefson nodded to Bobi to go ahead and call. Roberta telephoned a church and reported back that they use six. Dr.

72

Jefson watched Bruce for a reaction: Bruce was unfazed. "That's OK," he said, nodding. "It makes sense. Raymond is dead." Bobi cringed. "Six of us living and one of us dead," said Bruce. "Six candles."

"Bruce," said Jefson, trying to make eye contact. "Can you tell me what's going on?"

"I need to get the family all together in one place. I'm possessed by the Devil. I'm hearing voices from a woman. She knows everything, she sees everything, she's all-powerful. I'm trapped in time."

"What does that mean, Bruce, 'trapped in time'?"

"Déjà vu."

Bruce began reading from the Book of Revelation, then careened off into a diatribe about time going forward and backward, that all things are opposite. At some point in his splintered ramblings, Bruce confessed, "I am the Antichrist."

To Jefson, despite all the disjointed talk, Bruce did not seem violent.

"Bruce," said the doctor, "can I examine you?" He took Bruce's arm and wrapped the blood pressure cuff around his small bicep. Through this one point of contact, Jefson could feel Bruce's entire body thrumming with adrenalin. While taking his blood pressure, Jefson looked again in Bruce's eyes and saw what looked like fear. The blood pressure reading was 140/90, somewhat elevated from the norm.

73

"Bruce," said Jefson, removing the cuff and handing it to the nurse, "your blood pressure is a little too high. You need some medicine to bring it down."

"OK."

Senior offered this: "I have high blood pressure too, Bruce."

Jefson added for good measure, "It will also help you get rid of some of your tension."

The nurse rolled up Bruce's sleeve, then injected 25 milligrams of Modecate, a long-acting tranquilizer, into Bruce's protruding, blue vein. Bruce took a couple of deep breaths, then his eyes fluttered. Within minutes, he looked as if he were about to fall asleep. Together, Senior and Bobi breathed a sigh of relief. Bruce closed his eyes. The Bible sat next to him, open, on the couch. The ramblings, for now at least, had ceased.

Jefson talked with Senior.

"This injection should last anywhere from two weeks to a month. It'll help, but he'll need to take an oral tranquilizer daily. Here's a prescription." Dr. Jefson scribbled on a prescription pad, then ripped off the sheet and handed it to Senior.

"Let's get him in to my office soon, but before that, I'd like him to attend the Coquitlam Mental Health Centre before the end of this week." Jefson paused, "I think we may have to consider putting Bruce in a place where he can get some supervised help," he told Senior. Mr.

74

Blackman looked down at the floor and shook his head. Jefson continued: "I'm not telling you to do it now, but at least you'll have this if you need it."

Senior nodded, his lips pursed. Jefson had seen this before: parents doing their best to hold themselves together while they watched their children fall apart. He filled out a pink committal form, dated it December 16 and signed his name. "Here," he said, handing it to Senior. "If he requires hospitalization and won't go willingly, you can use this."

Before Jefson left the house, after approximately 40 minutes with the family, they confirmed that Bruce would attend the Coquitlam Mental Health Centre within the week.

"We'll make *sure* of it," promised Senior.

THREE DAYS LATER, 400 miles away, Bruce's sister Angela woke from a deep sleep at 5:30 a.m. to find a man standing over her bed. She screamed, waking her husband Fred. He was about to lunge for the stranger when Angela heard her brother's voice say, "Don't worry, Angela, it's just me."

"*Jesus Christ, Bruce*," yelled Fred. "You scared us half to death."

"God, Bruce, why are you here?" Angela asked.

"I really need to talk to you, Angela. Can I stay?"

Angela blinked and took three deep breaths to calm herself. "Go to the spare room. I'm going to try and get back to sleep. You go get some sleep too."

"I can't sleep anymore," said Bruce.

"Then go lie down and be quiet," said Fred. "Your sister needs her rest."

Via the sister-gossip-grapevine, Angela knew that there'd been something going on with Bruce back home, but she'd not experienced any of his strange behavior first-hand. Other than being shaken by his sudden, bizarre appearance in her bedroom, she wasn't overly concerned. This was Bruce, after all; happy-go-lucky, give-you-the-shirt-off-his-back Bruce.

An hour later, as Fred prepared for work, Angela joined him in the bathroom to pee. She was almost half-way through her pregnancy and was having to go to the bathroom more and more often, and more urgently. Fred was shaving, the hot water running a constant stream into the sink. She watched him slide the razor up his neck to his jaw and chin. She loved Fred's profile. He had perfect features — almost too perfect. Angela was probably the least attractive of the Blackman children, but she was still pretty. Next to Fred, though, she looked plain and common with her auburn hair that always frizzed. "My movie star husband," she called him.

"Why would your brother come up here in the middle of the night, and why didn't anyone from your family let us know he was coming?" Fred asked as he continued the shaving operation.

Angela remained on the toilet even though she'd finished. She shook her head, "Fred, I have no idea what's going on. Mom and Dad told me he was going through a difficult time and Bobi told me he's been acting crazy but I never figured he'd just show up here out of the blue."

"You're right about it being crazy," Fred said, soaking a facecloth in hot water, then wiping the remnants of shaving cream off his face. "Maybe I shouldn't go to work today."

"Why not?"

"I'm not sure I'm comfortable leaving him alone with you."

"Who, *Bruce?*" Angela practically laughed. "Bruce wouldn't hurt a fly. Don't worry, I can handle him." She stood up, walked behind her husband and wrapped her arms around his middle. She rested her chin on his shoulder and they looked at themselves in the mirror. Angela smiled. She would soon give Irene and Senior their first grandchild, and

Fred was the kindest man she'd ever met. Even with her younger brother facing some sort of personal crisis, Angela felt deeply happy.

"Have a good day at work," she told Fred, kissing him on his neck. She climbed back into bed, the covers forming a cocoon still warm from their bodies.

Later that morning, Angela walked into the kitchen to find Bruce sitting at the table, both legs bouncing, both hands drumming on the table. Angela yawned and said, "I feel like having an omelet. Do you want one?"

"I'll make it for you," Bruce offered. Angela tightened the belt on her robe then stretched her arms to the ceiling and yawned once more before she sat down at the kitchen table to watch. Bruce set about cracking eggs and whisking them together with other ingredients he would only refer to as "secret." Angela observed him from behind. He seemed all right, although his clothes hung off his frame and his skin was *so* pale, as if he'd lived in a cave his whole life. Angela always thought Bruce was the best looking of all the boys, but right now he looked and smelled like someone who had just come in from living off the streets. But Bruce was actually a pretty good cook: On hunting trips, according to Todd and Senior, Bruce often stayed in camp to cook the meals. Angela closed her eyes while Bruce hit the whisk on the edge of a ceramic bowl: *Bang, bang, bang, bang*. She heard the egg mixture sizzle a little when he poured it into the pan. When she opened her eyes, he stood before her, brandishing the omelet on a plate as if it were the finest gourmet concoction ever created. "Your breakfast," he announced, smiling, placing it before her with a flourish.

In that moment, Bruce looked happy. Right now, while he watched Angela eat her omelet, he looked as beautiful and guileless as when he'd been a child.

With her fork, Angela cut off a corner of the omelet and put it in her mouth. After just two chews, she grimaced in disgust. "Bruce," she said, forcing herself to swallow, "I don't want to hurt your feelings, but I don't think I can eat this." He looked panicked. "Try another bite," he insisted.

She put a small forkful in her mouth but this time the taste made her gag. "No, Bruce, I just can't eat it, I'm sorry. I think there might be something wrong with the eggs."

Gunner, the family dog, sat at Angela's feet, tongue wagging, his wide brown eyes fixed longingly on her unfinished breakfast. Angela stood and walked to the dog's dish, Gunner practically dancing on his hind legs in a circle by her side. She scraped her plate into his dish. Gunner finished it in three bites, tail wagging furiously.

Later that afternoon, Gunner fell into a deep sleep and wouldn't wake up. By evening, Angela was beyond worried. She shook the dog until he opened his eyes, but he appeared not to know where he was. Gunner's glassy stare looked past her and his tongue lolled out the side of his mouth. Angela didn't feel so hot either. Fred pulled Gunner upright and watched as the dog staggered into the wall, then fell onto his side. Over and over again, Fred tried to get Gunner to walk, but the dog was completely and utterly disoriented.

"Oh my God, what could be wrong with him?" Angela asked, rubbing her belly. At four and a half months pregnant, morning sickness was nothing new to her, but this felt different. "The last thing I fed him this morning was that omelet. Maybe he has food poisoning. Oh my God, maybe *I* have food poisoning!" Angela looked up at Bruce who was biting his nails, staring intently at the dog.

"Bruce?" she demanded, "what do you know about this?"

He just stared at the dog as it lay panting on its side.

"Bruce!" she shouted.

He looked at her with a face devoid of expression. He said flatly, "The dog wasn't supposed to eat the pills. You were."

"What?" Angela gasped, incredulous.

"God wanted me to give you those pills, because your child is going to do something. God made the doctor give me those pills so I could give them to your unborn baby."

In the shocked silence that followed, the only sounds were Gunner panting, and the slow drip, drip, drip of the kitchen faucet.

The silence seemed to go on forever until Fred exploded.

"Get out," he said, striding over to Bruce, fury reddening his face. "Leave this house now and don't come back. You could have *killed* your sister and the baby!"

Fred scooped up Gunner and took him to the truck. "Find out what those pills are," he called over his shoulder, "and how many he put in the omelet."

Bruce showed Angela the pill canister and its prescription label for Mellaril. She wrote it down. "How many pills?" she asked.

"Seven."

"Oh my God, Bruce. *The dog could die!"*

"They weren't meant for the dog, Angela."

Bruce heard the truck door slam. Fred came back into the house to get his wife. "How do you feel?" he asked her. "Are you all right?" Angela rubbed her belly and nodded. Fred turned to his brother-in-law. "Bruce, we have to get this dog to the vet or I'd stay here and eject you myself. You better be gone by the time we get back."

Bruce caught the next bus home.

Shortly after taking Gunner to the vet, Angela told Fred she felt something might be very wrong with the baby. Fred drove his wife to the hospital where she would remain for eight days. The doctors said they should be prepared to lose their unborn child.

WHEN DR. JEFSON learned about Bruce's impulsive trip to Quesnel, he was shocked that Bruce's family had allowed him to go at all, especially unsupervised. When Senior responded that Bruce had left without any fanfare or notice, Jefson was disturbed on a number of levels: the medication he'd prescribed should be doing a better job of evening out Bruce's erratic thinking, and his behavior should be more predictable than this now that his symptoms were being managed by medication. He told Senior, "Don't let him drive."

At an appointment on December 24, four days after his impulsive trip to Angela's, Bruce came to Jefson's office accompanied by Todd, Ricky and Senior. To Jefson, Bruce seemed calmer, and the fearfulness in his eyes was gone.

"How are you feeling, Bruce?" Jefson asked.

Bruce leaned back in his chair and closed his eyes.

"Bruce?"

He looked at the doctor. "I'm tired from the flu."

"How's everything at home?" Jefson asked to no one in particular.

"Better," said Senior, and Todd nodded in agreement. Ricky's right leg bounced and he chewed his nails.

"Ricky, what do you think?" asked Jefson.

"I dunno," answered Ricky, "I guess so." From conversations with Senior and Irene, Jefson knew that Ricky had become a source of concern to them: he was skipping school, drinking, doing drugs. Was it a reaction to everything that was going on with Bruce, or was it a typical 16-year-old rebelling against his parents?

Jefson looked at Todd who — even though he was Bruce's identical twin — bore little resemblance now. Short-haired Todd sat tall with a straight spine, his expression snapped to attention, his hands in his lap. Even in his off time he was still all military. Bruce's hair was long and greasy. He slouched, as if his shoulders were balancing a giant anvil, and his blue plaid flannel shirt looked as though it had been slept in every night for a month. They couldn't be more different.

"She did talk to me, you know," said Bruce. "I'm not making that up."

"I know you're not making it up, Bruce," said Jefson. "Are you hearing her now?"

"Not now, no. But I remember every word of it. Every word."

Jefson made a note that for the first time in his presence while talking about the white woman, Bruce did not seem anxious or frightened.

"Are you taking your pills four times a day?" Jefson asked.

"He better be," said Senior.

"I better be," echoed Bruce. "I better be."

Jefson did not press for an answer.

AS CHRISTMAS APPROACHED, Bruce obsessed over the family being together.

"Why do Angela and Fred have to be up in Peachland?" he asked his mother.

"Because," said Irene, "every year they alternate. This year they're visiting Fred's parents."

On Christmas Eve, Bruce called up to Peachland, a beautiful area in middle southern British Columbia, named for the fruit the town grew as its industry. "Fred," Bruce said, once he got his brother-in-law on the line, "Angela needs to come home. The family has to be together."

"She's not coming Bruce. "

"Let me talk to her."

When Angela took the phone, Bruce heard her sigh. "What," she demanded.

"Angela, the family has to be together. You need to come down here immediately."

"I'm not coming down and that's that."

"But Angela…"

"No! I told you. Let me talk to Mom."

"Angela, time is running out. Something is going to happen either on Christmas or on the thirty-first, but either way, you've got to be here with us."

"I'm hanging up if you don't let me talk to Mom."

"She's part of the star…"

Bruce heard a click. Angela had disconnected their call.

Later, Angela called and spoke with their parents. "Bruce," said Senior after he'd talked to Angela, "when did you take your pills?"

"My pills?"

Senior went to the upstairs bathroom and came down with the bottle of Mellaril.

"Take the goddamn pill, *now*."

"I don't want to."

Senior slammed his hand down on the kitchen table. "Bruce, I swear to God I will have them lock you up. Now, *take the goddamn pill*."

Irene filled a glass with water and brought it over. She handed it to Bruce who took it from her, never breaking the angry stare between him and his father.

"And I'm going to make sure you take every one of those pills, every day, if it's the last thing I do," said Senior, getting a little breathless.

"Honey," said Irene, putting her hand in the center of his back.

"My blood pressure," he said. "I need to sit down."

Senior made sure Bruce took his medicine, and Christmas came and went without incident. Bruce and Todd even went skiing at Grouse Mountain.

"How was he?" Senior asked Todd when they returned.

"He was fine, though he had to smoke a joint first."

"Well, I should tell you this now before you hear it from Bobi."

"What?"

"Karon and Robert have separated."

"What? Why?"

"Karon's trying to decide whether or not she wants to keep working or stop working and have children. She says she can't do that with Robert around. She gets too confused by her feelings."

"Wow, I am really sorry to hear that," said Todd. "Is Robert OK?"

"I haven't talked to him, but you know Robert. Whatever Karon wants, Karon gets. She's going to be staying with your sister Bobi."

"Well," said Todd, "when this family rattles off the track, we really go all out, don't we."

"I'm not sure that's something to be proud of," said Senior, running his hand through his salt and pepper hair. "But speaking of proud...Todd, I never tell you enough because I'm too wrapped in Bruce's problem, but the whole family is proud of you. I hope you know that."

WHEN CHRISTMAS CAME and went without incident, Bruce re-evaluated the situation. While he wasn't talking as much about his possession, he still heard the voice of the great white whore. He still felt possessed by time. He still fixated on the Book of Revelation. The other voices told him he was Zeus, because that rhymed with Bruce. On New Year's Eve, Bruce went to his appointment with Dr. Jefson alone.

"Dr. Jefson," he said, "Can you tell me what happened when we first met?"

"Are you having trouble remembering?"

"I can't really tell things apart. Like if I was sick, were the messages from sickness or were they especially for me?"

"What do you mean?"

"Well, like Todd and me. We're twins but we're opposite. Now, is that the truth or is that my sickness? No, it's the truth. So, if it's the truth, then isn't everything in my life supposed to be opposite?"

"Why would everything in your life be opposite?"

"Because the doctor told me I was rare."

"What doctor?"

"The one who said I was a mirror twin."

"That was a long time ago, Bruce."

"But I remember it. I remember that but I don't remember what happened yesterday."

"Sometimes the medication makes you forget things."

"I don't know if I'm here or if I'm dreaming."

"You're not dreaming, Bruce. I'm real. The chair you're sitting in is real."

Bruce stared at the doctor, who continued, "The good news is you're getting better. Just keep taking your meds and try not to worry so much."

IN EARLY JANUARY, Bruce returned to work as a swamper.

"So, love, how long do ye plan on stayin' *this* time?" asked Kevin, a short muscular Irishman who had yet to show up to work sober. "We missed yer wee little ass."

Bruce stared at him with such intensity that he could swear he saw the blood drain from Kevin's face. Behind Kevin, Bruce saw another worker, someone he didn't recognize, wiping at his eyes and nose, as if he were crying and trying to smear away the evidence. Bruce smiled. He could ruin any of these people just by looking at them, and now they knew it. They finally figured out he was Satan.

The men kept their distance and Bruce focused on his work. As usual, Kevin was on the lookout for women, and every time he saw one he'd whistle to the crew through the gap in his yellowed teeth.

"Lookee there!" alerted Kevin, and all the men turned to watch a young, pale woman in a black, ankle length coat cross the street behind them. Bruce saw her look at him and mouth the words, "You are Time." He quickly checked the faces of his co-workers. None of them registered anything but their typical horniness. If the great white whore was showing up in public, it meant that the end was getting closer.

The next afternoon, the sanitation crew was stopped because the garbage truck appeared to be overweight. Bruce and the crew knew that it was. This was a serious offense and that verdict almost always meant losing one's job. Bruce was eerily calm while the truck was weighed and

91

the finding announced: the weight was within the acceptable range. Immediately, the tension popped like a balloon. Kevin jumped up and down and danced a little jig. They all celebrated this close call with big sighs, laughter, and slaps on the back, except for Bruce, who had remained stoic through the whole ordeal. He knew this for sure: The truck had clearly been overweight, but God intervened.

It was another sign.

TWO YEARS EARLIER, Senior had applied on Bruce's behalf to Selkirk College in Nelson, 400 miles away in eastern British Columbia. Since Bruce was good with machinery, becoming a certified millwright would give him job options currently not available to him on his current non-career trajectory. Bruce hadn't participated in the process; he felt overwhelmed by the notion of having to try and succeed in school again.

Unexpectedly, an acceptance letter came in the mail in the second week of January.

"Bruce, look at this!" Senior said, wagging it in front of Bruce's face. Bruce grabbed it from him and read it, slowly, mouthing the words, his brow furrowed. Senior waited patiently, knowing it took Bruce longer to read than most people.

"Dad, I don't want to go."

Senior's smile disappeared. "Why not? This is a great opportunity for you. You're so good with engines and fixing things."

"I don't feel right about leaving. The family should be together."

"Bruce," said Senior, "Look, you can't be a part-time sanitation worker forever. Do you want to earn minimum wage for the rest of your life? Having certification will really make a difference in your career."

"But Dad," Bruce began. He stopped when he saw the hope in his father's face, a chance for his Dad to be happy. There was no point fighting it. And Bruce felt bad — he'd never seen his father so tired and stressed lately, as if he'd aged 10 years in just a few months.

"All right," said Bruce, "I'll go."

"We'll celebrate tonight!" Senior announced. Bruce went upstairs and lay down. *Bruce*, he heard in the distance. It was the white woman. *Bruce, it's coming.* The voice was faint, far away, quiet enough that Bruce was able to drift fitfully off to sleep for just a little while.

After napping, Bruce drove to his apartment on Lonsdale to gather some clothes. Jerry was there, surprised when Bruce walked in.

God, Jerry thought, as he quickly assessed his friend's condition. *What has happened to you?*

Bruce looked almost skeletal. His face was ghostly pale, except for the dark circles under his eyes. His hair looked ink-black, greasy from lack of washing. And despite the fact they were able to carry on a conversation, Bruce's mind seemed far, far away.

"What's up, Bruce?" Jerry asked. "Is everything OK?"

"I'm going to Nelson," he said, "I need some clothes."

"What's in Nelson?" Jerry asked, "Some hot chick?"

"I'm taking a millwright course," Bruce answered. He paused. "I don't want to go, but it means a lot to my Dad so I'm going."

Jerry watched Bruce's back as he stuffed shirts and pants into a brown paper bag. There seemed to be no thought given to the items Bruce was taking. He was grabbing aimlessly, haphazardly.

"Hey Bruce," Jerry asked, "want to smoke? You know, one last time before you go off and get smarter than the rest of us?"

As they smoked the joint, close-faced in the kitchen, Jerry

watched how his friend's face — so tightened by knots — relaxed. The familiar glaze over the eyes led eventually to a loose smile. "Aaah," Bruce sighed, exhaling smoke, "I guess it'll all work out."

Jerry smacked his friend on the shoulder. "You know it, man. It always does."

January 1983, eight days before the massacre

ON JANUARY 10, Bruce quit his job as a swamper and said goodbye to his co-workers who wished him well.

Two days later, Irene went to see Dr. Jefson alone.

"Mrs. Blackman," asked Jefson, "Where's Bruce?"

"I really need to talk to you alone, Dr. Jefson. May I?"

"Of course. Is Bruce OK?"

"He's having trouble making adjustments."

"What kind of adjustments?"

"We talked about moving the furniture around and he got upset."

"Is that all?"

"Well, he's been mildly obsessed the last few days."

"What do you mean?"

"He says things like, 'You better watch out, I'm the Devil.' Then he laughs."

Jefson nodded and Irene suddenly took off: "Dr. Jefson, I'm just at my wit's end. And it's not just about Bruce. Ricky is out of control and I'm angry at my husband all the time because he just won't…he just won't…well, he just won't handle things and when he tries to handle things he does them all wrong. He's either too lenient or too strict."

Jefson opened his mouth to ask a question, but she continued.

"We have so much debt and we can't seem to make a dent in it. We should never have bought this house. We've moved around so much. And now we're about to become grandparents and Angela's going to need support and what am I supposed to do? I work full time and I have the house and the kids and my husband and there's no time for me…"

Jefson finally gave up trying to ask questions or even clarify. He would later write in his notes "she proceeded to talk about herself and her family for the full hour, non-stop."

At the end of the session, even though he hadn't said more than a handful of words, Jefson said, "Well, I hope this has been helpful," and escorted Irene to the door.

"Oh," she said, as if the thought had just come to her, "Bruce was accepted into a millwright program at Selkirk College."

"In Nelson?"

"Yes."

"That's quite a distance away."

"My husband feels it will be good for Bruce to get certified in something, so he can get a better job."

"Well, that's good news about him being accepted, but I'd really like to talk to Bruce before he leaves."

Without acknowledging his statement, Irene walked through the door.

Two days later Jefson received a phone call from Senior.

"Dr. Jefson, he's not sleeping, and he's starting to talk about the Bible again."

"Has he been taking his medication?"

"I'm not sure. I think he takes it sometimes, but I can't be on top of him every minute."

Jefson could hear the defensive edge in Senior's voice; he paused for a moment before responding.

"Mr. Blackman, I strongly suggest that Bruce drop the apprenticeship program right now. Leaving home for a venture like this could significantly increase his anxiety and worsen his symptoms."

"This could have been such a good opportunity for Bruce," Senior said, then paused for a long time. "All right, I'll discuss it with him."

"Remind him he has an appointment with me tomorrow at two."

At 2:15 the next day, Jefson knew Bruce was not going to show for his appointment. The phone rang.

"Bruce Blackman on the line, Doctor," said the receptionist.

"Put him through." Jefson waited until he heard the line transfer. "Bruce," he said, "Where are you?"

"I'm getting ready to go to Nelson."

"Bruce, I don't think you should go. I'd like to see you before you depart."

"I've got to go," said Bruce, "I have to leave town."

"Bruce, please reconsider. It's not the right time for you to go."

"Dr. Jefson, can I call you once a week, you know, for support?"

"Of course you can, Bruce. You can call me whenever you need to."

"Can I have your home number?"

Dr. Jefson paused. "Bruce, this is the best number to call me at. The answering service can always find me."

"OK Doc, thanks for everything. Wish me luck."

"Bruce…"

The line went dead.

ON JANUARY 16, Bruce left for Nelson via bus. It was a long ride, but he had the voices to keep him company. They were all in high spirits, telling him that this trip to Selkirk College would unlock a door.

At a bus stop in Hope, an hour into the ride, a young woman boarded. Bruce watched her: thin, with waist-long, wavy blonde hair and a few freckles scattered across her nose. Under a frayed brown poncho she wore a white peasant top, two necklaces made of wooden beads and a crucifix around her neck. Her patchwork skirt looked handmade, and it was long enough to brush her ankles as she walked. Both wrists were banded in bracelets that jingled at the slightest movement. Bruce recognized the glassy look in her eyes. She smiled at him when she boarded, then walked right over to him and sat down.

"I'm Mary," she said.

"Bruce," he answered. "Where are you going?"

"Where am I going? Where have I been? There's a new planet in the sky."

Bruce felt his heart begin to race. "There is?"

"It gets in your dreams," she whispered, looking around. Then she tapped the side of Bruce's forehead with her index finger, "and it never leaves."

God, how does she know? Bruce wondered. "Tell me more," he said, enthralled.

"You look so worried," she told him. "So serious. Relax."

"I've got something I need to do. It's really important."

"Well, you'll have lots of chances to do it," she laughed. "I used to be afraid of death. But look at me," she smiled, "I died four times!"

"Four times?"

"Four times. Death is just another trip, you know? I'm supposed to meet you on this bus. That's what's supposed to happen. And you're supposed to meet me. We're supposed to meet each other."

Bruce nodded. "How did you die four times?" he asked.

"There's no death, really. I didn't even bleed when I died, because I was supposed to die. Just like I was supposed to come back. I died four times because they kept needing me. And then they sent me back here, and I just pick right up where I left off." She paused. "Do you believe me?"

"Yes," said Bruce, nodding. "I believe you."

Mary talked about things Bruce had never heard of, like teleporting, telekinesis, extra sensory perception. Bruce couldn't get enough of her. At Castlegar, six and a half hours later, they stopped for coffee. Outside of the diner, the night was cold and crystalline. In a field a few yards from the restaurant was a small pond that had frozen over. Under the ink black sky ripped open by a million stars, Bruce and Mary slid across the icy white surface, laughing and falling. Bruce watched how Mary's stray blond hairs were lit from behind by the diner lights. Her laughter sounded so unburdened, so pure. *She's an angel,* thought Bruce, *a messenger from God.*

They heard the unceremonious honking of the horn; the bus driver's signal that boarding would begin in 10 minutes.

"I need to use the can," said Bruce, running back to the diner. When he boarded the bus for the last leg of the trip to Nelson, Mary was gone. Disappeared. He spent the next 45 minutes between Castlegar and

Nelson, thinking about everything she had said to him. *She died four times!*

It was 8:30 p.m. when Bruce stepped off the bus in Nelson. He took a cab to his assigned dormitory. At the admissions office he gave his name, and they handed him a key. He looked at it resting in his palm.

The key, the key to everything.

He looked around his dorm room — a small bed, a tiny desk, a narrow closet and one overhead can light that buzzed. Bruce unpacked his clothes and rolled a joint. He heard stirring in the hallway and poked his head out to see what it was. Other people were arriving, pulling their duffel bags across the dirty gold carpet wearing thin from years of abuse. These would be his housemates and his classmates, but he wasn't ready to meet them yet. He smoked the joint then crawled into his bed, *no bigger than a coffin*, he thought. Staring up at the popcorn ceiling Bruce saw a vision: The Star of David, huge, glowing, and at each point, one member of his family. There were Todd, Bobi, Ricky, Karon, Angela. And Raymond, long-dead but waiting for them. And there was Bruce himself. His parents were there too. They'd been transformed into golden light, and together they formed the beautiful star. Bruce smiled. *They are the family of God.* He understood now how to ensure everyone took their place on the Star of David. The key to his dorm room was the key to the puzzle. It felt so good, finally, to know what he was supposed to do. But the feeling didn't last: Time was narrowing the gateway. He had to take action before it was too late.

In the morning, Bruce left his clothes and medicine — everything except the $400 given to him by his parents — and hailed a cab to drive him to the small airport in Nelson.

"There are no flights out until this afternoon," said a navy-suited woman behind the counter.

"But I've got to get home *now*. I'll pay for a private flight," Bruce said.

"Fine," she answered, looking him up and down, "but there aren't any pilots here right now. You might want to try Castlegar." She put a "Closed" sign on the counter and walked away.

Bruce sat down on an orange, plastic chair. There was no one else there except for a janitor mopping the floor. The voices were agitated; *Come on, come on, you know what you have to do. You're running out of time. The gateway is narrowing.*

Bruce found a pay phone and dialed the number for a cab. "Take me to Castlegar airport," he said to the driver when he arrived. The ride took 30 minutes, and Bruce sat in the back, staring out the window at the dirty snow banks lining the road, blurring into one long smudge of gray as they whizzed by.

The early flights from Castlegar to Vancouver had already left, but Bruce was able to book a flight aboard a small plane at 3:30. While he waited at the gate, the voices — all of them — competed for his undivided attention.

"The gateway is narrowing, you must capture Time."

"You are the Angel of Revelations."

"You are the Antichrist."

"You are Zeus."

"Save the universe."

"The Earth is a Satanic Star."

"Kill your family."

"STOP!" Bruce shouted. A few people turned to look at him. "Sorry," he said.

Bruce looked at his watch. He still had a couple of hours to wait so he went outside, huddled against the cold and smoked a joint. For a little while, the voices calmed themselves. With his thoughts now his own, Bruce decided to go back to his dorm, eat all his medicine, and kill himself.

While he was mustering up the nerve, he heard over the loudspeaker: "Flight 277 to Vancouver will commence boarding in 10 minutes."

When he landed at Vancouver International Airport, he walked outside the terminal to hail a cab. Bruce looked up into the rain and saw the last of daylight succumbing to a dark, cloud-choked sky. Under a streetlamp, a taxi cab sat idling, a white cloud of exhaust sputtering out the tailpipe. The raindrops on the windshield shone under the streetlight's beam, reflecting like diamonds. In his clarity about what he needed to do, Bruce now saw the world as a beautiful place, a place of wonder. It no longer frightened him. The voices were no longer confusing or scary. *Go on now*, they told him, *you know what to do.*

Bruce told the cab driver to take him home, but not to the actual address. He asked to be dropped off at the corner, about a block away. The 30-minute cab ride cost $40.00. Bruce took it from the remnants of the money his parents had given him. He gave the cab driver a $20 tip. Why not? Money wouldn't mean anything soon enough.

Bruce walked in the rain to his house. He stood outside on the driveway and looked at it a long time: A Spanish style home with an arched entrance...like a cave he thought. So many times he'd walked through that cave into darkness. Now, he was about to walk into light.

He paused before turning the front door knob. It was unlocked.

Bruce walked quietly toward the voices of his family. He snuck into the kitchen where his mother was serving dinner to Senior and Ricky who were seated at the kitchen table.

"Hi," he said.

Irene jumped, nearly dropping a plate.

"Bruce," she exclaimed, breathless, "you scared me to death! What are you doing here?"

He stared at everyone, expressionless. "I graduated," he said. Irene and Senior looked at each other. Ricky barely glanced up at his brother, focusing instead on the food that was fast disappearing from his plate as he shoveled it into his mouth.

"Sit down," said Irene. "We'll figure this out. Are you hungry?"

"No," said Bruce. He left the room quickly, as if he suddenly remembered he'd forgotten something.

"Bruce," Senior called after him.

"Eat some dinner first," Irene told her husband. "Lord knows this is going to be a long night."

CUSTODY

January 18, 1983
05:55

The conversations related here are verbatim and were given as testimony in court. The names and descriptions of the RCMP officers and the survivors have been changed.

RESPONDING TO A call of shots fired, Officers Watts, Bogan and Nichols proceeded on foot to the house in question, leaving Constable Darden behind to question the young man who had suddenly appeared out of the shadows. Darden adjusted the squelch noise on his radio as he walked the slender, small-framed man to the police cruiser a few yards away. Darden had been an RCMP constable for less than a year. A quarterback in college, he was still dedicated to his workouts and always had trouble finding off-the-rack shirts wide enough to fit his shoulders and chest. But even though Darden was accustomed to almost everyone else looking tiny in comparison, *this* young man was a mere wisp of a thing. A wraith. Darden was reminded of the Norman Bates character in the movie *Psycho*, except that this young man was even thinner and more harmless looking.

Rain drops bounced off Darden's flat-topped, police-issue hat. He noted that the suspect was mostly dry, so he couldn't have been walking outside in the rain for very long. It was hard to tell in the shadows, but Darden thought he saw dark, wet splotches on the man's shirt, and blood on his hands. Darden was still holding the man's wallet — the wallet that he'd been handed just a few moments earlier — when the suspect blurted, "So this is it. The big slam."

Darden asked, "Do you remember what happened?"

The young man shook his head as if to rid himself of the rain drops now soaking his dark hair. He was suddenly animated, his eyes wide and his talk fast. "I can't remember. I'm possessed by the Devil. I'm the Antichrist, and on the thirty-first, it's all over, man. The world's going to end. The big bang." He suddenly stopped and his expression changed from agitation to flatness. Darden was shocked by how quickly it happened. The young man recited in a monotone: "I'm possessed, my family is possessed, you're dead, I'm dead."

Darden opened the back of the police cruiser, took hold of the young man's bicep and said, "Get in the car, please." Once the door was closed and the suspect contained, Darden radioed Watts who would have by now reached the house in question. "Suspect states he's the Antichrist and the world is going to end on the thirty-first."

Darden paused for just a moment before he entered the police car, first tipping his hat forward to let the rain run off. He wrestled his frame into the car then turned, awkwardly, to read the standard-issue RCMP warning from a card. "You have the right to remain silent…"

The suspect looked out through the rain-speckled car window and into the night. Darden noted he was shaking violently.

Darden continued, "...Anything you say can be used in evidence. Do you understand?"

"Yes, I do."

"Do you remember what happened?"

"I can't, Officer. Really, the Devil's in me. It happened December third. It was called 'time through knowledge is death.' My twin brother has to die."

"How did you get the blood on your hands?"

"Shooting. I murdered my family."

At 06:09, Darden said, "I am arresting you for murder. You have the right to retain and instruct counsel without delay..." The young man fidgeted in the back seat while Darden completed the reading of rights. "...Do you understand?"

"Yes. My family is the only one with money. They bought me everything and I murdered them. Do you believe in the Devil? I'd like to phone Ottawa. I feel so awful but I *had to do it*."

"Do what?"

"I'm the Antichrist. I'm allowed one call. I have to call my brother — he lives in Ottawa. There's no way to get the death penalty, eh?"

Darden tried to keep him on track. "Where's the gun?"

"It was taken by Johnny, he's on the door."

Darden opened the wallet and found the suspect's identification: Bruce Alfred Blackman, 22 years old.

Darden wondered if Blackman was under medical care. "Do you see anyone?" he asked.

"Yeah, I see God all the time. Believe me, I'm insane."

"How many people did you hurt?"

"Six."

At 06:21, Darden radioed to the detachment that he was leaving the scene with the suspect and would arrive shortly.

The cruiser's headlights shone across the wet pavement like the moon on a dark, choppy ocean. As he pulled away from the curb, Darden watched in the rearview mirror as his prisoner took one long look back at the house on Spuraway.

"How do you feel?" Darden asked him.

"Like the world is going to end, man. After you do something like that in the name of God..." he trailed off. "No way you can kill me, eh? I should have killed myself. Why didn't I?"

Bruce looked out the window again as the shadowy world outside began to dissolve into a grey and drizzly morning. He hung his head and cried a little, then abruptly stopped. When Darden was able to turn around to look at him again, he was staring straight ahead, his face completely absent of expression.

They arrived at the detachment at 06:27. Darden removed Bruce from the car and escorted him to the breathalyzer room to be processed.

"All right," Darden said, "I'm going to ask you to please remove everything from your pockets and place them on the counter here." Facing them, on the other side of the counter, another constable watched closely. Bruce dug into his jacket pockets: He pulled out a box of matches and a small knife.

"Do you know what God's about?" Bruce asked. "Gets pretty narrow you know, pretty narrow."

"Take that thing off your head," Darden motioned to the headband.

As Bruce untied it, he said, "The big bang theory is what possessed me. Because we have seven in our family. The Antichrist is my sister. Todd and me are the key to everything, so what you just did by arresting me caused the whole thing." He laid the frayed and tattered band of leather on the counter, gently and — it seemed to Darden — with great reverence.

"I'm going to kill myself. My family is going to be shocked, the two that survived."

"Keep going," said Darden. "Your boots next."

"Everything is turning out perfectly. This is it man, I'm Jehovah Witness. God tells me it's time. How confusing." Bruce pulled off one boot and set it on the floor. "Life after death is like your own world. It's really strange, man. 'Let the seven thunders utter their voices,' which means the seven members of my family." He pulled off the other boot then handed them both to Darden.

"Your socks, please," said Darden.

"They claim I'm Chapter 10 of Revelations and I'm God. That's what the angel told me." Bruce pulled off both socks, then began to unbuckle his belt. "I love life, but this thing – *it possessed me!* If it's the Devil, look out, man. Fuck, *oh fuck!* Phone the doctor. He will really think I'm nuts now."

Darden took the belt. "Keep going," he said, "We'll call the doctor later."

Bruce shook his head as he dug into his jean pockets. "That's what she's saying — the world might end tonight, tomorrow, end of the month…If not then, then the Devil got me and I just murdered my family. Do you know what the tree of life is? Semen." He pulled everything out of his pockets and placed the items noisily on the counter.

"Look out, man. If I were you, I'd become Jehovah Witness." Bruce paused. "I had to do it man."

He looked around, then put both hands on top of his head, as if checking for something. "Can I have my head band back? It's my mark. It's my halo."

Darden interrupted: "Not right now. Take off the rest of your clothes, please."

"The doctor, he already knows everything. He knows I'm possessed."

As Bruce unzipped his jeans, he seemed to be considering something.

"Isn't that disgusting?" he said, shaking his head. "I was told they'd become everything. The universe. I wish I could die."

Darden said, "I need your underwear, too. Everything."

"Can I ask when the court date is? All my friends are gonna know, 'Hey! Blackman went nuts!'"

Bruce removed his jeans, then pulled his T-shirt over his head. Darden saw ribs and pale skin. Again, the smallness of the man surprised him. How could someone so petite kill six people without being overpowered by at least one of them?

Bruce said, "There's the beginning, then the end. That's what I was fighting against: The end."

"OK," said Darden, taking the jeans and shirt, "now I need that underwear." Bruce hesitated and placed his hands over his crotch. Darden assured him, "For evidence."

"Well, six counts…three hundred years or do I go to a mental hospital? My mom won't have to worry about her debts. The gateway is narrow. My brother and sister are going to hate me to hell. I got this jacket from the garbage man," he said, gesturing to the leather jacket on the counter. "That's where the Devil comes from — the scum of the earth."

Bruce looked at his hands. He turned them over, noting the dried rust-colored blood as if for the first time. "Blood," he whispered. "You're not supposed to bleed when you die."

Bruce quickly pulled off then handed his underwear to Darden who simultaneously passed him a pair of blue prison overalls. Bruce stepped inside them and practically disappeared. Darden placed handcuffs on Bruce's tiny wrists then walked him to a cell in the empty female ward. Once he'd uncuffed Bruce and locked him in his cell, Darden returned to the breathalyzer room to formally record the evidence seized and bagged:

06:00   wallet at car

06:30   at office seized knife, matches, one leather head band, 1 pair Dayton boots

06:52   seized one pair socks

06:54   one belt

06:55   one bag brown material, coins, keys

06:56   one pair jeans

07:03   one jacket

07:04   one shirt, one pair underwear

He initialed all of the evidence bag tags, and the officer on the other side of the counter boxed them for transport to the evidence room.

The officer on duty in the cellblock was R. W. Anderson who was preparing to end his shift. At 07:20, Constable Montgomery, another officer with less than a year's experience, arrived at the cells to relieve him. "Murder suspect," Anderson told Montgomery, gesturing with his head. They were out of earshot but not out of sight of Bruce. "He's saying things that don't make sense." Anderson said, speaking as low as he could without whispering. "Try to record as much information as you can." Montgomery glanced over his shoulder at the young man behind bars. Even from five yards away, Montgomery could see he was shaking.

"From what I've heard, it's a bad scene," Anderson added, intuiting the question before Montgomery asked it. "Clarke's over there

117

now," said Anderson, referring to their staff sergeant. Montgomery nodded. Anderson left the cell block.

As he settled into the worn-to-a-shine leather office chair — an old castaway from another detachment — Montgomery made a note that the suspect slept, "head turned to wall, wearing blue coveralls." Forty minutes later, Clarke walked in to the cell block.

Staff Sergeant Dumont "Dewey" Clarke was as solid as they came – physically and otherwise. He looked like a square block of concrete rounded off by meaty shoulders and the hairless top of his head. There was always something slightly rumpled about him, even though his pants were always pressed and his shirts ironed. It was almost as if the very act of walking into the detachment wrinkled his clothes and his spirit. He'd seen more than his share of what people were capable of at their worst. He rarely smiled, yet there was a warmth about him that made others feel safe in his presence.

"Take him up to Ident," he said.

Montgomery opened the cell door and said, "Wake up. We need to take you upstairs."

Bruce sat straight up, yawned, then rubbed his eyes. "Oh, man."

Clarke and Montgomery accompanied Bruce from his cell to the General Investigation Section (GIS)[9] office where he was swabbed for

---

[9] This section of RCMP law enforcement deals with the most serious crimes.

blood samples, fingerprinted and photographed. Clarke took Bruce into his office for an interview. Montgomery waited outside.

Montgomery sat in the hallway listening. He couldn't decipher words, but he could hear the variations in the volume of the voices: his staff sergeant's strong, steady speech and the responding voice of the accused as it dropped down, rose up, became emotional, angry, sullen. Then, the unmistakable, clipped tones of a conversation ending. At 09:00, Clarke opened the door. "Take him back," he told Montgomery.

Back at the cells, Bruce lay down on his cot and pulled a brown blanket over his head. Montgomery asked him: "Are you going to sleep?"

Bruce peeked out from under the blanket. "Yeah. Is that coffee for me?"

"No, it's mine," said Montgomery, wondering if he should give it to him or not. Would it make him more likely to talk? Bruce pulled the blanket back over his head and, according to Montgomery's notes, "drift(ed) to sleep." Five minutes later, Bruce pulled the blanket off his head again. He lay there for a full five minutes more, staring at the ceiling, then took a deep breath. Montgomery scribbled in his notepad, capturing everything, every detail. Three minutes later, Montgomery noted, Bruce cleared his throat then turned to face the wall. After 20 quiet minutes, he turned again and faced the officer. "I saw no emotions," Montgomery wrote. "He was lying there, but he wasn't sleeping. His eyes were open."

At 09:50, four hours after being arrested, Bruce sat up, wiping at his hands and asked, "Anyway, can I get to a sink, to wash off my hands?"

"I'll let you know in a minute," answered Montgomery. "I just want to check that out first."

"Can you tell me the time?"

"Ten to ten. I guess you're pretty tired."

"Yeah. Tired of everything."

Another officer entered the cell area, and Montgomery left to use the phone. When he returned, he asked his prisoner, "What's your first name?"

"Bruce."

"Well, Bruce, I checked with the fellow you spoke with earlier and he said he would be down as soon as possible to let you clean up."

"Mm hmm." Blackman flopped onto the cot.

"You're having a hard time sleeping."

"Is there any way you can turn the lights out?"

"No," Montgomery answered. "I'll be down here too so I need the lights on."

Bruce pulled the blanket over his head again and Montgomery wrote at 10:23: "Appears to be sleeping as snoring."

At 11:33, Montgomery and Clarke woke Blackman and took him to the breathalyzer room where he washed his hands twice: once at 11:40 and again at 11:50.

Back at his cell, he again pulled the blanket over his head and was quiet until 12:07 when he asked, "Excuse me, Officer, but can you tell me if all six people were killed this morning?"

"I don't know. I just got called down here to guard you."

"Can you find out for me?"

"Sorry Bruce, I wasn't at the scene so I don't know. You can ask the fellow you were talking to this morning."

At 12:18, Bruce was served beef stew for lunch. He picked at it, but eventually ate the whole serving. He asked Montgomery: "I guess you've never met someone like me before."

"No."

"Well, now you have. Do you think I might have a visitor?"

"What do you mean?"

"Could I get my brother to come and stay with me in the cells?"

"I don't think you can do that but when we get in touch with him we'll let you know if he is coming to visit."

"He's my twin brother, you know. He is also an Antichrist."
Bruce paused. "Do you think I could get a cigarette?"

"Well, I don't smoke and there are no cigarettes down here so
you'll just have to wait, OK?"

"Oh man!" Bruce mimicked a complete body spasm. "I'm a
chain smoker, so it's pretty tough since I haven't had a cigarette for a
day." Montgomery simply stared. Bruce smiled. "I guess we're heavy
smokers, we Antichrists."

When Montgomery didn't respond to his attempt at humor,
Bruce asked him, "Do you think you could get me a Bible?"

"Sorry, we don't have any Bibles down here."

"Do you think the world could end?" Bruce asked.

"I don't know."

"Maybe by the big bang theory?" Bruce lay on his back and
covered himself with the blanket. He spoke from beneath it, his voice
muffled and edgy: "Do you think you could try and get me some
cigarettes?"

"I can't right now as I'm the only guy down here. We'll see
when Ray gets back from lunch."

Fifteen minutes later, Bruce's disembodied voice spoke again
through the blanket: "You're not going to forget my cigarettes are you?

"Don't worry, I'll try and get a few."

"I've got six bucks. Maybe you could use that?"

At 12:57, Montgomery summoned another officer to stand guard. "I'm going to order lunch and try and find some cigarettes," he told his replacement.

"Here," said Montgomery when he returned to the cell. He passed Bruce two cigarettes. Bruce's hands shook as he took them.

"Do you believe in the Aztec Sun God?"

"I'm not familiar with that religion."

"All religions are the same."

When Montgomery's lunch was delivered, Bruce asked, "So, what's *your* lunch?"

"A burger."

"A cheesie burger for lunch," said Bruce, mimicking John Belushi from the *Saturday Night Live* skit.

"I think so."

Bruce lay down on the cot, under the blanket. At 13:45 he announced that he was being haunted.

"Oh?" Montgomery responded, chewing on his burger.

"I'm just thinking about the beginning. How Man started."

"Oh."

"I'm Adam and she's Eve. Or actually, she's Adam and I'm Eve. Either way, it doesn't matter. It sounds really bizarre, doesn't it?"

"Yeah."

Bruce stood up, cigarette in hand, then grabbed one of the bars of his jail cell. He motioned with the cigarette toward Montgomery. "When you get a chance," he asked, "could you get some cigarettes with my money?"

"Well, I don't know where your clothes and money are."

"It's been repossessed until I get out, right?"

"I think so."

Bruce was quiet for a moment. "I'm not going to get out for a long, long time."

Montgomery found a lighter and lit Bruce's cigarette through the bars. Bruce took one long drag before lying back down on the cot and exhaling noisily. He smoked the whole thing, then lit the second cigarette with the embers of the first.

"Man," he said, "do I ever feel bad. I guess you wonder what is wrong with me?"

"No."

Bruce turned over onto his stomach as he finished the last of the two cigarettes — sucking in every last puff, all the way down to the filter.

"Any chance you could get me another cigarette?"

"I had a hard enough time getting two butts for you. Why don't you ask the guy who's going to speak with you this afternoon? He's the boss."

At 13:45, Clarke removed Bruce from cells and returned him 30 minutes later. Bruce flopped down on the cot. "Cigarettes, cigarettes, cigarettes. Boy, I need a cigarette." He thrashed around on top of the blanket. "Well, the horror is all starting to come back now," he said, shaking his head back and forth. "Have you ever seen *Apocalypse Now*?"

"No."

"I've seen it about eight times."

Bruce was the most agitated Montgomery had seen him. Clarke quickly re-entered the room with a deck[10] of Player's cigarettes. Bruce was already tearing into it before Clarke had finished handing it to him through the bars. *"Thank you!"* Bruce whispered emphatically.

He pulled a cigarette from the deck, then paused while Montgomery lit it to ask, "Is this all out in the news yet?"

---

[10] The Canadian term for a pack of cigarettes.

"I don't know. I can't help you about that. I've been down here all day."

"Do you believe in praying?"

"Oh yeah, praying's good for you. Feel free to pray if you want."

"I do it all the time…to myself." Bruce began to pace back and forth in his tiny cell, then abruptly sat on the edge of the cot and smoked a cigarette with great flourish. Finished, he lay on his back and appeared to Montgomery to be praying. Then he was quiet for awhile before asking: "Do you think God could forgive me for what I did?"

"Yes, I believe so."

"If only my family would. I hope my twin brother and my sister Angela would."

"They will," said Montgomery. "Just give them some time."

Bruce shook his head. "I bet they're freaking out right now."

At 15:05, 10 hours after he was arrested, Bruce was removed from cells by Clarke and taken to a small room where he stood before a visiting Justice of the Peace, a middle-aged man with a kind face and thick glasses.

"Bruce Alfred Blackman," he began, "you stand charged that on or about the eighteenth day of January, A.D. 1983, at or near the District of Coquitlam, in the County of Westminster, Province of British

Columbia, you did commit first degree murder of Irene Katherine Blackman, contrary to Section 218 of the Criminal Code of Canada and against the peace of our Lady the Queen, Her Crown and Dignity." When the man said Bruce's mother's full name, Bruce felt as if he'd been punched in the stomach. *I killed my mother*, he thought. The Justice of the Peace continued, reading a total of six counts of murder, then remanded Bruce in custody until he could appear before a Provincial Court Judge the next morning.

The reading of six murder charges took less than three minutes.

Montgomery wrote that when Bruce was returned to cells he "appear(ed) a little upset." Bruce couldn't sit still. He paced, flopped down, sat up, smoked another cigarette.

Eventually, Bruce lay down again on his back. Montgomery noted the first overt display of emotion. "Appears quite upset," he wrote. "Eyes are watered."

In a trembling voice, Bruce asked, "Do you think I'll be allowed to see anyone?"

"Do you want to see friends and relatives?" Montgomery asked.

"Yes, relatives. I want to pray with my brother and sister for forgiveness."

"Well, you will have to ask the guard that when your brother and sister come to visit you."

Bruce paced in his cell again. "I wonder if God will ever forgive me for what I did."

Suddenly, he grabbed the cell bars and began to pray. Montgomery left him briefly to get a cup of coffee.

When he returned, Bruce asked, "Any chance I can get a coffee?"

"Here," said Montgomery. "I'll give you mine."

Montgomery's experience with murderers was, at this point in his career, confined to cases he'd read about in training. Based on bits and pieces he'd heard this day during all the back and forth of taking Bruce to Ident, then interviews and charges, Montgomery knew that the crime scene was, indeed, "bad," as Anderson had put it. "Grisly" is how it would later be described in a report to Crown Counsel[11]. Montgomery wondered if this prisoner had actually done it. He didn't look as though he were strong enough to even hold his head up very long, let alone savagely murder six people. Maybe there was an accomplice. That made more sense.

Bruce drank Montgomery's coffee, then asked if he could "take a piss." Montgomery accompanied him to the bathroom, watched him urinate, then returned Bruce to his cell.

"Good coffee, boss," said Blackman, smiling a little. "I think I better get some rest." Pause. "Do you know anything about law?"

---

[11] The Canadian equivalent of the prosecution, or the State.

"Yes."

"Will they get me a lawyer for tomorrow?"

"I think so."

Bruce lay on his back, then sat up for a cigarette. He appeared to Montgomery to be thinking hard about something, as if he were working out some problem in his mind.

Fifteen minutes later, he told Montgomery: "I have to take a shit."

Montgomery accompanied him to a well-lit stall and every 30 seconds asked, "You OK?"

Four long minutes later, Bruce emerged. Montgomery thought Bruce looked annoyed. *Maybe he couldn't go*, he thought. Before putting him back in his cell, Montgomery searched Bruce's pockets and found a plastic dinner fork with blood on the end of it. "Why is there blood on the end of the fork?" Montgomery asked.

"I tried to kill myself."

"What?"

"I just reamed myself," Blackman went on, "I was hoping I might bleed to death in a pool of blood."

Montgomery checked to make sure Bruce wasn't injured. He saw superficial scratches on Bruce's buttocks and near his anus, but no flowing blood. "I guess you're pretty depressed," Montgomery said.

"You'd be too, if you'd just killed your family. I just hope my brother and sister will forgive me."

"Give them time. They will."

At 16:55, Montgomery gave Bruce another cup of coffee and watched while he alternated between sitting and pacing. Bruce drank the coffee quickly, then requested another ten minutes later. As Bruce slurped on the fresh cup he asked Montgomery, "Ever try to kill yourself by bleeding to death?"

"No. Are you still bleeding?"

"No, you wouldn't give me enough time. If only my brother and sister would forgive me."

"Just give them time," assured Montgomery. "You just try and straighten yourself up."

"That will take a *long* time."

AT 17:34, BRUCE was taken out of cells to visit with a Dr. Hayes. When he was returned, 30 minutes later, Bruce was clearly rattled.

He could barely get the words out: "Boy, I really feel depressed." He shook his head back and forth; Montgomery could see the tell-tale quivering of his chin — tears were just a word or a moment away.

"Well, I feel sorry for you," said Montgomery.

"Oh man, if only my brother and sister would forgive me. *Oh, man!*" He burst into weeping — deep, raspy gulps for air, as if he were drowning. "Oh God!" he cried. *"Why did I do it?"* Montgomery watched as Bruce's entire body convulsed with sobs. When he could talk again, Bruce stated — almost as if to reassure himself —"If there is a God, He will forgive me."

"He will."

"Not if you're possessed by the Devil."

"He still will."

An hour later, Bruce asked for a pencil and paper to write his confession.

"Well, I don't think you should," said Montgomery. "I'm off in 15 minutes, so check with the next guard."

"Do you know any convicts?"

"Yeah."

"What's it like being a convict? Is it scary going to prison?"

"It all depends on how you can adapt to it."

"A lot of things scare me right now. Could I get a bath?" Bruce wrung his hands and moved his shoulders back and forth inside the prison overalls, as if he couldn't stand being inside his own skin.

"Well," answered Montgomery, "Not right now. Maybe at the next place you go to."

"Where will that be, a mental asylum?"

"Maybe. I don't know. What do you think?"

"Probably. They'll probably keep me locked up in a little box."

Dinner arrived; ham, potatoes and carrots.

Montgomery turned the shift over to Constable Nichols who had been at the murder scene when Bruce was arrested. Nichols had witnessed the aftermath first-hand. His hard stare at Bruce shut down any hope for chit chat. Four hours later, Constable Darden returned to the detachment to take over guard duty.

Bruce recognized him and was relieved to be in the presence of someone less intimidating. "Is my brother in town yet? I have to see Dr. Jefson about my possession." He paused. "I don't think I murdered. I think I delivered."

Darden wrote in his notebook.

"I'd like a pen to write my defence to my brother and my doctor," Bruce continued. "I'm scared of this possession thing. The big bang is going to happen soon. I am insane. Why did my younger twin die? Yesterday, I became an evil. Evils wobble but they don't fall down. It's going to end on the thirty-first. If not then, then the twenty-second. How about giving me back my pot? Have you ever tried pot?"

"No."

"It's really a bizarre drug. I don't recommend it. I can't kill, but I murdered because the Devil possessed me. Die before the thirty-first and you'll be saved. I am the Star of David. January thirty-first, it's going to end. There was always time. I didn't murder, I just delivered. I need that Bible, it is so important to me. You have until the twenty-fourth to die. You know what?"

"What?"

"I can't cry since December third. I have no feeling." Bruce sat on the edge of the cot with his hands resting in his lap. He was silent for a long time before he looked up at Darden and said, "I killed my father. Boy, he was ugly when he died. "

THE GATEWAY

January 17, 1983
10:30 p.m.

SENIOR WAS IN the kitchen when the telephone rang. On the other end was Dr. Jefson.

"Thanks for returning my call," Senior said.

"What's wrong?"

"Bruce came back from Nelson. He wasn't even there a full day – just went there and came back. He's…I don't know. He's going backwards."

"What do you mean he's 'going backwards'?"

"You know, regressing, going back to his talk about the end of the world again. All that big bang, Armageddon and Book of Revelations crap. Now he says he's possessed by the Devil."

"Has he been taking his medication?"

"I don't know. He says he left his meds at the dorm in Nelson, so he probably hasn't taken anything for at least a day."

"Do you think he should be admitted to hospital?" asked Jefson. Senior didn't answer. "Mr. Blackman, I want you to take Bruce to Royal Columbian Hospital right now. I can arrange for him to get his medication in the emergency room. I'll call ahead and do that as soon as we hang up." There was a long pause on the other end. "Mr. Blackman...are you there?"

"Well..." Senior hemmed and hawed. Jefson could almost see him at the other end of the telephone connection, walking in a tiny circle, an extra-long phone cord coiling around his body. "Dr. Jefson, Royal Columbian is four or five miles away, and it's so late already. I'll stay up and talk to him. I think I can keep him calm. Can he see you tomorrow morning?"

"Yes," said Jefson, "bring him in at 11:00. Make sure someone comes with him. *Do not* let him drive."

"We won't."

"Do you mind if I talk to him?" asked Dr. Jefson.

"Hang on," said Senior. He put his hand over the mouthpiece and called out to his son. "Bruce. *Bruce!*" There was no response. "Hold on Doctor, I'll go get him."

Senior placed the receiver on the kitchen counter and walked down three steps to the family room where Ricky sat on one couch watching TV and Bruce lay on the other couch, wearing big round headphones that were plugged into the stereo system via a long, black, spiral cord. Bruce bobbed his head to a beat only he could hear. Senior put a hand on his son's arm. Bruce opened his eyes and pulled off the headphones.

"Bruce, Dr. Jefson is on the phone."

Bruce put the headphones back on. Senior pulled them off. "Go up and talk to the doctor."

"I don't want to," said Bruce. "He can't help us."

"Bruce," said Senior, his voice no longer able to mask frustration, "*get* into the kitchen and talk to the Doctor and *do it now!*"

Bruce threw the headphones on the floor and stomped up to the kitchen. Ricky watched and shook his head. Bruce's behavior was aggravating, but it did have an unintended benefit: Their parents were so wrapped up in Bruce's drama that they paid little attention to Ricky who was able to get away with a lot more than he could have if their parents were on the ball. Ricky smiled and turned back to the television show.

In the kitchen, Bruce spoke into the telephone: "What do you want, Dr. Jefson?"

"Hello Bruce. Your family was surprised to see you back from Nelson so quickly. Did something happen?"

"Yeah," said Bruce, sarcasm oozing through the phone line, "I *graduated.*"

"After just one day?"

Silence.

"Bruce," continued Jefson, "are you having bad thoughts again?"

"A little."

Jefson's attempts to probe deeper were thwarted by Bruce's eerie detachment. Jefson would later testify that Bruce's answers were "curt" and that there was "a certain distance" to his responses.

"All right, let me talk to your dad again. Oh, and I'll look forward to seeing you tomorrow at 11:00, OK?"

Bruce handed the phone back to Senior and returned to the family room.

"Dr. Jefson," asked Senior, "What do you think?"

"He seems a little detached, doesn't he? How does he look?"

"Like he hasn't slept in weeks. He hasn't had a shower or brushed his hair. He says he can't go to sleep, but he looks like he could doze off any minute. He won't take off that headband of his either. I don't know what to do with him…"

Senior's voice trailed away. Jefson offered, "Mr. Blackman, think about the toll this is taking on you and the family. Why don't you go to Royal Columbian and get him medicated? At least then we can all have a good night's sleep."

The pause on the other end seemed to go on forever. "No, I think I can handle this one," said Senior. "It's only for tonight. We'll see you tomorrow then."

Senior hung up and took a deep breath, his hand pressing the receiver down into the cradle of the phone. *Just get through one more day.*

January 18, 1983

AS SOON AS he'd gotten home, and while his family ate dinner, Bruce snuck downstairs to the basement walk-in crawlspace where the guns were stored. The weapons were locked up of course, but that barrier was meant for intruders, not family members. Bruce knew where the key was hidden. From upstairs, he could hear his mother talking and the clanking of forks and knives on plates, but still, he held his breath and was as quiet as he could be. The freezer where they stored all the game meat from their hunts made a perfect table. Bruce grabbed a box of 30-30 ammunition and removed eight rounds, but as he reached for the gun, he thought about the noise it would make. Better to use the .22, he thought, and loaded two rifles. *I don't think I can do this*, he said to the voices spurring him on. *Yes you can, you can,* they hissed. Bruce took one of the .22 rifles and placed it on the floor near the stairs.

He stood there for a long time listening to the woman's voice: *The gateway is narrowing. You are Time. You are the Angel. You must liberate your family.* Behind her voice he could hear the malevolent

138

ones, the voices that told him he was the Devil, the Antichrist. He heard a dog barking — the Beast.

You are Time.

Bruce walked upstairs, arms hanging by his sides, head down. He walked past his family finishing dinner in the kitchen and went straight into the family room where he lay down — not to sleep — but to take stock. This was it. God had given him a key — the key to leave Nelson and come back to send his family into Heaven where they could hold the Star of David in place. Everything was ready, but there was one thing holding him back: he'd seen all the blood and guts involved in hunting. There was no way he wanted to do or to see *anything* like that with his own family.

But then he remembered what Mary said on the bus, that she had died four times and she didn't bleed once. "They needed me for something," he recalled her saying, "So I didn't really die. Not the way we think about death anyway." Maybe that was true — God needed Bruce's family up in heaven and He needed them *now*. The gateway to salvation was narrowing. When Bruce imagined killing his family, he saw them all turn into pillars of light before floating up to Heaven and meeting God. There was no blood or suffering. Everyone seemed really happy when he pictured it in his mind.

Still, he couldn't bring himself to do it.

Irene had called Bruce to come get some dinner. Four times.

"I've saved a plate for you," she shouted.

"I'm NOT HUNGRY!" he practically screamed in response to the fourth call. The first thing she'd asked when he got home was, "Where are your clothes? Where's the money we gave you?"

"I left everything in the cab," he lied, which prompted his mother to spend the next few hours calling every taxi cab company in Vancouver. Of course, she'd never find the precious clothes. They were still up in his dorm room in Nelson, waiting passively for an owner who would never return. "Where's the money, where's the money?" she insisted. Finally, Bruce pulled a rolled up wad of cash out of his pocket and smacked it into her open palm. "God, will you just STOP?" he pleaded. His mother had been both a source of support and complete angst to him throughout his whole life. He couldn't stand to hear one more word from her about the clothes that he'd left behind. What did they matter, anyway? She was too focused on material things.

"Bruce," she said, "you know how tight money is around here. We have so much debt…" Bruce watched her count the money and saw her face tighten when it fell far short of $400.

"Irene," said Senior, "just let it go. This isn't helping."

"But," she started.

"Let it go," he said, glaring at his wife, who looked like she was getting ready to climb onto an emotional carnival ride where she'd talk and talk and talk and talk, around and round in circles. It was almost like she couldn't help herself. She'd shoot out verbal vines that wrapped around anyone and everything within earshot, then chatter so much that the listener felt strangled at the end — even if they hadn't said a single word. Irene looked at her three men: her husband, who was frayed and frustrated; her last son Ricky who was now becoming a rebel; and Bruce, who was a mystery. She'd chosen one and given birth to the others. Why was her life suddenly so hard? To distract herself, she picked up a copy of the Yellow Pages and wrote down telephone numbers for more cab companies. She dialed the phone. Bruce went to the family room and put a cassette tape in the stereo, one he'd made of his favorite songs by *the Rolling Stones* and *the Who*. He'd learned long ago that the best way to avoid her *and* a lecture on loud music was to put the headphones on, then (and only then) crank it up. That's what he did, and at least for a moment, his mother and her nervous habits were obliterated.

Now and then he'd fling himself up from the sofa and storm through the house shouting "I am the Angel of the Revelations!" Senior followed him, sometimes patient, sometimes exasperated, but always exhorting him to "Sit down and talk about it."

At around nine p.m., Bruce ran upstairs. Ricky was in his small bedroom, still dressed. Bruce sat down on the little bed. "I have to let loose the four angels," he told his brother.

"What does *that* mean?" Ricky said, barely able to contain his mocking.

"The Four Horsemen of the Apocalypse. They are you, me, Todd and Raymond."

"Raymond's dead, or did you forget?"

"I know he's dead. He's the Lamb, he's Jesus Christ. That means we're all the family of God. We, the Blackmans."

"You're not going to start talking about jerking off again, are you?"

"Ricky, you don't understand. If you eat from the Tree of Knowledge, then you will see things the way I see them. Everything will make sense. You will see that when you die, you'll become a God."

Ricky turned his back to Bruce, picked up a brush from his dresser and ran it through his glossy, straight black hair. In the mirror's reflection, he saw Bruce reach down and put something under the bed. Bruce continued talking, quoting from the Book of Revelation, babbling about the end of the world, until Ricky told him to get out. Not just get out, but "*get the fuck out.*"

"Ricky," Bruce asked, "Do you love me?"

"Not right now I don't."

After Bruce left the room, Ricky waited until he heard Bruce's footsteps finish their descent. Then he heard the muffled sound of his parents and Bruce talking. Only then did Ricky reach under the bed to see what Bruce had put there.

The downy hairs on the nape of Ricky's neck stood straight on end.

It was a hunting knife.

Why in the world would Bruce put a knife under his bed? To kill him with it later, while he slept? Ricky's hands shook a little as he turned the knife over and over, its blade glinting in the light. He'd seen Bruce use this knife to rip open and eviscerate deer. Ricky felt his dinner shift a little in his stomach. He hid the knife in his closet, inside a shoe, then walked downstairs. His parents were in the kitchen, talking.

"What is it, Ricky?" asked his mother.

"I need to ask Dad something."

"OK," she said, "but it's time for you to go to bed. You've got to get up for school tomorrow." She ran her hand through Ricky's hair. He pulled away, disgusted by her touch. His mother still treated him like a kid. Irene was unfazed. She leaned in to kiss him knowing he would grimace and swat at her like a fly. It was her little game. "I'm going to bed, too," she said, managing to almost get a kiss planted on the top of his head. "Goodnight."

"Dad," Ricky whispered to his father as soon as she'd left the room, "Bruce hid his hunting knife under my bed."

"For what?"

"I don't know, but he was talking his end-of-the-world talk again. He's scaring me, Dad. Why would he put a knife under my bed?"

"I don't know, Rick. Where is it now?"

"I hid it in my closet."

Senior put a hand on his youngest son's shoulder. He'd never seen Ricky so rattled. Usually, Ricky behaved like any rebellious 16-year-old boy — bored, disinterested and disdainful, no matter what was going on. Now, he looked the way he used to when he'd run to his father, afraid of the lightning outside. "It'll be OK," Senior said, "I'm going to stay up with him."

"Then I am too," said Ricky. "I don't want to sleep in my room. I don't want to be by myself if he comes in there."

Senior couldn't really argue. Who knew what Bruce would be up to as the night wore on? "OK," Senior said, "you can sleep on the sofa, but you still have to get up for school tomorrow."

"Mom will wake me."

"Go brush your teeth."

Ricky bounded upstairs and Senior took a quick look around the kitchen. There was Bruce's knife sheath on the counter. Empty. Also on the counter, next to the toaster, was a butcher-block holder full of kitchen knives, all accounted for. He stared at it for about ten seconds

144

before opening the oven door, picking up the block and pushing it all the way to the back of the stove.

Ricky came back downstairs, fully clothed.

"Did you brush your teeth?"

"Yes."

"Why aren't you wearing your pajamas?"

"*Dad,*" he said, indignant, "I don't wear pajamas anymore."

"You don't?" Senior smiled.

"Daaaad," Ricky said, smiling too.

"OK, Son, goodnight. How about a kiss?" Senior smiled.

"If you promise to buy me a Mustang for my birthday."

"Fair enough. No kiss. Goodnight. Turn the TV off in half an hour."

Senior knew Ricky would fall asleep with the TV blaring, but it didn't matter. If it made him feel safer to sleep with the lights on, closer to his father's watchful eye, whom did that hurt?

Senior sat in the kitchen with his head in his hands. The roughness of his cheeks reminded him that he'd gotten lax about shaving. He hadn't washed his hair in awhile either. Bruce's ceaseless drama had disrupted everyone's routine. Even Senior and Irene were bickering

145

more than usual. Ricky needed a good kick in the ass but Senior worried that it might be an over-reaction brought on by his tension over Bruce. Senior sat there for awhile, breathing in and out and thinking about how much the family had travelled around, all the places they'd lived. Bruce had always complained that was the reason he'd done so poorly in school. Could that be that true? In trying to provide for his family, had Senior actually harmed some of them irreparably? There were times, like right now, when he felt tears well up in his eyes. His throat hurt with the effort of holding them back.

With the exception of the TV noises from the family room, the house was dead quiet. Irene's footsteps overhead had stopped, finally. She'd done the last of her walking back and forth from bathroom to closet to bathroom and back. Senior rubbed his eyes and stood up. He walked over to the stairs above the family room and snuck a couple of looks below. There was Bruce sprawled out across one of the sofas, his hair unbrushed, the soles of his dirty socks moving to the beat of music. And around his head was that woven leather headband that never seemed to come off anymore. Yet Bruce – for the first time in a very long time — seemed almost content with the headphones snug around his ears and his eyes closed. While one foot tapped a rhythm in the air, his fingers tapped a rhythm on his chest. Senior tiptoed down the three stairs and turned off the television. Ricky had already covered himself with a blanket and was fast asleep. It was 2:30 a.m.

Senior went back to the kitchen and picked up that day's edition of *the Province* newspaper. It was likely that at some point looking through it he'd see a picture of Irene: She was literally the poster child for the newspaper, her smiling face on billboards and buses all across town. *How ironic*, thought Senior, *she never even has a chance to read the damn thing.* From somewhere inside the house, Senior heard a clock ticking. Otherwise, the house was as silent as a tomb. His turning the pages of the newspaper sounded incredibly loud; the crackling of the paper unnerved him.

Suddenly, Bruce burst in and shouted *"Wormwood!"*

Senior jumped to his feet and felt his heart seize for a moment. *"Jesus H. Christ*, you just about gave me a heart attack!"

Bruce clutched a Bible in both hands. He scraped a kitchen chair across the floor to where his father was standing and started reading: "And I saw a new Heaven and a new earth; for the first Heaven and the first earth were passed away; and there was no more sea."

Senior breathed in and out, trying to calm down. Best to just let Bruce rant until he veered off to something else, which he always did.

"Dad," he said, "I am possessed by the white woman. She says I am the Angel of Revelations. Wormwood is here. The big bang. The family has to be together."

Bruce flailed one arm in the air while reading and re-reading verses from the Bible. Then, suddenly, he stopped. His wild-eyed expression went from evangelical ardor to complete passivity. Senior grabbed his chance. He took Bruce by the arm and led him down the hall.

At 3:00 a.m., in the living room — a place they almost never used — Senior sat Bruce down on a curved, floral patterned sofa.

"I know you're going through a hard time," Senior said, "but you just need to relax. I know you're worried about the world — hell, we all are — but you can't fix it yourself. You need to just kick back, let things be."

"That's what Dr. Jefson says," Bruce offered, his face slack.

"And he's right, Bruce, he's right. You used to be so laid back. Remember? Do you think you can be that way again?"

"And I saw another mighty angel come down from Heaven, clothed with a cloud, and cried with a loud voice, as when a lion roars, and when he did, seven thunders uttered their voices." Bruce recited it dully, staring at the floor, until he got to the part about the seven thunders. Then, he stared at his father with such intensity that Senior, for the first time, felt his whole body prickle with fear.

"Bruce, I'll stay up with you all night if that's what it takes. Tomorrow we'll see Dr. Jefson together, OK?"

"Our family is the family of God. You have to believe me. Only we can save the universe."

"Bruce…"

"I'm going out for a smoke," said Bruce, animated once more. He launched himself from the sofa and fled to the back yard. From inside the breast pocket of his jacket he fished out a plastic baggie containing one joint and some loose leaves. In the other pocket he found his plastic butane lighter.

The night was entirely still. The only sound was the strike of the lighter; the only light the little flame. Bruce couldn't remember a darker night, even when hunting in the wilderness. He stood out there in the cold, in the drizzle, and inhaled deeply. One breath of the night air, one toke off the joint. He smoked it all the way down to the twisted end of the rolling paper, ate it, then chewed on the remaining leaves. It wasn't long before he felt much, much better.

Inside, Senior checked on Ricky again who was huddled under a blanket, snoring lightly. Even though he was 16 already, he was still so small, so *young*-looking. Senior remembered when he was born, and the happiness they all felt when Ricky emerged squalling and kicking, and the grief when his twin brother Raymond emerged lifeless and blue. Senior remembered all of his kids' births: No matter what was going on his life, no matter what burdens were pressing down on his shoulders, seeing one of his newborn children filled him with a joy that couldn't and would never be replicated by anything else.

Senior sighed as he folded the top of blanket under Ricky's chin. It wasn't likely that Bruce was going to sleep. That meant Senior would be staying up too. Well, might as well make the best of it. He found a cross-word puzzle and settled down at the kitchen table to solve it.

Thirty minutes later, Bruce sauntered back in. Senior looked up and saw that Bruce looked different. His whole body seemed loose and liquid, as if at any moment he might strike a tai-chi pose of serenity. Most of the lights in the house were off now, but the light from the hallway framed his son's head, almost like a halo. In a weird way, Bruce looked angelic.

"Dad," said Bruce, hovering at the base of the stairs that led up to the kitchen, "Do you love me?"

"More than you know."

"No matter what?"

"No matter what."

Bruce paused. "Thanks. You know....for everything."

Senior watched Bruce shuffle back to the sofa and his headphones, then returned his focus to the crossword puzzle. Perhaps the worst had passed.

AT 04:45, IN the house on Spuraway, Bruce made a telephone call to his sister Bobi. "Something is about to happen," he told her.

150

"What is it Bruce? What are you doing?"

"I have a knife."

"What do you mean you have a knife? Why do you have a knife?"

"I was talking to Ricky."

"Oh God, Bruce, don't do anything stupid."

"You and Karon need to come over right now, and don't bring John."

Roberta heard a click on the other end. "Bruce? *Bruce?*" He'd hung up.

Roberta's fingers barely worked as she dialed the phone number for Dr. Jefson. Across town, the ringing jerked the doctor out of a deep sleep. He looked at the numbers on his bedside digital clock: 04:49.

"Yes?" he said, squinting as he turned on the beside lamp. "Who is this?"

"Dr. Jefson, this is Roberta Davies. The family wants Bruce committed." She sounded out of breath and panicked.

Jefson sat upright in bed. "Has something happened?"

"He has a knife," she said, "We're going over there."

"Roberta," said Dr. Jefson in his most measured voice, "I want you to call the police."

There was a long pause at the other end. Evidently, indecision ran in the family. "No," she finally answered. "I don't want to upset my father. We're going over there now. I'll let you know what happens." The phone line went dead. Jefson made some notes on the pad next to his bed, and then went back to sleep.

After calling his sister, Bruce put the headphones back on. He listened to Roger Daltry: "I can go anyway, way I choose/I can live anyhow, win or lose/I can go anywhere, for something new/Anyway, anyhow, anywhere I choose."

And then, blasting in his ears with a booming bass track was the Rolling Stones song, "Slave." "Do it, do it, do it...don't want to be your slave. Do it, do it, do it, do it, do it, don't want to be your slaaaaaaaaave."

And then he heard the voice again saying, *It's time to do it, Bruce.*

"I can't," he whispered, shaking his head, "I can't kill them."

Do it.

Bruce pulled the headphones off his ears and stood up. He walked downstairs and picked up the rifle. Looking at it in his hands, he shook his head and said out loud, "I won't."

And then, suddenly, every feeling went away, as if the Devil that possessed him had erased him from the earth. A new voice, a voice out of nowhere, said *Here it is. Here you go.* His heart began to pound. The lyrics kept on in his head — "do it, *do it, do it,* DO IT..."

Bruce gripped the rifle in his hands, knowing his mission, but still not able to carry it out. The voice — the voice that had been guiding him all this way — said *I'll take over.*

He felt a surge of adrenaline at the same time he saw the vision — the vision of each of his family members up in Heaven, holding the Star of David in place. He ran up the stairs, turned left and saw his father's surprise.

"Bruce!" Senior shouted as he rose to his feet, raising one hand to protect his face. *"DON'T!"*

Bruce leveled the gun and fired.

CONFESSION I

This is a verbatim tape recorded interview taken the same day as Bruce Blackman's arrest. The statement is presented exactly as given. All RCMP officer's names and identifying features have been changed.

January 18, 1983

STAFF SERGEANT DUMONT "Dewey" Clarke was the man in charge of the General Investigation Section (G.I.S.) of the RCMP's Criminal Investigation Division. On the morning of January 18, he visited the crime scene on Spuraway. Because he would be interviewing the suspect within the next hour, he gleaned as much information as he could from the officers present and with his own eyes. In his twenty-plus years on the force, Clarke had seen a lot. So much, in fact, that he wished his memory would begin to fail. After his cursory visit, and as he exited the house on Spuraway, he wondered how one person could have committed such a gruesome slaughter. Clarke hadn't seen anything like it in his entire career.

Back at the detachment, Clarke prepared a tape recorder for an interview with murder suspect Bruce Alfred Blackman, who had been in custody for approximately one and one-half hours. Clarke walked to the cell block and, along with Constable Montgomery, removed Blackman from his cell. They accompanied him to be fingerprinted and photographed. Clarke noted the smallness of the man, made even

154

smaller-looking by the oversized blue coveralls drooping off his bony frame.

Blackman's hands and fingernails were swabbed for blood evidence before he was fingerprinted. Blackman was compliant as his mug shots were taken. He was brought into Clarke's office and seated. Clarke pressed the red "record" tab on the tape recorder and began.

08:05

"O.K., as I told you Bruce, my name is Staff Sergeant Clarke. I'm stationed at the Coquitlam detachment here, and you understand that you are arrested for murder, do you? The officer that brought you back to the detachment informed you of that, right? And he also informed you that it was his duty to inform you that you have the right to retain and instruct counsel without delay. Do you understand that?"

"Yeah, I do," answered Blackman.

"Did he give you that warning?"

"Yes, he did."

"Just to make sure we have it on the record, I'm going to give you that warning again, OK?" Clarke repeated that anything Blackman said could be used in evidence. "Bruce, do you understand?"

"Yes, I do."

"OK, now can you tell me…?" Clarke began, but Bruce interrupted.

"It's just that I feel so bad for what I've done, but really, I've been totally possessed, totally possessed. I mean, I'm supposed to…" he seemed to search for words, and finding none, said, "Oh, I don't know what I did, I don't know what I did. Believe me, I feel very bad about doing it, but I was possessed."

"Can you tell me what you did?"

"To my family?"

"Yes."

"It all started December third when this little voice came out of nowhere. I'm a very good, clean, God-loving person. I love everything, but I seen [*sic*] it possess me, yesterday, claimed that it was telling me different ways, like there was one, one girl he married, she died four times, supposedly this is what it's claiming anyways."

"What significance is December the third, Bruce?"

"That's when we got started. That's when I was possessed."

"Was?"

"My doctor, he knows this. Dr. [Jefson]."

"Is he a doctor in Coquitlam?"

"I don't where he's a doctor at."

"Where do you go to see him?"

"In Vancouver."

"Is the doctor…?"

Bruce burst in, nearly tearful: "I love my family very much, very, very much and it is very important to me, very important to me…"

"You're telling me that you killed your family, is that right, Bruce?"

"Did I? I never killed them. The thing that was with me did. I never did it."

"Something made you do it then?"

"Something definitely made me do it. It was trying to tell me that I had to do it. Ever hear of the Star of David?"

"Yes."

"And then we have this satanic stuff, the regular stuff. You draw a star like this, like the Satanic Star and the Star of David, like this." Bruce drew two big stars in the air in front of him. He continued: "The Satanic Star is supposed to represent all…and the Star of David is supposed to represent three and she's half of it."

"Who was home with you last night in the house there, Bruce?"

"Who was home with me? Mom and Dad."

"Who of your family members were there?"

"Me, my Dad, my Mom, my younger brother Richard who I love very much, Bobi, Karon and John."

"Who are Bobi, Karon and John? What relation are they to you?"

"Bobi and Karon are sisters, and so is my little brother Rick, and John is Bobi's husband and I don't love – I don't like murder. I've been a very, very good, very clean type of person but this possession thing that's gotten into me…"

"When did it get into you Bruce? When did it first come upon you?"

"December 3, 1982."

"Tell me about that."

"Well, first of all it came on the edge of the Tree of Knowledge. Now everybody wonders what is the Tree of Knowledge, why is there anything and why there is an earth. This [sic] is all the questions and I say the only nightmare that I'm living is my reality. What if I die? I don't have nothing [sic], but from what I did, I threw my…" — Blackman's voice dropped and Clarke could not decipher his words — "…supposedly that we are living right now. I saved the heavens from the big bang theory, supposedly because that's where everything came from, eh? The big bang theory. I'm so scared. I am *so scared*. I don't know what's going on. I know that my family is definitely a key in this and in my possession and I wish to believe them all, every one of them. Every one of them."

"Last night, was your family up all night with you?"

"Yes."

"Why were they dressed?"

"They were up all night with me."

"What were you doing during the night? Were you talking, or what was going on?"

"I was possessed. I was waiting for the world to come to an end. Honestly, I thought the world was going to come to an end at 12:00. In fact, this morning I thought it was going to come at 12:00 but everything, everything has happened totally by prophecy. That's what happens with me."

"But the end of the world didn't come, did it?"

"No, but it states that it's gonna."

"Where does it state that?"

"It states that everything began so everything must end as in the big bang theory, so…oh, I don't know." Bruce stopped abruptly, as if he'd suddenly run out of words. He sighed, the sound perfectly audible on the tape.

Clarke changed course: "We found two rifles in the house. Who do they belong to?"

"One belongs to me and one belongs to my father."

"What is your weapon? Is yours the .22?"

"Yeah."

"What's the other gun?"

"What other gun is that?"

"There were two guns there."

"They were both .22s. I think they are. I wouldn't want to make any noise. I didn't want to bother anybody. In fact, as soon as I finished doing all this, I wanted to die myself because that was a big part of it but you see the living part of my family is going to hate me. They're going to hate me to hell, they are. They have no right to be mad, and I can't blame them at all.

"What remaining family do you have, Bruce?"

"My sister…and there's my twin brother... You know, they tell me — these little voices — that if [my sister and brother] are Satan and Antichrist and that I have to talk to them on the death. I got to at least tell them what's bothering me. I have to let them know before they damn me further. Does this make sense?"

"Not particularly, not to me. You know, if it makes sense to you I guess it must make sense to you, but I can't rationalize it myself, Bruce. Tell me, last night, was your family sitting up with you? Talking with you?"

"My father was."

"Where was the rest of your family?"

"In bed. Sleeping."

"And what happened between you and your father?"

"He was just up because he was worried about me. He was wondering what I was doing and I was wondering what I was doing, and then all of a sudden — bango! — it came to me: Kill, you must kill in order to save the universe. Not save the world — who cares about the world — save the universe, because this is what beginning is. It's the big bang theory.

"O.K., this came to you, Bruce, when you were talking with your father where? Where in the house were you sitting?"

"I was sitting in the living room."

"And only you and your father were up at this time? Tell me what happened."

"I hate what I did."

"Tell me how it happened. What did you do?"

161

"How did I do it?"

"Yes."

"I can't remember it all, Sir. I can't remember how I did it and I don't want to remember how I did it."

"Did you kill your father first?"

"Tonight I can't remember, honestly, that is all blank to me. I don't want to remember it so it's just kind of thrown out of my mind, because of this thing that's possessed me. You know what? I'm really scared. And if you think that I'm scared from murdering my own family that I love very much, you're wrong. It's not that, it's my possession that I'm scared of. I'm scared of my possession, oh." Blackman paused and breathed in and out as if he'd just sprinted a mile. "I don't know what's going to happen to me."

"Do you recall any of the details of this morning?"

"Do I recall them?"

"Yes, tell me what happened as far as you can recall sitting there talking with your father. Did you have an argument with him?"

"No, I didn't have any arguments with him at all. They kind of sensed I was going through an emotional problem. They sensed this, they know of the problems that I was going through, but they don't understand."

"When you were talking with your father, did you get up and go get the rifle and come back?"

"I can't remember how I got there. Really, my mind is totally blank on this. I think it is trying to reject this. It's trying to reject my thoughts."

"You're responsible for the murder of the six members of your family though, Bruce."

"This soul is. What about my spirit?"

"Physically, you did it though."

"Physically, but what about mentally? This is what I'm wondering: did I really murder them or did I save them? "

"Well," Clarke began, trying to reason, "That's only…"

Bruce cut him off. "Because of time, because time possessed me to do it. I had to do it."

"You say time possessed you? Then why was it necessary to do what you did last night?"

"I had to capture time, not me, but my family. My family was the key to time and I had to capture this time because Jesus Christ was supposedly my little brother — he's a twin and was robbed — his spirit was robbed when he was little, before he was even born and that's why he could walk on water and do all sorts of miracles, but without this how would — without time how would he be able to remember anything?"

Clarke tried to bring him back to the present by asking him an easy question. "What faith are you, Bruce?"

"Jehovah Witness."

"Do you go to the Jehovah Witness Hall normally?"

"I went there for a couple of weeks of help, but no, I haven't gone. I usually don't go to church. I usually keep my mind very, very open on everything I listen to, usually, and the music — like it was total déjà vu, but it wasn't telling me — it wasn't telling me that it was telling me. Now I know that I was going to be caught by the police because I am the living prophecy of my Saviour. Believe me, this is a problem within me relating to my family and time."

"You say you went to the Jehovah Witness Hall or you spoke with somebody?"

"Mm hmm."

"Who?"

"I spoke to — I don't remember the guy's name. That's the only drag about it. I was trying to talk to him about the Tree of Knowledge. You see, the Catholics think the Tree of Knowledge is an apple; Jehovah Witnesses think that it is a pear; but what is the real Tree of Knowledge?" He paused, as if making an effort to order his thoughts: "She told me that December third there would be just me, because only God would know what the Tree of Knowledge really be [sic]. Could a man seeing that if he eats it he'll be able to record all time, what's gonna happen from the beginning to the end and that was it. It was gonna be no more."

"This was on December..." Clarke asked.

Blackman interrupted him again: "There would be a new beginning, not a..."

Clarke interrupted Bruce: "This was on December the third you went to see this person? Where was it at, Bruce?"

"I don't know where it was at. This one woman that I was talking to, she died four times. This is what she told me. She said that there is a new planet out there. 'A new planet?' I asked. 'Oh well, it gets your dreams.' 'Well, what's this about your dreams, tell me more, tell me more.' I was asking her all these questions, I don't know why I'm asking these questions but everybody else in the room, they couldn't understand this except for me and these guys in front of me, they said 'Wait 'til you get to the door. There's a woman out there called Direct Mary or Detect Mary. I think she's really good looking or she's supposedly a whore'."

"You were talking with her on the bus?"

"And this is what her name was, the woman that I was talking to was Mary, and so I said dee, dee, Dee-tect Mary, Detect Mary on what? Detect Mary on death. What am I saving? I'm saving death. I don't know, I don't know what's possessed me. But it's telling me that death is the answer because once they die they become everything."

"Is this why you killed your family?"

"This is why I killed my family because they are part of everything. They are part of the end, the deal that we made it or break it, we broke."

"How long have you thought you were going to kill your family?"

"Just this morning."

"When did it come to you? When you were talking with your father?"

"Well, actually, it came to me before, once before, but I just threw it out of my mind. I said no, there's no way I can kill, there's no way I can kill, so I threw it out of my mind. Finally, this morning it said 'you must, because you have to capture time, you have to capture a part of your family, and if you don't capture this part of your family, then everything is going to die, as in the big bang theory.' No-one believes that there was a beginning. Well, there is a beginning but they don't believe on [sic] how it's going to end. They think that I'm imagining this, this is telling me that that's all wrong, it's going to be to Heaven, where we began. Where we came from."

"Where are you getting all your theory from, Bruce?"

"From 'it.'"

"From where?"

"From 'it,' the thing that possessed me."

"When it spoke with you?"

"Yeah, because it's saying that it is part of me, it's part of my life. It is the Devil, it is God, it is everything."

"And it spoke with you this morning. What did it say?"

"It said 'Kill, capture time'."

"Was the rest of your family in bed except for your father and yourself?"

"My little brother was sleeping on the couch."

"Downstairs?"

"Yeah, watching TV."

"How did your father get downstairs?"

"I don't know how. No idea. I carried him."

There was a sudden, piercing screech, and Bruce jumped. *"What's that noise?"*

"That's the tape recorder."

"It's called feedback."

"Right."

"The feedback into time."

"You put your father downstairs you say?"

"Yes."

"Beside your brother?"

"Yes."

"Do you recall anything else?"

"No recall. That's it. That's all. I told you everything."

"Was one of your family outside at one point in time?"

"Yes, outside my body."

"No, I mean outside the house."

"No, they were outside my body always, trying to tell me something."

Clarke sighed and clicked his pen several times before continuing. "I'm talking about the physical aspect of this. Did one of the members of your family leave the house this morning, during the time that this episode was going on?"

"No, because I just came in today, tonight, from a plane. I took a plane all the way from Nelson. I was supposed to be going to school there. I went there to say that I graduated and I was going to become God. I don't want to become God, I never wanted to become God, but this is the thing that's gonna possess. That's the beginning, unfortunately."

"You've been away from home for some time, have you?"

"Yes."

"How long?"

"I've been away from home for two, three days. Two days."

"Where were you?"

"Nelson."

"With somebody?"

"I was staying in the dorm."

"What kind of a dorm?"

"I was supposed to be taking a millwright course. This is also another part of time that I was supposed to experience with."

"O.K., you're taking a millwright course, were you?"

"Yes, I was, but I didn't even go to it."

"You went up and came back home?"

"'Cause they gave me a key and then, you know, I had my plane ticket and I can show you the number and she also told me about this monk, and she said that this monk…"

"Who told you that?"

"This thing in my brain. This thing in my brain told me that."

"The 'it,' eh?"

"The 'it.'"

"And you and your father didn't argue?"

"Me and my father, we had a few arguments, but he was trying to understand me, and I was trying to understand him. Now, together, we don't understand each other."

"Did you shoot all the members of your family?"

"Did I?"

"Yes."

"No, I didn't."

Clarke recognized that Bruce was misinterpreting. He backed up. "No, I know…"

Blackman reminded him: "My mental self…"

"I'm saying your physical self," asserted Clarke. "Is that the way you killed all the members of your family?"

"I hate using that word, because I did kill them. "

Clarke opened his palms and offered Bruce a half-smile: "I would like to tone it down but unfortunately, I don't know words to use that express it less than what it is."

"I don't know. I don't think I killed them. I think I liberated them. I hope I did."

"Now that we've talked for some time here, can you recall how it took place in the house? Did you murder your father first?"

"I can't recall that. I can't remember that. That's all blank. That's all blank, and I really don't like talking about it because it's just like a nightmare, like I am the nightmare. In the beginning."

"Had you planned to do what you did before this morning?"

"No, I didn't. It all came onto me, just all."

"While you were talking to your father?"

"Mm-hmm. I told my little brother everything. Told my family every bit of them that they were, I told them, I tried to reason with them but they couldn't understand because this is the total thing. It possessed me because I am Jehovah, supposedly."

"How long have you been a Jehovah?"

"I've been a Jehovah Witness for over a year and a half, two years. Two years now."

"But you haven't attended."

"But no, I haven't attended, but I read everything that they put out. But you see, what I read from there I get different interpretations from. And then when I go down there to talk to them, I'm still their opposite. Why am I their opposite? We — playing this game called Dungeons and Dragons — it's a game with your mind, right? And here I had my God (inaudible) before I was really able to call what God wants, that that was my opposite — God — opposite, opposite of what, opposite of time. It's a riddle. It said 24, it said 24, what's gonna happen? I don't know what's gonna happen. Maybe it's the twenty-fourth of this month."

"You say Dungeons and Dragons?"

"Yeah."

"Tell me about it."

"Dungeons and Dragons is a game that people use to play with their minds because this is the heaven or this is the hell, one of the two."

"How old are you now, Bruce?"

"I am 22 years old now."

"You're not employed at present?"

"No. I don't want a job, I don't want anything, except for maybe a cup of coffee. Can I get a cup of coffee, please?"

"We'll get you something to eat and drink."

"I suppose I should fast so I could die." Bruce paused to consider this alternative. "Hmm, that would be a good idea. Yeah, I think I'll do that instead. I don't want to eat anything."

Clarke wanted badly to figure out a way to move past the place in questioning where they were stuck. He tried a slightly different approach: "As a police officer investigating this, naturally I'm trying to find out all the facts I can concerning it because I'm going to have to write reports on it, and we're going to have to try and ascertain what took place in the house."

"Yeah, you're just looking for the facts and the reality of what's happening, right now, or what happened."

"That's what I have to do," said Clarke. "I've spoken with you here about what has possessed you."

Bruce answered, almost pleadingly, "I'm telling you it's a mental [*sic*] that I have and that my family's going to hate me, this physical family's going to hate me. They don't know that they are the Devil. I have to do that myself."

"I've listened to you here now and there's no question in my mind that something has possessed you as you tell me."

"Definitely, definitely."

"Because this isn't the thing that people do."

"Definitely. People don't do this and believe me if this is the truth, if there is not going to be any death, or if there's not Armageddon, I think Armageddon's gonna come no matter what, something's going to come. But if death does succeed and that we can capture time, then this is really strange."

Clarke did his best to try again. "Can you tell me about the physical aspect of this morning? As a police officer, I'm being practical and I have to…"

"Honestly, Officer, I can't remember much in the confusion. I really can't. Like I've been always considering myself the last of the hippies. Now, what are the hippies? Aren't hippies the person that's really spiritual, like really, but I call myself the last of a dying breed. This is what I call myself; I am the last of a dying breed of hippies. Now, why am I a dying breed of hippies? Because all hippies die."

"I don't know, I can't tell you that Bruce."

There was a long pause before Bruce offered: "What you're trying to do picture out is the reality, isn't it?"

"Right," answered Clarke.

"That's what I'm trying to picture out right now. I'm trying to picture reality. It's so very, very difficult for me because I'm a mass murderer."

"There were only seven people in that house; yourself, and your six family members?"

"My Mom and Dad."

"There was no-one else there?"

"That's right. There was [*sic*] seven spirits. I must have done something. I must have done something."

"What do you mean, you 'must have done something'?"

"Mentally, I get all sorts of weird pictures."

"What were you and your father talking about?

"What was I trying to tell him? I was trying to tell him about death."

"What was he saying to you?"

"He couldn't — he's exactly like you. You're trying to get the reality side of it."

"He was trying to help you."

"Yes, and I couldn't help myself."

"Had you spoken with the rest of your family members during that time that you'd just come home?

"Ummm, yes."

Clarke paused again before he asked, "What did you discuss with them?"

"I discussed this exact same problem that I had with them. But you see Karon, Bobi and Ricky, if they do possess the Heaven, then those parts of the Heaven will not come in but they could be devoured by this hidden big bang."

"Where are you reading this stuff, Bruce? "

"I'm reading it in my mind."

"This isn't in any book?"

"Yeah, Chapter 10, the Book of Revelations. If you have a Bible, I really wish that you'd check that Chapter 10 in the Book of Revelations, I really would. Why don't you look for one right now? Because it is really important. That is my whole life. Chapter 10."

"Who directed you to this chapter?"

"It. Time. Time is a riddle; everything has a riddle to it, even life itself. Doesn't it sound truthful, though?"

"I find it hard to understand, Bruce. I guess maybe your dad did too, eh?"

"Yeah, well, everybody did. I'm a murderer – I murdered my whole family so, so maybe this thing could win. I love life, but that that's all there is gonna be to it. I don't understand."

"You're pretty confused, eh?"

"Very confused. Dazed and confused, and I'm very cold. I'm always shivering."

"All the time?"

"Uh huh. You should have seen me at home. Shaking like a leaf."

"Have you ever had any doctor's help? A psychiatrist or anything?"

"Yes, I was seeing a psychiatrist…"

"Did your family send you to him?"

"Yes, and I was supposed to see him today at 11:00 in the afternoon. They wanted me to see him last night but I just said, no, no, no, I can't, I can't, I want to just stay up 'til 6:00, I want to see what tomorrow's going to bring me. And then I find out: Death. What's tomorrow going to bring me, what is tomorrow, what is the thirty-first going to bring me, what is time going to bring me?"

"So your father sat up with you trying to comfort you, did he?"

"Yes, he did."

"And he wanted you to go and see the doctor last night?"

"Yes, but they know who they are, they know who they are."

"Did the doctor…"

Bruce abruptly interrupted him: "They always damned God, too. *They always damned him.* I never damned him. Never, ever."

"Who damned him?"

"My family."

"How?"

"Well, just saying God damn it and Jesus Christ, just like everybody…They go 'ah, shit,' or 'ah, God damn it,' and I've never been like that. I've kind of – well, to an extent, but I try to control myself when I know it's going to happen because this is all my big, wicked nightmare and I'm still living it."

"How long did you and your father talk?"

"Me and my father talked 'til 4:00 this morning, fifteen after four, I do believe, and then I just wanted to sleep with it and then I just can't remember what happened."

"Was your father still there when you woke up?"

"No, I wasn't there. This, this is why I can't really remember what's really happened. This is like a picture to me; everything is just like a picture to me."

"So you say you and your father spoke 'til 4:00 in the morning?"

"Mm hmm."

"And then you fell asleep?"

"Yeah, and this is when time possessed me to do what I had to do."

"When you woke up…"

"I was totally possessed."

"Do you recall waking up?"

"Do I recall waking up? Yeah, I can recall waking up just before you came down and got me. That's when I woke up."

"When I came down and got you from the cells?"

"Mm hmm, that's when reality just kind of kicked into me: hey man, what is happening?"

"Do you recall waking up at home when you were talking with your father? Or did you go to sleep there?"

"I don't know, I don't know. My twin brother…has to be a key in this. My twin brother…"

"Was the rest of your family in bed and just you and your dad were talking during the morning hours?"

"What I can recall through my dream, yeah. I've gone totally insane. I swear, I must have in order to see things pictured like this, like a picture, like I'm not really here, I have no feeling, you know, like I can be on the other side of me, feel my spirit. It's really strange."

"Your father couldn't understand these things that you were talking to him about?"

"No. He's probably with us right now looking at me going...going..." Bruce trailed off and dropped his gaze. "I don't know."

"What was your father saying to you when you were talking this morning? What advice was he giving you?"

"He was giving me [the psychiatrist's] advice."

"What is that?"

"Reality. Just let it kick back, don't worry about it, just let all this get away from here, and now I have to phone up Satan and the Antichrist."

"That's your brother and sister you're referring to?"

"Yeah, I'd like to phone them and tell what happened, from my lips. They're going to hate me, they're going to hate me to pieces, but I have to because supposedly I am love, I am the heart of the universe. This is like a devil's cult, isn't it?"

"I don't know."

"I must talk to you like a hippie."

"No."

"Do I talk to you like a normal person?"

"No."

"I don't know what's happening to me."

Clarke paused. He'd been talking to Bruce now for almost 45 minutes and decided he'd not get much further.

"I think I'll take you downstairs again now, Bruce," he said.

"Can I get a blanket, please?"

"Sure."

"If it's no trouble, I'd just like to sleep."

"Maybe you and I can speak later?"

"Sure, I look forward to it."

"O.K."

"I guess you're going to get in touch with my family?"

"Yes, we'll have to advise them of what has taken place. Perhaps that's already been done now, I'm not sure. Is there anything else you want to say before we go back downstairs, Bruce?"

"Give them my love."

"O.K. There's nothing more you want to say to me at this time?"

"Tell them that I'm really sorry and that I am experiencing time. You must say that. You gotta tell them that they gotta trust me and they gotta put their heart with me because I'm so scared. I'm so scared."

"O.K. Bruce, we'll talk later on then if you want. If you want to get a hold of me…"

"Can I wash my hands?"

"Yes, we'll go downstairs."

"I just hope I'm allowed to wash my hands."

"No, that's fine."

"I wasn't allowed to wear my clothes. I'm here naked. These pants are made for two people that aren't even here."

"Yes, we had to do that naturally because we have to preserve evidence as you know and we don't mean to do anything other than we have to give you a pair of those coveralls to wear and hopefully we can get some clothes for you here. Before we go back downstairs, is there anything else you want to say before we leave here, Bruce?"

"Give my sister my love. Say that really, by the heart, the same with my twin brother. Tell him that he is a key to me. Tell him I'd love to speak to him in private. Tell him he must come here and speak to me in private."

"O.K. This interview is now terminated at 08:45."

Clarke stopped the tape recorder and escorted Bruce back to cells.

He did not allow him to wash his hands.

SLAUGHTER

January 18, 1983

AT 04:50, PROPELLED by the sureness of his task, Bruce grabbed the rifle he'd loaded in the basement, bounded up the stairs and turned to shoot his father. In the kitchen, Senior lurched upright from where he sat at the kitchen table and shouted *"Don't!"* as he placed his hands in front of his face. The first shot sliced through his palm, into his cheek. It was not a fatal wound, but a deep one. He staggered forward and, for just a moment, felt warm wetness when he stepped into a pool of his own blood. Bruce shot at him again and missed. *"Son!"* Senior pleaded. Bruce shook his head to focus, and re-aimed. He pulled the trigger three more times before Senior was down, and dead.

Ricky woke suddenly at the first shot. It took four seconds for him to get oriented, but he knew by the way his stomach lurched that something was wrong.

"DAD!"

Ricky bounded up the three stairs to the kitchen where his father lay in a widening skim of blood. He turned to his left. There was Bruce, pointing a rifle directly at his head. BAM! Ricky saw the flare; the hot bullet grazed his chin and earlobe. *"FUCK!"* he screamed and ran for his life back to the family room.   At the top of the stairs, Bruce leveled the gun and fired. Ricky hit the wall, then fell in a heap.

Upstairs, Irene woke to Ricky's scream. *"Dad!"* she heard, then gunshots. *Oh my God*, she thought, was her husband killing Bruce? Irene's body felt paralyzed in the darkness. She'd left a light on in the walk-in closet so that Senior could find his way if he'd managed to come to bed. As her eyes adjusted to the dim light she listened for what came next.

Silence.

"Honey?" She swung her legs over the edge of the bed to place her feet on the floor. Below, Bruce heard the movement and looked up at the ceiling. He bolted up the stairs, two at a time. When he flung open her bedroom door, Irene was running for the bathroom, her back toward him, naked except for white panties and white socks. When he shot her in the back, she hit the wall and fell backward, toward him, mouthing words that made no sound except for a faint hiss and some gurgling. Bruce took a deep breath to calm himself while he watched his mother on her back, struggling to breathe. He walked over to evaluate her. She raised her arm against the rifle but it did no good. He shot her one more time in the head. The gurgling stopped.

Bruce had seen the look of dead things before. You could always tell by the eyes. His mother was dead, that was for sure. But there was blood, and a lot of it. Didn't Mary say that you don't bleed when you die? Bruce grabbed his mother's housecoat and tried to dab the blood from around her head but he couldn't stand the vacant look in her eyes. He took the housecoat – a kimono, really; one of those exotic, indulgent gifts only received at Christmas – into the bathroom. He thought about rinsing it out, but spied his jean jacket vest hanging on the door. He dropped the kimono and grabbed the vest, put it on. But it was comically big. He'd lost so much weight the thing looked ridiculous. And anyway, now there were bloody handprints all over it. He removed it and placed it on a towel bar. With one last look at his mother, he walked downstairs.

There was his father heaped in the kitchen, the floor covered in a film of blood like a red skating rink. Bruce froze. *Dad!* he squeaked, the Devil inside him retreating a little. Bruce began to cry. "What did I do, what did I do?" he whispered, wringing his hands. Then the voice said *They're coming, clean it up.* So he grabbed brown towels from the laundry room — less likely to stain — and started mopping, but blood kept seeping out of his father. *Take him downstairs*, the voice commanded. Bruce — with a superhuman strength brought on by the ragged coursing of adrenalin through his veins — dragged his father down the basement stairs and into the games room. When he dropped him to the floor, Bruce looked at Senior's face – a hideous grimace of pain and fear. Bruce had never, ever seen his father look that way in life and it made him sick.

As Bruce trudged back up the stairs, he glanced over his shoulder. His dad looked so lonely laying there. Bruce marched to the family room, grabbed Ricky by the arms and dragged him downstairs where he laid him next to their father, face down. Bruce shoved the two of them together, so close that their heads and shoulders touched. "That's the way they should go up to Heaven," Bruce thought, "As one."

Up in the kitchen, the chair where his father had been sitting oozed blood like a living thing. Bruce grabbed a paper towel and wiped off the seat, then took the chair downstairs. He sat in it, gazing quietly at Senior and Ricky. His brother looked peaceful, almost asleep, but his dad…Bruce couldn't stand it — the startled, rolled back eyes, his dad's rugged face contorted by terror. Bruce ran back upstairs, pulled a section of plastic carpet runner from the hallway then used it to cover his father's face and upper torso. Better, he thought. He gathered one last look, then left them.

Upstairs, the voices spurred him to work furiously at cleaning the blood off the kitchen floor and the counter tops. He did this like an automaton, wiping with the towels until they were sodden, then rinsing, then wiping, then rinsing, until the voices said, *They're here.*

Bruce reloaded the rifle and waited. He heard a vehicle pull up outside. The garage door was open, and he knew that's how they'd all enter. At the front door, he held the rifle and his breath, listening to his sister Karon saying, "Go on ahead, my shoe is coming off." He heard Bobi's voice, and her husband John's too. *Dammit!* They brought John, even though he'd told Bobi not to.

Bruce snuck out the front door and came up behind Karon in the garage as she was trying to adjust her backless shoes. When she turned to face him, he saw the look of surprise on her face — a face beautiful even without makeup.

"Bruce?"

He shot her in the head. She fell forward, landing on her right cheek and smashing her glasses. Both shoes came off her feet.

John turned and gasped. For a moment he looked like he was going to run, but there was no-where to go. "Hold on there Bruce," he said, trying hard to control his panic. "Come on, let's talk about this. Give me the gun." As John walked toward him with palms up, Bruce heard his sister Bobi crying from inside the house. John was with him in the garage now. They locked eyes.

Bruce lowered the gun for a moment and, when he did, John bolted outside into the night.

Bruce chased him, spurred on by the fury of the voices. He shot at John's head, but missed. Bruce fired again and hit him in the left shoulder. "Help! *Help!*" cried John as he rounded the corner of the yard. Bruce stopped running, aimed the gun and fired. John crumpled to one knee. Bruce pointed the gun down at the ground and strode over, indignant. *"You,"* he hissed, "you're the Devil." John tried to stand on his wounded leg, but went down again. *"Get up,"* Bruce shouted, *"Get in the house!"* John, a man three times the size of Bruce, rose then fell, rose then fell, staggered his way into the house, aided in part by Bruce kicking and pushing him from behind.

"I told them not to bring you," he said calmly, "But here you are. That must mean you're supposed to die, too." In the laundry room just past the entrance to the garage, John collapsed to both knees. Bruce shot him in the face and head. Not just once, but over and over again.

Despite six gunshot wounds, John was still breathing. *Fucker!* Bruce shouted, then ran to the garage to grab a hammer. Returning to where John lay wheezing on his side, Bruce raised his hand, and with every bit of force left in him, smashed the Devil's face until it was mush.

Roberta had seen the carnage inside the house. She ran outside to hide, then heard her husband shouting for help. By the time she could summon the courage to go back in, she saw her brother attacking her husband with a hammer.

"No, Bruce," she pleaded, weeping. She thrust her hands over her husband's face, but it was too late. John's face was unrecognizable. One of the blows struck her finger.

Bruce glared at her with awful, glittering eyes, and she knew she was next. She ran, pumped full of a fear that was primal, one that made her feel almost superhuman. She could outrun this crazy man.

But Bruce was feeling supercharged, too, and Bobi couldn't elude him for long.

The grass outside was slippery from the rain. She kept losing her footing and stumbled, but recovered. Bruce grabbed her arm. They were about the same size – slim and slender – but he suddenly had an otherworldly strength. Her arm felt like a little sausage and he was squeezing it to burst.

"No, no, not me. *Not me Bruce! Not me!*" Roberta's last hope was that she'd be spared; that Bruce would feel some flicker of mercy earned by her allegiance to him. He let go of her arm and punched her in the face. She staggered backward. Bruce leveled the gun at her and shot it twice. He fired once more for good measure, but the gun was empty. He tossed it into the grass.

His sister lay there in the rain. Even in the dark he could see that emptiness had overtaken her. He closed his eyes and breathed. In and out, in and out. He'd done his job. The voices were gone. He grabbed his sister's arms and dragged her into the garage, dropped her between the two parked cars. Her head cracked when it hit the concrete. Bruce hit the "close" switch on the garage.

He paused to let his breathing return to normal. Then he surveyed the surroundings. The scene laid out before him was part one of the plan. Part two would come in the next few hours and days when he could get close enough to Todd and Angela to finish the job.

As he walked past Karon — her body half in the garage and half in the house — he thought she might still be breathing. Bruce went downstairs and grabbed the Marlin rifle he'd loaded earlier then shot her again, once, behind her ear.

There was nothing else to shoot. Bruce walked to the family room and looked at the place where Ricky had fallen, marked by a deep pool of blood at the base of the stairs. With great care, and slowly, Bruce leaned the rifle against the stairs, the butt end in Ricky's blood, the muzzle pointing upward, toward Heaven.

It was a shrine to his family.

Bruce stood in the hallway and listened. John was still breathing, a sound like someone blowing into a soda through a straw. Bruce was tired, but he picked up the hammer and hit John a few more times. "Come on, why won't you die?" he asked.

His sister Bobi answered with a gasp. Bruce jumped. *"Shit!"* he squeaked, "you scared me!" He walked over and nudged her with his toe. She didn't move but he could hear her struggling to breathe. Bruce raised the hammer and hit her twice.

Then the voice said, *Go. Go find the others.*

Bruce took a moment to straighten his headband — his crown of thorns. He looked in a mirror before leaving the house. He'd done it. He'd saved the world. What he saw reflected back was exactly what the great white whore had told him: Bruce Blackman had become God.

"I'll be with all of you shortly," he called out to the silent house. "I just have one more thing to do."

CONFESSION II

January 18, 1983
Approximately 6 hours after the massacre

AT AROUND 11:30, Staff Sergeant Clarke and Constable Montgomery escorted Bruce to the breathalyzer room where they took him to a sink. Blackman was quiet as he filled the basin with water. He soaped his hands, then rubbed them the way he would as if trying to warm them on a cold night, until they were covered by a mass of soap foam tinged pink. He rubbed and rubbed, then soaked, then rubbed, finally draining the water from the basin while he rinsed with clear water to banish every last trace of blood and soap. Montgomery gave him paper towels and Blackman used a stack of them to dry his hands. Just as they were about to return him to his cell, Blackman asked if he could wash his hands again, and repeated the procedure. Clarke thought, *It's going to take a lot more than this to wipe away what you've done, son.* He watched Blackman's small frame hunched over the sink, earnestly focused on re-cleaning his hands. Something about Blackman's size, his politeness, his apparent sincerity, evoked in Clarke a fleeting sense of sympathy. Whether through interrogation, medication or time, Blackman would eventually remember what he'd done that morning, in all its gruesome detail. Clarke wondered if it wouldn't be better that he never remembered. That would be the humane thing.

After returning Blackman to cells — and before part two of the interrogation — Clarke received more details from the crime scene. He learned, before talking to Blackman again, that at least one of the victims had been brutally bludgeoned about the face and head. Clarke thought again about the smallness of Bruce Blackman, about his cooperative demeanor, his good manners. The "please" and "thank you's" that came at the beginning and end of every request. How could this quiet boy, who professed to love his family, be capable of such savagery?

1:40 p.m.
This is a verbatim transcript of the second interrogation

Clarke pressed the red "record" button and began: "O.K., Bruce, I've told you here we got a hold of your relatives."

"Mm hmm."

"And you asked for your brother in particular when he comes."

"The reason why I asked for him is because he's my twin brother. He's so very close to me."

"Yes."

"I hope he can understand me." Blackman sighed.

193

"OK, I've asked if you would give me a written statement, and at this time now Bruce you claim that you don't want to put anything in writing. You're not...you don't..."

"I'm mentally very distracted, mentally."

"Can you recall anything else? You said that you would recall something else if you would have a sleep and you've been down in the cells now and you had a rest. Can you tell me anything further that physically happened at your home last night?"

"The Star of David."

"I mean physically, Bruce, what took place? You and your father were in the living room speaking, talking?"

"Yes, we were talking about..."

Clarke interrupted: "You weren't arguing, so you've told me. You were just talking about..."

"My possession."

"Your possession. Can you tell me what took place from the time when the talking ended and what you physically did in the house this morning?"

"I was just up, up, up all the time. I was always up. I couldn't sleep because of this possession that I had."

"Yes."

"And finally, I just kind of left myself and then next thing you know I was doing really bizarre things."

"What do you mean by bizarre things?"

"Well, why would a man kill another man? Now, is that him in his own state of mind or is he out of this world somewhere? Is he doing something that he should be doing? Is it wrong to kill or is it right to kill and this is the thing that possessed me. Is it wrong or right? Now I know that it's wrong."

"OK, now I would like you to tell me physically what took place. Did you, when your father…"

"I can't remember." Blackman said, his tone abrupt. "I really, really can't remember it because every time, as time drags on, it just becomes more dated and more dated and more dated."

"Do you recall being picked up by the police officers near your home?"

"Faintly. I don't even know what they look like."

"Do you recall being outside of your house?"

"Do I recall being outside? I can recall being picked up outside, down by the school. Almost down by the school."

"From the time you and your father were talking until the time the police officers picked you up, tell me anything that you can recall during that period of time."

"Not much. Not much of anything."

"You and your father were the only ones that were up in the house?"

"Yes."

"Your mother and your sisters and John Davies, is it?"

"John, yes."

"Yes. They were all sleeping?"

"No. I think John and Bobi and Karon came over from North Van."

"What time did they come over at?"

"Around 5:30."

"Why did that happen?"

"I don't know."

"Someone must have phoned them, did they?"

"Yes, that was probably me. You see I can't remember this. It's all like a picture."

"So who came over? John?"

"My sisters. Both my sisters."

"Both your sisters and John came over from North Van. Was that in the early morning hours?"

"Yes, very early."

"About what time?"

"I can't remember. About 4:30."

"So prior to that it was just your mother, your father and yourself in the house?"

"My mother, my father, and my little brother Ricky."

"And then your two sisters and John Davies came in the early morning hours?"

"Mm hmm."

"And you don't recall the reason that they would have come over?"

"No, I don't recall it."

"Do you recall talking with them on the phone?"

"Everything's just blank. Everything's just blank. I can remember it, if I really think, but what I'm trying to do is trying not to remember because it's so horrible."

"Well, I appreciate it is and like I say I would like you to tell me about it, once, if you could really remember for me so that it would…"

"Clear things up?"

"It would clear things up so that we would know." Clarke felt momentarily hopeful. It sounded as if Blackman might have found a thread of reality to hold on to.

"That's all. Everything that I told you. The Star of David possessed me. The Star of David. Now how could a star possess a person?"

"I don't know, Bruce, I couldn't tell you. But what I'm mainly trying to clear up in my own mind now is that you've told me these things and that you are possessed. What I'm trying to clear up is how it physically occurred and you say your father was up. Were your two sisters and John Davies also up? Were they awake?"

"My sister and John Davies, early in the morning...no, I don't think so. I think I had to wake them up."

"You woke them up?"

"I must have."

"From the time when your dad and you were talking in the living room, can you *really* try and remember for me and tell me exactly, physically, what happened in the house? It's important for us to know because we know what's happened and we would like to know the circumstances and how it came about. We know that — you've told us that you were possessed, but what I'm trying to get out of you here now is *how* did it happen? What, who was up, and how did you go about it? In what manner?"

"How did I go about it? I don't know how I did it. All I know is that I did it."

"You know that you killed…"

Blackman completed the sentence. "…six people."

"You remember doing that?"

"Why did I kill six people though?" Clarke watched Blackman's brown eyes begin to shine with tears. They spilled out, running down his cheeks, as Blackman began to cry.

"I don't know, Bruce."

"I don't know, either." Blackman sniffed, wiping at his nose. "The Star of David, it was the bug in the star. It's something out there. Or is it something with the universe? I don't know. I'm scared. I'm scared for you, I'm scared for me, I'm scared for everything. I'm scared about everything because of this thing."

"During the time that you were doing the act that we're speaking of, was this thing talking to you?

"No, I was in a dream, but believe me, I'm not in no dream now."

"You're much more alert now than when I spoke to you earlier."

"Definitely, definitely much more alert."

"Than this morning?"

"Oh yeah, like I'm all of a sudden here, and I picture 'hey man, look what I'm doing, look what I did, why did you do that, why?' There's got to be a reason why, and I'm trying to search within myself. Why did I do that? And it's so…" Blackman trailed off. He shook his head in disbelief. "I don't know, I really don't know."

"Do you recall anything about how you did it, how you went about it? Was it a planned thing? Did it just all of a sudden as a spur of the moment come over you?"

"Definitely a spur of the moment."

"You hadn't planned this."

"No, it just all of a sudden — bango — it was there, 'hey, do this.' I wasn't even doing it — well, it didn't even seem like my body was doing it. It all of a sudden just said 'here, here you go.'"

"You didn't plan on having your sisters and John Davies at the house this morning?"

"No."

"Was it the fact that there was a group of people there that caused you to do it?"

"A group of people?"

"Well, your family — a lot of family was there. Did this seem the time to do it or why would you do it when there were so many people there?"

"Don't ask me, I don't know." Blackman squirmed in his chair, his tone agitated. "I need another cigarette. Can I get a cigarette?"

"I can get you one as soon as we go downstairs. We'll get your money and I'll buy you a…"

Blackman interrupted: "I smoke too much. Now, does it really matter if I smoke at all?"

"Do you use drugs at all?"

"Yes, I have."

"Do you drink?"

"No, I don't drink. I smoke marijuana."

"You weren't drinking last night?"

"No, I wasn't drinking last night. I smoked a joint."

"About what time?"

"I had one rolling paper left, so I smoked a joint and then I ate some."

"You ate some? Did it have any effect on you?"

"I don't know. That's why I can't remember."

"How long have you been smoking marijuana?"

"Since I was in Grade 8."

"About six years, seven years."

"I'm 22, so it must be seven years or so."

"Is that all the marijuana you had was just one joint and then you ate some?"

"Yes, yes."

"Was that in front of your father?"

"Did I do this in front of my father?"

"Yes."

"Smoke a joint in front of my father?"

"Yes."

"No, they never cared for marijuana. They always thought it took you out of this world and I think that that's what it was."

"You think this is what's bothered your mind? The marijuana?"

"It probably was."

"So you had this prior to your talk with your dad?"

"About what?"

"The marijuana. You had that prior to speaking with your dad?"

"Did I have that prior?"

"Yes." Clarke made a note that Blackman was having a hard time concentrating. He couldn't follow the conversation.

Blackman: "I was speaking to him all night."

"When did you have the joint then? When was that?"

"I guess it must have been around 1:30 or 2:30 or 3:30."

"You just excused yourself then and went outside?"

"Yeah, I just walked outside after telling him I was going out for cigarettes."

Clarke paused. He decided to change course.

"Do you recall at all loading the weapons? The .22's?"

"No, I don't. I don't recall it at all."

"Where are they kept in the home?"

"They're kept downstairs in the games room, down by where we keep all the meats and that — the freezer, the food. We have the freezer and then we had the gun for hunting. My dad reloads his own bullets and that."

"Do you recall going down there and...?"

"No I don't recall. No, I don't recall it at all. I can't even recall me shooting them, because that just seems like a dream."

"Yet you tell me you know that you did it?"

"Now, because I'm here. That's the only reason why I know that I did it."

"How do you know that you did it?"

"Because of the occurrences in time."

"You recall doing it?"

"Yeah, when there's questions brought up about it."

"You can see it in your memory, can you?"

"When certain points are brought out, yeah."

"Are there any points I can bring out to make it clearer to you so that you can tell me how it occurred, what physically happened? Not the fact that you were possessed. I know that, you told me that, but the way it occurred?"

"I think the reason I was possessed was from that joint. If you ever talk to any hippies, I talked to you on the tape before, they all smoke dope and they're all thinking that once you smoke dope, you see God. You're talking to God and then you're a part of God. This is the reason why I became a hippie, because I like talking to God. Now I feel — now

I know what God is, God being marijuana. Oh man, why did He make this world go crazy?"

"I don't know, Bruce."

"Maybe we should get rid of marijuana altogether on this bloody planet. It's a wicked drug."

"After you had that joint last night, did you feel any differently than any other joints you've ever had?"

"No, I felt the same as I ever...oh, no, I did. I *did* feel different because I ate some and so it was like a more intense stone."

"Have you ever eaten it before?"

"Yes, I have."

"Did you feel differently this time?"

"Did I feel differently this time? Well, because I smoked one joint and I ate some."

"Have you ever had the thought cross your mind before to do anything of this nature?"

"Never. Well, something brought it up to me and of course, I'm a very honest person, and so the first thing I say...I say everything that feel to my Mom and Dad and so, as [the psychiatrist] would say. Have you talked to [the psychiatrist]?"

"I'm trying to get a hold of him. But you were going on and saying that you're a very honest person and that…"

"Definitely, I am a very honest person."

"And I asked you the question, had it ever crossed your mind before. Has it?"

"To murder?"

"Yes."

"Never."

"You've never…"

"I've never thought of murdering before which is like a sudden occurrence, like bango, you had to do it and I was stoned out of my mind when I did it, I swear, I must, I was out of this world. I was out on something. It was like a big, giant acid trip."

"What did you do, simply leave your chair and go get the gun?"

"Yes."

"Do you recall that?"

"Do I recall it? I can recall sleeping in the living room."

"Was your father there?"

"And I can remember getting up."

"Yes, go ahead."

"And walking downstairs and then when I came up, everything happened."

"Tell me about it."

"I just came up with the gun totally loaded and I just started shooting — *phoo, phoo, phoo…*"

"Who did you shoot first?"

"My father."

"Where did you shoot him?"

"I can't remember. I can't remember."

"Was he awake?"

"I think he was talking to me."

"Who did you shoot next?"

"I can't remember, I can't remember at all, I don't want to remember it, I don't want to remember it."

Clarke tried to be as gentle as he could be: "I would like you to remember it just for my sake, just for the record."

In the long pause that followed, Clarke waited for Blackman to speak.

"I can't remember. I know that I was talking to my father."

"You do recall shooting your father, do you?"

"Yes I do, because I was talking to him."

"How many times did you shoot him?"

"I don't know how many times I shot him. I don't know how many times I shot any of them. I don't. All I know is that they're all dead."

"And there's no doubt in your mind that you did it?"

"No doubt in my mind at all and I feel very, very, very bad about it. This is it, I think…How many years is it for murder? Can I ask you that?"

"Well, I'm not the judge, you see. I can't tell, you but…"

"Average."

"I can't even speculate on what might happen."

Blackman paused, and appeared to be thinking.

"When do I see the judge?" he asked.

"It won't be today."

"Probably be tomorrow?"

"You'll be remanded by a justice of the peace today, into custody. Probably tomorrow. Is there any more that you can recall, Bruce?"

"No, there isn't. I don't want to recall any more."

"I realize you don't want to recall it, I know that. The only thing is it's important for me to have you recall it to me on one occasion for the record of what took place."

"Yes, I realize that, and as you know I am a very honest person and I don't lie whatsoever."

"No, I don't imply that whatsoever. I know that you're telling me that you're having a hard time recalling what took place. I believe you. All I'm asking you to do is search your memory as best you can so that we are able to have an account of what took place, because we're seized here with investigating the incident. You appreciate that, eh?"

"Yes, yes I do appreciate it."

"And it's incumbent upon us to ascertain, the best we can, what took place. That's the reason why I'm asking you. You've told me that you've done it, there's no doubt in our own mind that you've done it, and everything is consistent with that. The only thing that I'm searching for now is any other details that will give us what we need."

"Hmmm. I can't recall."

Clarke pressed on. "When you left the house, can you recall where the bodies were in the home?"

"No, I don't."

"Do you recall struggling, or any conversation with any one of the six people during the time that this took place?"

"John, I was talking to John."

"What did John say to you?"

"He said, 'come in, let's talk about it,' so I came in and I talked to him about it."

"Was that before the incident with your father?"

"Yes, no, that was after."

"After you had shot your father."

"Yes, I think so."

"And you would have had the gun in your hand at this time?"

"Yes, I think I did. Yes, I did. John is a very understanding man."

"Do you recall anything else? Any conversation or any struggling with any one of the members of your family?"

"No, I don't."

"Can you give me any estimation of length of time that it would have taken place over?"

"No, I don't."

"It happened very suddenly and very quickly?"

"Mm hmm, mm hmm."

"If you were to estimate, how long would it have taken place in?"

"I can't remember, I can't remember, I don't want to remember. It's just a nightmare. I'm living in a nightmare."

"Would you want to talk with me again, Bruce?"

"Sure, if you really want. I'd like to talk to my twin brother."

"Well, you will be able to talk to him. The phone isn't a good method of talking with him and he will come out here and we'll tell him that you wish to talk to him."

"Can I be with him? I gotta hug him. I gotta say sorry to him. I gotta say sorry to him."

"Well, that's down the road. We'll see."

"Can I go back to my cell?"

"Certainly. Is there anything you want to say before you go back?"

"Yeah. I need some cigarettes. Players filters."

"All right." Clarke noted Bruce's cigarette request, then asked if he had anything more to say.

"If there's a God," he answered, "I'm sorry."

EVIDENCE

TWO WEEKS LATER, Staff Sergeant Clarke walked into his office to find his desk cleared. The haphazard piles were gone. Replacing them was a thin stack of papers awaiting his approval and a cardboard wine box full of files set exactly in the middle of his industrial green, formica-topped desk. Everything else had been stacked in neat piles on the floor behind his chair. Gladys, his secretary, was no doubt the person who'd done the arranging; it was her way of saying, 'you have a report to write and you better get to it'.

Gladys. She'd been his administrative support in one way or another since the sixties. But in her case, longevity and experience had not combined to equal any measure of competence. She was a horrendous speller and Clarke had to proofread everything before he could agree to attach his name to it. Yet, whatever scab had hardened over Clarke's heart after twenty-plus years in law enforcement, it wasn't thick enough to allow him to fire her. Every time he thought about it, every time he resolved to cut her loose, he softened. Clarke knew she could never find — and certainly never sustain — gainful employment anywhere else. So, he endured her typos and spelling mistakes and tried

213

to ignore the prodigious amounts of White-Out[12] crusting the pages of every report he signed.

Clarke sat down, his chair objecting with the same little screech it had since its first day placed into service. Gladys had brought olive oil to work, claiming she could silence "that annoying squeak". Even the maintenance department had performed their handyman incantations on it, but nothing worked. *The chair doesn't want to be here either,* Clarke thought.

On top of the small pile of papers to his left was a memo Clarke had dictated for Crown Counsel[13] with an update on when he'd have his full report ready. Clarke scanned it for errors; miraculously, the memo read clean until the last sentence.

"Gladys!" Clarke shouted.

The clack of unsteady typing in the other room stopped, and soon Gladys peeked around the door frame. "Yes, sir?"

Gladys wasn't her real name. Her real name was Marjorie, but in 1964 Marjorie became an unfortunate victim of alopecia and lost all her hair, including her eyebrows. She'd immediately begun wearing a brown, frumpy wig and painting on eyebrows so arched they made her look both surprised and horrified. During this same time the television series *Bewitched* aired. In her new get-up, Marjorie was the spitting

---

[12] A substance like Liquid Paper, used to make corrections on typewritten pages.
[13] The Canadian equivalent of the prosecution, or "the State."

image of the nosy neighbour Gladys Kravitz. The resemblance was uncanny, and everyone started calling Marjorie Gladys instead. Nearly twenty years later, they still did.

"Gladys," said Clarke, "do you really think it's appropriate to have a wine case front and center in the detachment office?"

"No-one comes in here except me and you," she said, "and anyway, it's the perfect size for all those papers. It'll help us keep everything together. I brought it from home."

"I'm glad to hear you didn't bring it from the break room."

"Is that all?' she asked.

"Look at this memo you typed," he said, holding it out across the desk.

Gladys reached toward and took it from Clarke, the same little choreography that had played out between them for years. She scanned it quickly, her eyes moving back and forth across the page. When she finished, a sheepish smile lit her face. "It's why I put it on top," she said. "I didn't have to use White-Out once! Aren't you proud of me?"

"Read the last sentence."

She quoted, "'*It will most likely be another week before I can sort through the details of the grizzly scene.*'"

"Gladys, were there any bears on Spuraway?"

"There were bears at the crime scene? That wasn't in the news."

Clarke sighed. Why did he even try anymore? "Gladys, the word 'grisly' is not spelled with two zs."

"It's not?"

"I bought you that dictionary for a reason."

"A dictionary is only useful if you know how to spell the word in the first place," she countered. "Anyway, who cares? You know what I meant and they know what you mean."

Clarke had decided that "anyway" was Gladys' favorite word. She used it as a noun, a verb, an adjective, a conjunction, an exclamation and an epithet — whatever the occasion demanded.

"Take it with you," he said, nodding at the memo in her hand, but she simply stood there, staring at him. Waiting.

Oh, just give it to her, he thought. "G-r-i-s-l-y."

"An 's'? That doesn't even make sense. Anyway, I never would have found it."

Gladys scurried out of his office and Clarke stood up. He reached into the wine box and extracted five file folders containing different reports. There was the investigator's extensive narrative covering the probable course of events and forensic evidence to uphold the theory. There was the crime detection laboratory report from the firearms section. There were the autopsy reports, a catalog of witness statements, and hand-written notes from the various members[14] who'd guarded Blackman in his cell. Heaviest of all was an album containing photographs from the crime scene. He'd not yet seen those.

Clarke's job was to stitch all the different threads together into one cohesive blanket that would cover the events of January 18, 1983.

He laid everything out before him, took a deep breath and sat back down. From the top right desk drawer he retrieved a yellow legal pad, a blue pen and his dictating microphone. While he decided on his plan of attack — which report to tackle first — he looked at a piece of paper detailing Blackman's criminal record.

1978 May 22 in North Vancouver. Charge: Possession of a Narcotic. Conditional discharge and one year probation.

1983 January 18 in Coquitlam. Charge: Murder (6 counts).

Clarke shook his head. That was the steepest trajectory he'd ever seen. From simple possession to mass murder? It didn't make sense. It didn't make any sense at all.

Last week, Clarke had made some notes after consulting with Crown Counsel at the court house, and with psychiatrists at the Forensic Psychiatric Institute, (a place known as "Riverview"), where Bruce was being held. There were some discrepancies between Bruce's version of the events, the eye witness accounts, and the forensic evidence. Clarke

---

[14] The term 'member' refers to an officer of the Royal Canadian Mounted Police.

would have to sift through the files to find six critical needles in the haystacks of information. Those were what he needed to sew everything together. He would have to determine with as much certainty as he could — and back it up with evidence — the following:

Were there, indeed, two separate killing sprees?

In each incident, who was attacked first and last?

What time(s) did the murders occur?

What occurred between spree #1 and spree #2?

How many and which of the bodies had been bludgeoned after being shot?

Did Bruce Blackman murder all six victims and did he act alone?

Clarke read the witness statements first to get a fix on the time. William T. had called police at 05:53 hours saying he'd heard gunshots and what looked like two males shouting and running in the yard of the house across the street. Another witness, Luther S., witnessed what he said were "two males" fighting in his yard. Luther heard the words, "Not me, Bruce, not me," then two quick shots. The timeframe was about the same as William had reported to police. Clarke made a note on his yellow pad, "Last shots approx. 05:50."

William said that after he'd called the police he saw a young man exit the house, then ran outside and told the two officers approaching the Blackman home that the person who had just walked out of the house was the person now being questioned by the other officer still stationed at the police cars. Clarke made another note: "From last shots to apprehension 10-15 min."

A portion of those fifteen minutes would have been consumed by Bruce dragging one of the bodies into the garage and performing his last acts of violence upon the victims in the house. There would not have been enough time to have executed anything but the most cursory wiping down of evidence, certainly not the protracted clean-up effort detailed in the investigator's report. That meant that the first three victims — Mr. and Mrs. Blackman and young Ricky — would have been killed earlier, with enough time in between killings that Bruce was able to make a significant effort to clean up the blood.

Now Clarke had to determine the order of attack. In one of the interrogations, Bruce had told Clarke that during the second killing spree he'd killed Roberta first, but that did not jibe with the witness accounts. William T. saw two men arguing. One of the men, he said, was much bigger in size than the other. That would rule out Roberta, since she and Bruce were both very slight of build. It must have been Bruce and John Davies. Clarke made a note, "Male Davies and Blackman seen first."

Luther S. claimed he saw "two men fighting" in his back yard before the last shots were fired. The two men, according to Luther, were almost exactly the same size. Even with longish hair, Roberta could have — in the dark — been mistaken for a young man. Another witness stated that he also saw two shapes fighting, but the voice crying out for help was that of a woman. William said he observed one man dragging another shape into the garage. That must have been Roberta who was found between two cars, on her back, with her arms above her head and her jacket pulled up over her face. The autopsy revealed mud on her hands and the side of her face, as well as blades of grass stuck near her chin. Her car keys were found in the witness' back yard; her shoes were partially off her feet; and, the stud to her back jean pocket was ripped, consistent with her being dragged. When all these details were pieced together, it appeared that John Davies was attacked before Roberta, but what about Karon? Her body was found face first, her arms by her sides and one hand still clutching a purse, as if she had simply pitched forward where she stood. The investigator believed — and Clarke concurred — that Karon was the first one killed during the second spree. Bruce had snuck up on and shot her before she'd had time to react.

Bruce had also told Clarke and the psychiatrist that he'd used the hammer to bludgeon Karon, but no evidential marks were found on her body. Clarke looked again at the autopsy report. Roberta had sustained several cracks to her skull and jaw. While some of those injuries could have occurred when Bruce dropped her head to the concrete, it was feasible that he'd hit her a few times with the hammer. Clarke made another note: "Hammer likely used on both Davies."

Fixing the time of the earlier shootings proved more difficult. There was only one witness to have heard the first set of shots fired. Vernon P. stated that at about 05:00 he heard a woman scream and then a crack like a gunshot. This would have been eleven minutes after Roberta telephoned the psychiatrist. If this witness was correct — that the scream was from a woman — that had to be Mrs. Blackman. The time between Roberta's call to the psychiatrist — 04:49 — and when Vernon P. heard a woman scream — 0500 — was a mere eleven minutes. After calling his sister, Bruce would have gotten the weapons together and then quickly murdered his prey. He would have done this hastily, relying in part on the element of surprise.

But who was shot first?

Clarke relied in part on Bruce's memory for the answer to this question. It was possible that Ricky could have been the first one attacked; if Blackman, Sr. had tried to intervene, Senior would unquestionably have been killed in the process. But there was no real evidence of struggle, of a father trying to protect his youngest son. No furniture upended, no bruises or contusions on Bruce that would have resulted from wrestling with his father.

Blackman, Sr. had been fired at multiple times. Bullet casings and slugs had gone all over the place, indicating, perhaps, that Bruce was at least initially hesitant as he began his attack. Ricky, who was sleeping in the family room below the kitchen, would have awoken at the first shot and been on his feet by the second and third ones. By the time he ran up into the kitchen to see what was happening, he would have immediately been fired upon by Bruce, the first bullet only grazing him superficially, the final one fatal when Bruce shot him in the back of the head as Ricky ran down to the family room to hide. Upstairs, Mrs. Blackman would have been awakened by the first shots.

Clarke thought about her up there, in the dark, ripped out of her slumber, knowing something ghastly was happening, but with no way of knowing what. Did she know she was in peril, or did she freeze? Her fallen body in the master bedroom lay only a few feet from the bed. Bruce must have been all the way at the top of the stairs before she tried to flee into the bathroom.

Irene had been shot in the back. The bullet entered her lung which accounted for the blood spatter on the en-suite shower wall. The second shot, the one that killed her, left unburned gunpowder on her left shoulder. Bruce had to have been looking in his mother's eyes when he shot her point-blank in the head.

At this, Clarke leaned back in his chair. He'd seen cases where young men had either killed or threatened to kill their fathers, a not uncommon expression of adolescent rage. But a son killing his mother? It rarely happened and it was one of those sobering, awful crimes that no one ever wanted to acknowledge.

Poor Irene, up there alone, so afraid. Clarke rocked back and forth in his chair, listening to its anguish: *ree-ee, ree-ee, ree-ee, ree-ee...* He opened the top left hand drawer of his desk and looked at the deck of Players cigarettes he'd bought for himself when he'd gone to get Bruce a carton. Clarke hadn't smoked in 10 years, but it had been a hard-won victory. When he'd stopped smoking, he'd started over-eating. When he'd conquered that demon, he started drinking. Now sober, he had no vices and no sense of humor. It seemed a completely unfair trade-off.

222

Clarke pulled the book of crime scene photographs toward him and placed one hand on the top. He'd seen thousands of these things and yet this one was different. This one, he knew, was going to wreck him for good. Clarke reached into the drawer and pulled out the deck of Players. He peeled off the cellophane wrap. Its bright crackle shot him through with a little surge of adrenalin. He popped open the deck and inhaled. Long and slow.

He waited for a signal.

Something in his brain switched back on. He couldn't go one more minute, *one more second*, without sucking on one of those things so hard his whole face might cave in around it. He grabbed his plastic butane lighter — something he kept on hand to sear stray threads off his uniform — pulled a cigarette from the deck, stuck it in his mouth and lit it. Somewhere along the periphery of his awareness, he heard Gladys' typing stop.

Clarke took a long, deep, *committed* drag off that cigarette and then began coughing with such sincerity that Gladys bolted into the room, arms flailing. "What is it, what is it?" she screeched. "Are you having a heart attack?"

When she saw the smoke curling from the cigarette in his hand, her painted eyebrows nearly flew off her face. Then, they obediently followed her furrowed brow line into harsh slashes. To Clarke, she looked just like a jack-o-lantern. In the midst of his coughing fit, he began to laugh.

"You're *smoking?*" Gladys hissed. "Don't you remember what we went through when you quit last time? *What are you thinking?*"

She was right, but for whatever reason, Gladys had never been moved by evidence. She could be mistyping the most graphic description of a decapitated victim and still be humming a tune. Oh, for her innocent kind of detachment, Clarke thought. He, unfortunately, was doomed to care.

Clarke coughed again – three more spasms into his left fist — and waved her away with the right hand holding the cigarette.

"Oh," Gladys growled, *"Anyway!"*

She looked so *personally* offended, he thought, as she stormed out of the room.

IT WOULD TAKE several more days before Clarke could finish his report. There was so much information, so many small details that had big consequences. In the midst of piecing things together, Clarke placed calls to Bruce's remaining siblings Todd and Angela, and to the brother-in-law Robert, to ask if they had any other information to offer. Clarke could tell by the monotone of their voices that they'd been knocked numb by grief. This was one of the many parts of his job he hated — intruding on people's worst and saddest moments. But Clarke made a note that all three became instantly animated when asking about what was next for Bruce. There was no mistaking what was in their voices:

Fear at what might happen to them if he were to be released. All three of them asked Clarke for assurances that Clarke couldn't offer. Robert, Karon's husband, was the most vocal. "We want him put away forever, somewhere far, far away." Robert had dropped off at the detachment Bruce's white Bible and a cassette tape. Inside the Bible – which was as big as a telephone book — Robert pointed out where Bruce had written the names and telephone numbers of the surviving family members in the pages of the Book of Revelation. Bruce's voice on the cassette tape was a rambling, repetitive, sometimes incoherent recitation of Chapters 10 and 11 of the Book of Revelation and how each of the family members related to those sections.

"He means to finish the job," said Robert. "I don't doubt for a minute that he will if gets the chance."

As Clarke made his last sweep of the evidence, he was troubled by a number of items, mostly relating to the span of time between killing spree #1 and spree #2. Bruce had made a cursory attempt to clean up around Mrs. Blackman, and a long, protracted effort downstairs. Why did Bruce feel the need to erase evidence? Why did he drag the bodies downstairs to the games room? Ricky would have been fairly easy to relocate, but Mr. Blackman was a big, bulky man. Bruce had said during his interrogation that he'd carried his father downstairs, but Bruce weighed a mere 128 pounds. Mr. Blackman, according to the autopsy report, weighed more than 220. Even dragging his father – first down the three steps from the raised kitchen, then down the main stairs to the basement – would have been neither easy nor quick. So why do it? Was he trying to hide the bodies and blood from his sisters? If so, wouldn't that indicate he was thinking rationally at that point? Cleaning up the blood and hiding the bodies might indicate that Blackman had not only premeditated the murders of Roberta and Karon, but understood that what he was about to do was wrong. Clarke also noted in the lab report that no fingerprints were recovered from any of the rifles, or from the hammer. While Clarke believed Bruce had killed his first three victims at the behest of voices, he was having trouble buying that the voices were still present when Karon, John and Roberta were ambushed.

What would have set him off? One of the pieces of evidence seized from the Blackman home was the pink committal form the psychiatrist had signed upon his first examination of Bruce. Did Bruce find those commitment papers and become enraged? Had his father threatened to put him away for good?

And then there was the plastic carpet runner Bruce had placed over his father's chest and face; a classic sign of remorse. Was it possible for Bruce to have been "possessed" off and on during this whole awful debacle? Clarke didn't know enough about the psychotic mind to draw any conclusions, but these details would nag at him for years.

He pulled the book of crime scene photos toward him with one hand at the same time he opened the upper left drawer of his desk with his other.

His cigarettes were gone. In their place were ten packs of Juicy Fruit chewing gum.

"Damn you, Gladys," Clarke sputtered.

He unwrapped and shoved 3 sticks of gum in his mouth at once and chewed furiously to release the fake, yet oh-so-addictive sweetness. He savored the taste for a full minute before flipping open the album.

Clarke had been to the crime scene, but his time there was brief, just enough to give him the visual information he needed to conduct his interrogation of Bruce. On his way out of the house he'd crossed paths with coroner Brenda Bolin as she went about her duties. He liked Brenda — she was bright, efficient and professional, yet warm and always smiling amidst the grimness of her job. But on the morning of the Blackman murders, Clarke saw her brown eyes glittering as if filled with tears. Later, by the time news reporters shoved microphones in her face, she was once again composed, always the professional. But what she said to the press would go down in history as one of the great understatements of the year, Clarke thought. A reporter asked her, "What's it like in there?"

Bolin answered: "It's the worst thing I have ever seen."

The booklet contained hundreds of photographs. Every bullet casing, slug, footprint, fragment, blood spatter…every single thing that could have any possible relevance had been photographed by officers diligent and sombre in their work. There was a photograph taken in the crawlspace storage area — the place where the guns were stored — of a box of large calibre ammunition set atop a freezer. It appeared that a number of rounds had been removed. Had Bruce intended to use one of

227

the high-powered hunting rifles? Clarke remembered Bruce saying something like, "I wouldn't want to disturb anyone. I wouldn't want to make any noise." Was that why he switched to the .22s? Clarke flipped through the pages and stopped when he reached a photograph marked Exhibit 16. It was a small fragment of something lying next to John Davies' bloodied hand. Clarke checked the Crime Detection Lab report. Exhibit 16 was the fragment of a tooth. In another photograph, quite a distance away from the body, Exhibit 45 was a fragment that looked like lead. The lab report stated Exhibit 45 was "not the type of material used in bullet manufacture. It appears to be consistent with the type of material used for dental fillings." For the contents of the tooth to have travelled that far from the body, the blow to the face must have been delivered with stunning force. Clarke thought again about the smallness of Bruce Blackman. His quiet demeanor. The attack on Davies was so vicious, so unrelenting, and so *powerful* it just seemed to Clarke impossible that Bruce could have done it. Bruce had said all along that he *didn't* do it, that the "thing" in his brain did. But how? How could Bruce summon a demonic strength he didn't have?

Clarke opened a file to the autopsy report on John Davies: six foot one, two hundred and one pounds. Bruce had stated during his interrogation that John was trying to "talk to him" during the killings. No doubt, thought Clarke, John was attempting to distract Bruce long enough so that Roberta could get away, and maybe — just maybe — John thought he could convince Bruce to hand over the gun. Witnesses reported seeing Bruce pushing and shoving a larger man to his knees and demanding he go in the house. Why did Davies not simply turn around and overpower his attacker?

The autopsy revealed an entry and exit wound to Davies' left leg. The entrance was from the rear, indicating that Davies was shot from behind. Both knees bore clear abrasions. Bullet wounds were also evident to Davies' left shoulder as well as entry and exit wounds to the soft flesh between the left shoulder and the neck. The entry wounds to the shoulder were also from the rear. There was another bullet entry wound to the side of his head just above the left eye, as well as gunshot residue, indicating a near-ranged shot. A separate bullet had sliced through the left side of Davies' mouth.

"Jesus," Clarke muttered.

A handwritten note stapled to the autopsy report explained that the medical examiner confirmed the wound to the leg would not have caused Davies to be unable to walk, but that the shot to the shoulder would have incapacitated his left arm. Still, thought Clarke, Davies could have thrown himself onto Blackman, knocking him down by sheer incompatibility of weight. Was John continuing to lure Blackman away from Roberta so that she could get away for good? The rest of the autopsy report revealed that Davies had sustained 11 "paired puncture wounds, consistent with having been administered with the back of a claw hammer." Some of the blows were struck with such force that the skull cap was punctured and the brain perforated.

Clarke sat with this: John Davies had been shot six times and struck with a hammer 11 times and yet he still lived. Clarke closed his eyes at the thought of what Davies had endured — the terror, the pain, the unspeakable suffering. To live through all that, only to die when help finally arrived? Clarke spat his gum into the trash can.

The photographs from the kitchen showed blood spatter covering the curtains, the ceiling, the light fixtures and two walls. There was a photograph of blood-soaked cookies that had been retrieved from the trash can. Mr. Blackman must have been eating those at the kitchen table when Bruce burst in. As much as Clarke was unnerved by how Bruce had killed his mother, he was equally disturbed by the way Mr. Blackman died. The autopsy could not determine for sure whether Mr. Blackman had been shot three or four times because it appeared that the first wound was a defensive one. That meant the shot to his hand and cheek may or may not have been the same. Based on the blood trajectory on Mr. Blackman's hands, it was probable that he was upright when first shot. There would have then been two or three more shots fired, Mr. Blackman no doubt aware, at least up until the second shot, that his own son was killing him. Clarke thought about *his* own son, Darren, with whom he'd had his share of shouting matches. Darren had hollered on more than one occasion: "I HATE you! I could just KILL you!" The truth was, for Clarke, the feeling was sometimes mutual, but they would have never in a lifetime acted upon the threat or even come close. Clarke tried to imagine what it would have been like to see Darren coming at him with a rifle. When he pictured it, Clarke's throat ached.

The autopsy report noted two other items. One was that there was very little blood remaining in Mr. Blackman's body. The inside of one of his lungs had to be scraped in order to get a usable blood sample. The other item of note was that Mr. Blackman had "a large callus" on his right hand. Clarke flipped through some other papers and saw that, in life, Mr. Blackman had been a heavy duty marine engineer, the callus no doubt a product of years and years of bringing old, broken, rusty things back to usefulness with a few expert turns of the wrench. In his mind, Clarke could see the callus. He could see the Blackman children playing with it the way Clarke had played with own father's various scars and bumps when he'd been a kid.

Several officers had engaged in conjecture that Bruce had an accomplice, but there was simply no evidence to back that up. Not a shred of it. In a way, Clarke wished that Bruce *did* have an accomplice. It would have made the whole thing a little easier to accept. Bruce may have been truly and completely sick when he killed his family, but who out there in the general population would or could ever feel compassion for him? The only reason Clarke did was because he'd seen the young man in the hours after the murders, when adrenalin, regret and horror had reduced Bruce down to his most basic essence. And that essence was a troubled young man who loved his family, who had good manners, who was cooperative and scared and lost.

Clarke found himself wishing — although he would admit this to very few people — that Bruce had committed suicide at the scene. What Bruce was about to go through in the tortuous aftermath would be a

231

worse and more relentless punishment than death could ever be. And the toll that would be taken on the lives of everyone involved: the police officers giving evidence of the horror they'd seen; the jurors — people so unfamiliar with violence that they might be irretrievably ruined by what they'd hear and see; the witnesses, asked to dredge up what they'd spend the rest of their lives trying to forget; the survivors, who would forever have a hollow place inside them where everything they'd known and loved had been viciously carved away. The ripples kept going: It was impossible to predict how many lives would feel them. Clarke wondered at his own coldness at wishing Bruce's death, but better to have seven funerals and be done.

Gathering up the papers on his desk, Clarke found a statement made one of the treating psychiatrists that on December 31, just two weeks before the murders that he — the psychiatrist — had referred to Bruce's case as "a blow-out which sealed nicely." Clarke was speechless. He looked further and found another note from January 14 — four days before the slaughter — where the doctor had spoken to Mr. Blackman. "I received a call from Mr. Blackman regarding 'regression,'" it said, "but I don't recall going into specifics." *Don't recall going into specifics?* Clarke felt like slamming his fist through the wall. *I should set Bogan on this guy*, Clarke thought. *What an asshole.*

Clarke looked through the photographs one last time to ensure his report covered everything. He found something he'd missed on the first pass: Down in the games room near the bodies of Mr. Blackman and Ricky, there was a table. Set upon the table was a board game called

232

"Risk." The irony of it, thought Clarke. He closed the book and shoved it away from him. He would never look at it again.

Into the microphone he dictated the conclusion to his report.

"It is abundantly clear from the interviews with family, friends and the psychiatrist, that Bruce Blackman needed psychiatric care and incarceration in a mental institution. All the signs indicated this; however, it appeared that the family tried to deal with this youth on their own grounds. The most important aspect of evidence is the fact that Bruce Blackman gave a voluntary statement in which he admitted to the murders of the six family members. Although he refused to face reality and identify the order in which he killed the victims or how he killed them, Bruce Blackman takes full credit for the tragedy. His surviving brother, sister, and his brother-in-law have all expressed great concern and fear that if Blackman were to escape, that he will try to 'finish the job,' and kill them. They have asked that he be incarcerated in a hospital outside of the province."

Clarke closed all the file folders, placed everything back into the wine box, stood up and walked out of his office.

"Gladys," he said, "the report for CC is ready. Let's make sure it's ready for me to sign by Thursday."

"It's Monday," she said. "I'm sure I can have it ready for you tomorrow."

"Thursday will be fine. I won't be back in 'til then."

233

"Why? What's wrong?"

"Nothing. I'm going to take a few days and visit my son."

JUDGMENT

All testimony presented is verbatim.
For ease of readability, ellipses between segments of testimony have
been eliminated.
No names have been changed.

IT WAS STANDING room only on January 19, 1983 when Bruce
Blackman made his first appearance in provincial court. Situated inside
a row of trailers that served as the temporary court house while a new
building was under construction nearby, the small room nearly burst its
seams trying to contain reporters, onlookers and the twenty or so people
who were scheduled for first appearances.

Judge Kim J. Husband presided over court that day. He was a
tall, thin man with a grayish cast to his skin and a perpetual frown that in
the right light could make his face look like a prune. Everyone who'd
been in court with him noticed. Crown Counsel Pedro DeCouto, a young
prosecutor with Latin features and a pleasant, boyish grin, called the
Blackman case. He made an application under Section 465 of the
Criminal Code of Canada seeking a psychiatric remand for observation
of the accused. He also sought a ban on publication on the proceedings
to ensure that Blackman retained his right to a fair trial. During this first
appearance, Blackman was represented by duty counsel[15], who agreed

with the request for a ban. The duty counsel, round-faced and shaped like a snowman, also requested an order to clear the court room. DeCouto disagreed, citing the public's right to attend court. "Nothing has been presented to indicate that the public ought to be cleared out of the court room," DeCouto stated. Duty counsel told the court, "My client does not want the press in the courtroom."

Judge Husband agreed to the ban on publication, but denied the closing of court.

DeCouto gave an overview of the events as they were known to have unfolded in the early morning hours of the day before. He called as his only witness Dr. Gary Hayes, who had examined Blackman at the RCMP detachment after his arrest.

Dr. Hayes was a general practitioner and had been practicing medicine for three years when he was asked to examine Blackman. On the witness stand, Hayes described Bruce Blackman as "quiet, cooperative...a fairly small fellow and certainly didn't appear threatening at all." Hayes examined him for 35 minutes and noticed some "fairly major defects" in his mental status: a flattening of affect; a conviction he was possessed by a devil; he was experiencing hallucinations and hearing voices of the Devil telling him what he should do. Hayes also testified that Blackman admitted that he "loses control of his mind on these occasions. In the last 24 hours he said he had been heavily possessed and was under total direction from the Devil." Hayes

---

15 The Canadian equivalent of a legal aid lawyer.

stated that Blackman also exhibited something called "perseverance of thought," and this was the idea of seeking forgiveness from the Lord through his brother and sister who were still alive. "He constantly said that if he could just get their forgiveness, he would be much better and the Devil would be gone, and he would feel all right then. He said it at least 20 times in the half hour."

Hayes also testified that Blackman admitted to the use of marijuana and said that he'd smoked one joint and ate some prior to going to bed the previous evening. In examining Blackman, Hayes had found no evidence to suggest Blackman was under the influence of any chemicals.

Hayes testified that Blackman had been under the care of a psychiatrist for the past six weeks. It was Hayes' opinion that Blackman was mentally ill.

"No further questions, Your Honor," said DeCouto.

"No questions for this witness," said duty counsel. Hayes was excused.

Judge Husband issued a psychiatric remand for Bruce Blackman and scheduled him to reappear in court in 30 days.

ON FEBRUARY 9, 1983, Bruce Blackman made another appearance in Provincial Court before Judge Husband. Attorney R. J. Levenson had replaced duty counsel as Blackman's attorney and would continue to represent him in the coming months. Pedro DeCouto, continuing to act as the prosecution, stated that he wished to proceed on Section 465(3) of the Criminal Code: a hearing to determine whether the accused, Bruce Blackman, was fit to stand trial. The Judge agreed.

Dr. Philip Harvey Adilman, an expert in the field of forensic psychiatry, was called to the witness stand. Adilman had conducted eleven interviews with Bruce Blackman dated January 19, 24, 25, 26, 31, and February 1, 7 and 8, 1983.

Adilman testified that Blackman had resided under "constant attention" at the Forensic Psychiatric Institute of British Columbia — Riverview — a sprawling brick-and-columned neo-classical landmark with its own dark history. Periodically, Blackman would be moved from his private room to other parts of the ward; specifically, the day room and the TV room. "Constant attention," explained Adilman, meant that a nurse was continuously in attendance outside Blackman's room or with him in close proximity when he was elsewhere on the Institute grounds. This constant attention was in effect 24-hours a day, as Blackman was considered a suicide risk.

Adilman testified that he saw Blackman within 30 or 40 minutes of his admittance to the Forensic Psychiatric Institute, a day after the murders, and at that time, Blackman's thinking was "very unclear" and he "did not make any sense." Blackman "professed many delusions and was hearing voices." Adilman diagnosed him as suffering from a schizophrenic-like illness, probably schizophrenia. (At that time, the Diagnostic and Statistical Manual III [DSM3] — the official guide to diagnosing mental illness — reserved the diagnosis of schizophrenia for a person who'd had the illness for a period of six months.) Adilman made the diagnosis of schizophreniform, a form of schizophrenia which had all the signs and symptoms of the disease except for the six month criteria.

"Psychosis is classified as a major mental illness," he told the court, "A break with reality to the extent that mental function is impaired in the areas of perception, thought, feeling, action, and how one relates to one's environment."

In the first week to ten days of Blackman's incarceration at Riverview, he showed evidence of thought disorder. His state of mind, however, had improved since then.

Adilman discussed the nature of Blackman's delusions, particularly the religious ideation and the obsession with the idea of opposites. "Hallucination is a misperception or a false perception," he testified. "Rather than getting cues from one's senses in the environment, one gets the cues from internal sensations. Blackman claims he hears voices when he watches TV — he hears the Devil's voice. His moods fluctuate dramatically — laughing and giggling quite inappropriately as he was talking. Abruptly, he would change, become silent and depressed, sad, tearful, again giggle. Other times he would appear quite stoic."

The doctor described Blackman's overall mood recently as "more of sadness, tears, remorse," and "staying pretty well to himself.

The giggling and laughing and inappropriate response has not been noted in the last week to ten days."

"His grasp of reality is minimal," Adilman testified, though "in the structured setting of the hospital it has improved. If he were not in such an environment — i.e., a court room — he would decompensate relatively quickly to his former state."

According to Adilman, Blackman had also made references to suicide attempts, and wrote a letter stating he did not want to live. It was Adilman's opinion, therefore, that Blackman required care and treatment in a mental health facility because he was suicidal and at risk.

After cross examination by Levenson, Dr. Adilman was excused as a witness.

As his second witness, DeCouto called Dr. Derek Eaves, tendering him as an expert in psychiatry and forensic psychiatry. Dr. Eaves had examined Blackman on four separate occasions: January 19, February 1 (twice) and February 8. The total time he spent with Blackman was three and one-half hours. Eaves' conclusion was that Blackman was suffering from "schizophrenia with some features of depression evident."

Eaves testified that in addition to hearing voices of a white woman and the devil, Blackman also said he heard "the voice of an ex-girlfriend screaming."

"The development of his symptoms have [*sic*] been over the past two or three months," said the doctor. "They came on with considerable intensity and they were extremely intense when he was first admitted to Forensic. There's been some improvement but without continued treatment he would relapse to his former state."

In cross examination, Levenson questioned the doctor more deeply about the voices heard by Blackman.

Eaves responded: "He has heard voices which indicate he should kill himself. [He is] constantly preoccupied by these thoughts. [He feels] a considerable amount of sadness, remorse."

Eaves also testified that Blackman had stated to him, "I'd like to know what's going on in my brain. Something made me do it. Something did it for me. I'd like to know, I really would."

Once Levenson had finished his cross examination, the Doctor was dismissed as a witness. "No further witnesses, Your Honour," DeCouto said.

"Calling Dr. Roy O'Shaughnessy, Your Honor," said Levenson. "I'm tendering this witness as an expert in the field of psychiatry with specialized training in forensic psychology."

O'Shaughnessy confirmed the findings of Adilman and Eaves, and stated that Blackman was "suffering from a major mental illness. The auditory hallucinations are of the command type — he feels he must do what the voices tell him to do."

O'Shaughnessy testified about Bruce's recent demeanor, particularly his withdrawal which "appeared in greater frequency when any kind of emotionally upsetting material was discussed, including his family" and the charges against him.

O'Shaughnessy's diagnosis: Schizophreniform psychosis.

After a brief cross examination by DeCouto, Dr. O'Shaughnessy was dismissed and no further witnesses were called that day.

In DeCouto's submission to the court, he cited R. v Roberts from the B.C. Court of Appeals, Vol. 24, and asked Judge Husband to make a finding under Section 543(6), that Bruce Blackman was not fit to stand trial.

Based upon the evidence presented, Judge Husband was satisfied that the accused was suffering from a severe mental illness, that he was not capable — by reason of insanity — of conducting his defence at a preliminary hearing, and "pursuant to Section 543(6) of the Code, [I direct] the accused be kept in custody at the Forensic Clinic until the pleasure of the Lieutenant Governor is known."

DURING HIS MONTHS at Riverview, Bruce improved. The voices diminished. Unreality gave way to actuality. The fervor he'd felt so strongly — the conviction that he was a hero saving the world — dissolved little by little with each dose of anti-psychotic medication. The irony was that as Bruce's mind was knitting back together, the memory of what he'd done was tearing him apart.

In a brief court appearance on April 26, 1983, Bruce Blackman was found fit to stand trial. He had stabilized and, according to his doctors, was now capable of understanding the court proceedings and would be able to instruct counsel. Following the verdict, he was returned to the Forensic Psychiatric Institute where he continued his medication therapy of injectible fluphenazine decanoate, 25 mg, every two weeks, and 10 mgm of Haloperidol, by mouth, at bedtime. A court date was set for the fall.

ON NOVEMBER 2, 1983, inside a modern, glass-roofed courthouse in New Westminster, British Columbia, the Blackman trial began. Outside the court house, rain fell sporadically. Wind gusts rattled loose the last of the dry maple leaves still quivering on almost-bare branches. The clouds overhead were thick and bruised and seemed to hang over the court house, unmoving. They would stay there a full three days.

Bruce Alfred Blackman, neatly dressed in a brown leather jacket and white shirt, was brought before Justice L. G. McKenzie and faced a jury of seven men and five women who sat poised to make one decision and one decision only.

Was Bruce Blackman insane at the time he committed the slaughter of his family?

As the prosecution, Pedro DeCouto represented the Crown, with Barry Sullivan as co-counsel, and R. J. Levenson continued his representation in defence of Bruce Blackman.

In a scenario unusual to court proceedings, both the prosecution and defence agreed that at the time he committed the murders, Blackman was unable to appreciate the nature of his actions. Nevertheless, a trial ensued that lasted three days and required numerous witnesses. (According to a 1985 article in *Vancouver* magazine, a local attorney said that except for the sensational nature of the crime, it never would have gone to trial otherwise, the fact that the accused was mentally ill so obvious as to negate the need for a public hearing.)

In the dark-paneled court room, the Clerk called the proceedings to order.

"Will the prisoner stand? In the Supreme Court of British Columbia, Oyer and Terminer and General Gaol Delivery, Her Majesty the Queen against Bruce Alfred Blackman. Bruce Alfred Blackman stands charged: That count one, that he, the said Bruce Alfred Blackman, on or about the 18th day of January, A.D. 1983, at or near the District of Coquitlam, in the County of Westminster, Province of British Columbia, did commit first degree murder of Irene Katherine Blackman, contrary to Section 218 of the Criminal Code of Canada and against the peace of Our Lady the Queen, Her Crown and Dignity. Bruce Alfred Blackman, how do you plead to this charge, guilty or not guilty?"

"Not guilty."

The Clerk read the remaining charges; identical except for the names of the deceased. Bruce's response was the same for all of them: "Not guilty."

The Clerk introduced the jury.

"Prisoner, these good persons who shall now be called are the jurors that are to pass between our sovereign lady the Queen and you at your trial; if, therefore you would challenge them or any of them you must challenge them as they come to the book to be sworn and before they are sworn and you shall be heard. You may be seated."

The jury of five men and four women was impaneled and sworn, without challenge, then dismissed until later in the day.

With the jury out, Sullivan asked Justice McKenzie whether a voir dire[16] would be necessary. A voir dire is a "trial within a trial" to determine whether or not statements made by the accused in custody were voluntary. Blackman had already admitted that statements given by him were made voluntarily, so the defense was willing to waive the voir dire if the Justice felt that was appropriate.

After a short break, the jury was recalled and announced their Foreman. In a long and sometimes confusing explanation of their role, the Justice reminded them that the issue at hand was whether Bruce

---

[16] In Canada, a voir dire (Latin for "to speak the truth") is used for a number of purposes, including determination of the admissibility of statements given in custody. In the United States, a voir dire is used as part of the jury selection process.

Blackman was insane at the time of the murders. That was the only question on the table.

"There is really only going to be one issue that is going to trouble you, and that is the issue of insanity. [N]o person can be found guilty of a criminal offence if he was insane at the time of the commission of the offence. That idea is incorporated in the Criminal Code of Canada in this language: '16. (1) No person shall be convicted of an offence in respect of an act or omission on his part while he was insane. (2) For the purposes of this section a person is insane when he is in a state of natural imbecility or has disease of the mind to an extent that renders him incapable of appreciating the nature and quality of an act or omission or of knowing that an act or omission is wrong. (3) A person who has specific delusions, but is in other respects sane, shall not be acquitted on the ground of insanity unless the delusions caused him to believe that in the existence of state of things that [sic], if it existed, would have justified or excused his act or omission. (4) Everyone shall, until the contrary is proved, be presumed to be and have been sane.'"

The Justice explained at length that the jury members were to put aside their own personal definitions of insanity, and to focus on the law. "You must decide the case solely on the evidence. You must not bring into this court room any preconceived notions about the case or about the law. It may be that you will have heard or read about the events at an earlier time and that you may have certain predispositions as a consequence of that."

He revisited over and over the responsibilities of the jury, explained the notion of presumption of innocence, and the definition of culpable homicide. Satisfied that he'd communicated their duty to them, he dismissed the jury until the next day.

Sullivan addressed the court on the voir dire: "My learned friend and colleague," he said — referring to DeCouto — "will be leading two witnesses, My Lord. One is a constable who had a conversation on the street outside the Blackman residence in Coquitlam early in the morning on January the eighteenth, the date of the offences, and secondly he will be leading a long statement in a conversation between the accused and [a staff sergeant] of the RCMP."

The constable was called to the stand as the first witness in the voir dire. He related the sum of his conversations with Blackman at the scene, during transport in the police cruiser, and at the detachment. The statements were ruled admissible, and — given the Crown and defence position that every other statement would follow the same path — the Justice agreed there was no need to call further witnesses on the voir dire.

Sullivan mentioned to the court that he would be filing an admission of facts — 14 of them. It was agreed that the jury would be provided with a transcript of the recorded conversation with the staff sergeant who took Blackman's statement.

Court was dismissed until the following day.

ON NOVEMBER 3, 1983, co-counsel for the Crown, Barry Sullivan, addressed the jury, and encapsulated all of the evidence they would hear during the course of the trial.

Exhibit 1 in the case was an "Admission of Fact" filed by Bruce Blackman's attorney. It contained 14 items that would not be contested by the Defence:

1. Bruce Blackman caused the death of his mother, Irene.
2. Cause of her death was gunshot wounds.
3. Bruce Blackman caused the death of his brother-in-law, John.
4. Cause of death was multiple gunshot wounds and multiple skull fractures via hammer blows.
5. Bruce Blackman caused the death of his sister, Roberta.
6. Cause of death was a gunshot wound to the head.
7. Roberta also sustained multiple fractures caused by blows to the head.
8. Bruce Blackman caused the death of his sister, Karon.
9. Cause of death was double gunshot wounds of the head.
10. Bruce Blackman caused the death of his father, Richard, Sr.
11. Cause of death was multiple gunshot wounds.
12. Bruce Blackman caused the death of his brother, Richard, Jr.
13. Cause of death was a gunshot wound to the head.
14. All conversations were voluntary.

The first witness called was the crime scene photographer who had taken extensive photographs and created the crime scene diagrams. The jury was given a booklet of graphic photographs and diagrams to follow along with the witness's testimony. While looking at the pictures, several jurors put their hands over their mouths.

Other witnesses to testify before the court on November 3 were the arresting officer, the staff sergeant who interviewed Blackman twice, Bruce's Lonsdale Avenue roommate, and the psychiatrist who had first treated Blackman a month before the murders. Also taking the stand that day was Karon's husband who closed his testimony with an odd statement.

DeCouto asked, "From all of your association and knowledge and being part of the Blackman family, what was the relationship of Bruce with the family?"

"The family loved Bruce."

"And what about Bruce and the family?"

"He loved them too, a lot."

"And this continued right through until January 18th?"

"It continues even now."

"Sorry?" asked DeCouto, taken by surprise.

"It continues even now."

ON NOVEMBER 4, 1983, outside the court house, small patches of early snow clung stubbornly to the grass just now starting to turn brown for hibernation. Inside, the Blackman trial was winding down. There were four final witnesses to call, all of them doctors who would testify about the accused's mental state.

The first witness called by the Crown was Dr. Adilman, who had testified at Blackman's fitness hearing. He was asked to provide the jury with an explanation of the different kinds of mental disturbances.

"For example," he began, "there is something called a neurosis. A neurosis is a minor mental disturbance where the major manifestation is anxiety. In that particular type of condition there is no break with reality. A second form of mental disturbance is a personality disorder where there are maladaptive patterns of behavior, sometimes which get people into repeated difficulty with the law. There is no break with reality. These people don't have a conscience or a very good sense of what is right and wrong, but there's no break with reality. And then there is a major mental illness which we refer to as psychosis and the major symptom of a psychosis is the person's inability to recognize reality, to deal with reality, to communicate properly in a realistic term. And psychosis invariably, because of the unreality, exhibits disturbances in an abnormal way in thinking, in feeling, in perceiving things, and then there are several types of psychoses. One type is called schizophrenia and schizophrenia is a psychosis which is a break with reality where there is a disturbance in thinking, behavior, mood, and there may be gross misperceptions.

"Under schizophrenia itself, there are several types of schizophrenia. One type is referred to as paranoid schizophrenia, and

[this] is a disorder which is characterized by the presence of persecutory or grandiose delusions often accompanied by hallucinations and disturbances in thought. Now there are various kinds of delusions, and a delusion is defined as a false belief that is firmly held despite objective and obvious contrary proof or evidence that it is wrong and to the person who is deluded or who has a delusion it makes perfect sense. They cannot be argued with and told that what they're thinking is silly. Now the various kinds of delusions that we have are, for example, a bizarre delusion, and that's a false belief that is patently absurd or fantastic, and then there's a delusion of control, a delusion that a person's thoughts, feelings or actions are not his own, but are being imposed upon him by some external force, and then there's a delusion of grandeur, exaggerated concept of one's importance, power, knowledge or identity. Then there's the delusion of persecution, a delusion that one is being attacked, harassed, cheated, conspired against. Then there's the delusion of reference – delusions that events, objects or behavior have a particular and unusual meaning specifically for that person. And then there's a religious delusion, a delusion involving theological themes. So there are various types of delusions that are all false belief. And then there is that which is called a hallucination.

"Now normally we respond to things that we see or that we hear from other people, but a hallucination is a false sense of perception and it occurs in the absence of any relevant, external stimulation to the senses. And there are different types of hallucinations. For example, there's an auditory hallucination which is an hallucination of sound. And then there's a command hallucination which may be obeyed at times creating

251

danger for individuals or others. So in schizophrenia you have then a disturbance in what we refer to as thought content, and you have a disturbance in perception which is an hallucination, and then there is also a disturbance in the actual thinking process.

"Normally when we talk, our conversation starts at one point, ends at another and has a logical conclusion. In schizophrenia the thought disturbance can be very marked and it is the hallmark, actually, of schizophrenia. Schizophrenia actually has been defined as a disturbance in thinking.

"There is one other aspect of schizophrenia that's important and that is a person's 'affect' or feeling or emotional tone. Normally when we see something funny, we laugh. When we experience something sad, we cry. People with schizophrenia have a disturbed emotional sense and sometimes they laugh and giggle in a most inappropriate fashion. Their responses are sometimes flat or blunted with no emotion."

Bruce's attorney, Levenson, interrupted the witness: "Let me ask you this, Doctor. If someone has a major psychotic illness like schizophrenia as you've defined, do the symptoms that you have outlined here, do they manifest themselves necessarily at all times, every minute of their life, or may the symptoms be there at certain times and during certain conversations and not there during other times and at other conversations during the course of a day, say?"

"Yes," Adilman answered, "that is one of the manifestations, that a person who is suffering from schizophrenia doesn't necessarily exhibit all of these symptoms all of the time, twenty-four hours a day. A lot depends on, for example, the type of question that one asks someone who is schizophrenic. Sometimes you ask them their name; they will tell you their name. Where it becomes most evident is if you talk to them in a very open ended way (like) 'tell me what's happening,' and then the disturbance will manifest itself."

Dr. Adilman continued to answer questions related to the onset of Blackman's condition — from the hunting trip up until the murders — which he termed "phase one". "Phase two" consisted of the interviews and reports and investigations from the nineteenth of January through and up to the ninth of February.

"OK, begin your evidence on that [second] phase," directed Sullivan.

Adilman continued: "Mr. Blackman was admitted at 11:50 hours on January the nineteenth, 1983, from Port Coquitlam and I first became involved with (him) on that date and I began an interview at 12:30 p.m. on January the nineteenth. Now Mr. Blackman was acutely psychotic on his admission to the Forensic Institute and he displayed evidence of auditory hallucinations, illogical and non-goal directed speech including a formal thought disorder, evidence of grandiose and bizarre religious delusions and his affect was inappropriate and it's in this context that I would like you to view the material that I'm going to present.

"On admission, Mr. Blackman was routinely seen by the nursing staff and was admitted according to standard procedures. His mood was fluctuated; at times he was happy to be relating his story, then he would become very quiet and solemn. When talking about his religious convictions he would speak with great exuberance and joy. From the nursing note, Bruce feels that he...

> '[S]aved his family from death as they were the Antichrists. He saved them from death as the world will come to an end on January twenty-fourth, 1983, or January thirty-first, 1983 — then there will be a new beginning. Since all the family isn't dead there are still three Antichrists alive; his brother, his sister and himself. He is convinced that he did the right thing. Everything revolves around the Satanic Star and the Star of David.'

"From the nursing report:

> 'When he listened to the radio and TV when there [were] religious programs on, that there [were] specific messages directed to him. He constantly hears voices — the voices talking to him about the Tree of Knowledge, that the tree is actually one's own semen; therefore, he had to eat his own semen. The voices tell him that he is God and God is Time. He has seen a vision, a spirit, the white woman who is mentioned in the Bible — the whore.'

"The report continues,

'He feels that he is being persecuted constantly by the Bible. Further, his brother is one of the Horsemen of the Apocalypse — he must ask his sister to commit suicide by taking sleeping pills as she is one of the Antichrists. He stated that all of his family were now happy because they were in Heaven.'

"When I began my interview with Mr. Blackman I had seen him in the admitting hospital office on one of the wards at the hospital. I informed him that I was a psychiatrist and would be forwarding a report to the court. I informed him that the material he would give me would not be confidential and that he was free to say whatever he wanted to or not. I asked him if he understood this and he said, 'I'll tell you anything.'

"As I entered the examining room, I noticed Mr. Blackman was sitting with an open Bible on his knees. He was talking without paying much notice to my presence. He was wearing hospital pajamas and a housecoat. I introduced myself and he stated, in a spontaneous fashion:

'What my new name —you're not going to understand this. When I murdered my family — I was in a blue suit when I murdered my family — I'm black — never see prophecy — I am loved. Everybody liked me — this they possessed me — it murdered my family.'

"I noticed then that he closed the Bible and stated,

'I read it — I thought I was a good teacher — I'm God.'

"There's a delusion, and the speech that he was making was not making any sense. He began to laugh quite inappropriately at this time, which I noted as inappropriate affect. [He] then continued:

'You'll find out — I have to keep my eyes on everything – the thirty-first — the end — take [sic] seven days for the world to be in end.'

"He was laughing again.

'I'll end here. Everything else end here — half of the Star of David — found the wrong half.'

"He continued, smiling,

'Well, go ahead. You be the teacher.'

"He is commenting on me.

'Writing all I say. If I'm insane or not — I'm just possessed. Time — not God — God's God, nothing else, but Time — you should have realized this — time possesses me.'

"He then sat back on the chair. I asked him his name and he stated, 'Bruce Alfred Blackman.' He added, 'My grandfather's name was Alfred.' I noted that he was sitting back, somewhat remorseful looking. I asked him what his age was and he stated,

'Twenty-two — October 24, 1960. Do you believe in Haley's Comet? — It will come in 1984 — it will be Wormwood —

256

that's the thing that will come — that will be it. It will kill us —
all mankind.'

"I mentioned that he stated that he had murdered and then he
stated,

'I can't say anything about it — it's awful — I should have
never done it. They are least living in Heaven now. I'm always
in Heaven. Time possessed me. Everything I'm living is déjà-vu.
This is déjà-vu. I never knew — know it now — because of this
star — Satanic Star. There is a beginning and an end. In the
beginning there is the end because God is the beginning and the
end.'

"I asked him where he lived and he stated, 'I live here now.' I
asked him where that was and he stated, 'The Forensic Medical Building
— I don't have a home — any home. I murdered my family so they can
experience God.' I then repeated again that I was a psychiatrist and
would be reporting my findings to the court and asked him if he
understood this. He replied, 'I'll tell you everything — you don't have
to live because of the Wormwood. I'm not a murderer — Time is the
murderer.' I asked him to tell me about this and he stated, 'It's all
written down on a piece of paper I wrote this morning.' I asked him if I
could have the paper and he stated, 'Yes, take the Bible and study and try
and understand my possession.'"

Levenson asked, "Did you take that piece of paper?"

"Yes."

257

"And did you bring it along with you today?"

"I have copies, I have the original."

The pieces of paper containing Blackman's writings were entered and marked as Exhibit 8.

Sullivan: "And this Exhibit 8 that we just entered, Doctor, was a letter that Bruce Blackman had written when you first interviewed him on January the nineteenth?"

"Yes, it was," Adilman replied. "It was with him. Originally, he didn't want to give it to me, but he wanted it mailed to his brother and sister and I suggested that maybe he let me read it first, which he did."

"Now, I don't want to go through this word by word, but (are) there any comments that you would like to make about this particular letter and direct the jury and His Lordship's attention to?"

"Well, I think the second page, 'I am Chapter 10,' is pretty vivid evidence of a delusion, a false belief. I think that if you study the contents you can see how disjointed, disorganized, totally nonsensical these pages are. He refers constantly to his family, his mother and father, all the children, on various points of the star which he called at varying times the Star of David or the Satanic Star. He talks about the world coming to an end.

"It's very interesting, on about the fourth page, midway down where he says, 'You and [sister] are the Devil and the Antichrist and the gateway is very narrow. [Brother] October 24th, seven days, October 31st [sister].' Throughout this entire testimony you will hear various numbered sequences all related in some way to number seven. October twenty-fourth, interestingly enough, ends up to be Bruce and [his brother's] birthday. October thirty-first, his [sister's] birthday, and that is referred to: seven. I'm not very familiar, Your Honour, with the Bible, but I did do some reading and found number seven a very important number in the Book of Revelation as is number 24... So I think that's something to keep in mind.

"This first letter basically, I think this is the one that talks about his wanting [his brother] and his sister to commit suicide. Again, here's the picture of the star. On the next page there are more stars and then the Four Horsemen of the Apocalypse as you will hear later are to represent the two sets of twins. And then this other star that says starting and ending and then again seven days, this was presumably the Satanic Star which he — I think you will hear later that towards the end of this last page he shows marked confusion where he's talking about 'detect Mary.' Detect Mary ended up in later interviews to be a young woman he met on a bus on his way to school in Nelson which I will refer to later, and she talked about dying and coming back four times. He referred to her as 'detect Mary' because he felt that she could detect things. And then the last page is just a plea to [his brother].

Sullivan: "And then the diagram that he did, one where the diagram of the Wormwood and son, death and big bang theory, that's a theme that comes up again?"

The Doctor answered, "I guess this is a depiction of the — we didn't really discuss in detail what this picture was. This could have been a star, Wormwood, I don't know."

Justice McKenzie stopped the proceedings. "I think perhaps we should take a break and then perhaps another break before the morning's over. It's a rather long morning."

Court adjourned for a break. Bruce Blackman, quiet and compliant, was taken by sheriffs out of the courtroom through a door that led to confinement.

WHEN COURT RESUMED, Adilman was recalled to the stand. Sullivan asked him, "Is there another comment you wish to make arising out of the interview you had with Bruce Blackman on the nineteenth of January?"

"Well, yes," Adilman answered. "From that interview he had told me that he was studying a millwright course in Nelson and then I asked him what happened. He said, 'I decided to come home and murder my family. I never did it. Time did it. A third of the heavens are going to come in on us and devour everything.' I asked him about the voices in the first hour and he told me that he heard the voices and that he was hearing the voices of the seven thunders. At that point I asked him if he knew what he did was wrong and he stated, 'I was living in déjà-vu, through time.' I asked him if it was wrong what he did, and he stated, 'Definitely — thou shalt not murder — Jehovah's Law — 'cause I am

260

Jehovah.' I asked him what happened with this incident and he said, 'I was trying to save time.' I said to him how, by killing, he was to save time? He answered,

> *'Because you save the universe — no I don't understand what went on. I understand one thing — we are going to die, everyone on this planet is going to die. I have to tell the Pope that I always thought that the Pope was the Devil — 1984...'*

"He was singing at that time, '1984, 1984.' My impression at that time at the conclusion of the interview was that Mr. Blackman was a 22-year-old male who looked disheveled, pale during the interview; he was cooperative and very verbal. He gave information spontaneously; he was oriented in all three spheres: time, place and person. He said he heard voices. His conversation was illogical and non-goal directed. There was evidence of a formal thought disorder and tangential thinking — going off on a tangent. He exhibited evidence of delusional thinking ...and of a grandiose nature were the delusions he professed to be God and Jehovah. His affect was inappropriate, he was preoccupied with religious matters and that the world was going to end. I made a diagnosis of a form of schizophrenic illness and at the conclusion of that interview, quite spontaneously, he said to me,

> *'I wish I never did what I did, but it improved it all. The whole Bible is coming to me; all religions are coming to me, because that's the beginning. The family is the end. Time is the beginning. There are three Antichrists left: my sister, my brother and me. Can I go to sleep?'*

261

"I said that he could and he began to cry. 'I murdered. No one will understand. No one person. Oh no, what was it in me?' I asked him if he wanted to tell me more about what happened. He said he didn't want to talk about it. He was escorted to his room.

"I then saw him again on the twenty-fourth of January and part of the interview he told me that he was possessed and I asked him to tell me about it and he stated, 'Chapter 10, Book of Revelations.' I asked him to explain this. 'There is time, no longer, verse six. That's what Satan told me. I heard him and saw him last night. He's got me, he's got you too.' I asked him when all this came about and he said, 'December three, because God's coming.' Further from that interview I asked him if he was insane and he stated, 'Yes, I have to be. Why would I murder my family?' I asked him why and he stated, 'I told you, the Devil, because God said I shall not murder and I murdered.' I explained to him that that didn't seem to make much sense and he stated, 'That's the first commandment — that doesn't make sense?!' I asked him why he did murder and he said, 'Because the devil possessed me.' Throughout this second interview his responses were very erratic; he continued to be deluded and irrational. I asked him again in the second interview if he was experiencing auditory hallucinations, God or the Devil's voice. He says, 'I always hear them.' He then stayed silent for a moment and I felt that it would be difficult to continue, but then he said, 'Now I'm the Devil. Now I'm the Devil.' My impression at the second interview was that he was still psychotic, still suffering from loose associations and now feeling that he was the Devil. On the twenty-fourth, later in the afternoon he stated,

'There is nothing to discuss. I'm possessed, plain and simple. Satan — I am the Devil — the thirty-first — it's over for me, for all of you — the big bang theory.'

"I saw him again on the twenty-fifth. An excerpt from the twenty-fifth stated,

'Satan's got me. He's got me. I want to see my brother and sister. They'll never want to see me again because of my insanity. The Devil, he says I'm insane.'

Sullivan: "Let me stop you right there, Doctor, just very briefly. Up until that time, had Bruce Blackman received any sort of medication whatsoever administered by yourself or others for the condition that he was experiencing?"

"No."

"And when is the first time that he began to receive, if at all, any medication for the illness he had?"

"On the twenty-eighth of February, 1983.

"All right, thank you. Continue."

Justice McKenzie asked, "During this period of time, Doctor, I would assume that he would be totally deprived of any alcohol or drugs also?"

Adilman: "Yes. He was in a side room and on constant attention, twenty-four hours a day, because he began to think of suicide and we had a nurse with him at all times and he was in a private room at all times. I asked him when he realized what had happened and he stated, 'When I was arrested.' I asked him how he felt before that and he stated, 'That I was possessed by the Devil — he's picked a lot of people.' 'Before you were arrested you didn't know what you were doing?' 'That's right.' Again, my impression was that at the end of that interview that he was still thought disordered and delusional. He seemed to be getting depressed and I, as I said, put him on special or constant attention. Now, on the twenty-sixth I saw him again and he stated the following — I have also another piece of his writing, Your Honour, that starts: 'I don't want to live!'…"

The paper was marked and entered as Exhibit 9.

The Doctor continued: "On the twenty-sixth I asked him if he could explain to me what happened to him over the last little while regarding his charges and he stated,

> 'Because time possessed me, buddy. I live by prophecy. Everlasting hell, because I'm Satan. How would Satan like to live? He doesn't want to live. He possessed me — Satan. It's me committing suicide or murder. The Devil told me to do it. The Devil made me do it, through time. He possessed me in December, because 1982 goes forward, 1984 goes backward. It goes backward and forward by eleven months, which is the date of my possession, be it December and January.'

"This is a clear example of gross thought disorder. I asked him to explain this and he stated, 'Time,' and he spelled it out:

'T-I-M-E. Time doesn't have to go backwards. What happens if I die? You ask why I murdered. The Devil made me do it by possessing me.'

"I asked him if he knew what he did was wrong and he stated, 'When you're possessed, how could I stop myself?' He continued later in the interview, 'Today is the twenty-sixth – I'll never see February first.' At this point he began to talk about suicide. He went on, 'I'm very depressed.' After a short silence I asked him if he could tell me a bit more about how he was feeling and he stated, 'Little voices in my mind that told me to kill it, when I killed my family. It's unfortunate, isn't it? I told my family I was possessed. They're asking themselves right now. They want to see me. They have to have time for themselves.' My conclusion was that he still remained mentally ill and unable to sustain a logical conversation.

"On January thirty-first we have another letter; this again is very bizarre with stars and a whole conglomeration of stars, trying to explain the big bang theory."

Sullivan asked the Doctor if the content of this letter was similar to the others. When it was determined that there was no new information contained in the writing, they moved on. Sullivan asked, "Is there anything else you wish to say about the interview you had with him on the thirty-first of January?"

265

Adilman: "Well, just before I had seen him there was a nursing note...

'The five points of the pentacle will rush inwards as of twenty-four hours, January 31, 1983, as time is running backwards.'

"He spoke about the Book of Revelation (and) stated that 'I killed my family,' and also that 'Time killed my family, not me.' And then he was convinced, 'I think I'm going to die tonight, I know it. I just know it. 12:00 tonight I'm going to die – my possession.' And then throughout that day he was pleading with me to have his brother and sister with him because the end of the world would surely happen on the thirty-first of January. He was continuing to hear voices and just to give you an example of how he misinterpreted things, he had been watching the television for a while and I asked him if he was getting messages from the T.V. and he stated, 'I get my own interpretations from them. They may be singing a song that might be anything, and then I get my own interpretation.' I asked him if he could give me an example.

'I can't think of any interpretations, but last night, Smokey and the Bandit, Smoke and the Bandit. He was going to come and smoke. Smoke up everything. My whole body, my whole spirit, 'cause he's the bandit. He and she — she's everything, man, absolutely everything. The whole fucking universe, man, tonight's the night, man. I'll never see my brother and sister again. I got to phone them. I'd like to watch the world end with them. I'd like them both to be with me 'til twelve tonight.'

266

"Dr. Eaves saw Mr. Blackman on February the first. On the seventh,

> *'I don't know why I killed them. I thought the world was coming to an end. What else do you want to know? I don't know what I did, man.'*

"I then later asked him [on the seventh] about the voices and he stated,

> *'The voices, save the universe. I told you everything. I guess it isn't death, is it? There's life after death. Maybe they died on the thirty-first. Maybe it wasn't me and you. It was them — all the dead people. Maybe they died on the thirty-first. I don't know, man.'*

"Again, he was unable to sustain the logical conversation. He was returned to court on February the ninth and the judge, after having heard psychiatric evidence, found that Mr. Blackman at that time was not fit to have his trial, and that brings us to…"

Sullivan interrupted: "So throughout the period from January the nineteenth on his first admission [to the hospital], to the point where you've taken us now — February the ninth, 1983 — would it be fair to say that the [same] theme and your impressions of him continued throughout that entire period of time?"

"That's correct."

"Now, let's briefly go through a period of time from February the ninth, and you've told us that he began to receive certain medication on February the twenty-third?"

"No, the eighteenth."

"And tell us what is the anticipated effect of the medication that he was given on February the eighteenth, 1983?"

"Well, the medication is to minimize anxiety, improve attention, improve concentration, to work on the actual psychotic process and that's why these drugs are called anti-psychotic medication, in the hopes of improving the thinking, the voices and the delusions."

"All right," said Sullivan, "So let's continue on a little bit from there and I'll turn it back over to you again, Doctor, to highlight some of the things that happened in that brief period."

"Throughout the month of February he was still very fragile. On the twenty-eighth I made a note that he was improving, but he could quickly revert to his bizarre material. On March the first, I had a two session interview with him, two different times during the day. He was better and I wanted to try and see if I couldn't reconstruct with him what had happened and so I saw him from 11:34 in the morning to 12:22 after lunch and then again from 1:34 to 2:17 p.m., and I can read you some highlights from those interviews.

"He had explained to me that he was working for the District of North Vancouver as a garbage [man], he was a swamper, and that he had suddenly quit that job because he had gotten a new job. He had applied to attend Selkirk College in Nelson and he was on the waiting list to take a millwright course [and] he got word that he was accepted and so he quit his job towards the fourteenth or fifteenth and was preparing over the weekend of the fourteenth, fifteenth, and left for Nelson on the sixteenth, which was a Sunday. I asked him why he came home and he stated,

> *'I was all mixed up. The voices were telling me things. The voices said I had a key, a key of my dorm. They gave me my graduation key. The voices said, you graduated, go home. It was a female voice, the white woman.'*

"He claims that he obeyed the voices. He added,

> *'The voices kept saying, go home, you graduated. My diploma was a key. It was actually a key to the dorm room.'*

"He acknowledges that he never attended a class while at Selkirk College."

Adilman proceeded to lay out the relatively quick trajectory of Blackman's illness, beginning with references to statements made by Blackman's roommate, as well as Blackman's brother-in-law who had testified in court the day before. While Blackman was cooperative in terms of making statements, Adilman noted, "I wrote that Mr. Blackman appeared to be responding to the treatment he was receiving, some medication, but I still kept him on constant attention. There were memory gaps at that time. He was preoccupied and could not

269

concentrate too well. He would repeat questions that he asked me from the day before and was extremely anxious and quite depressed and he was now feeling the impact of what had happened. [It] was finally getting to him. He was becoming more and more sad."

Sullivan: "So would it be fair to categorize that this is the first time that we have heard that some of the symptoms of the illnesses that you've told are beginning to diminish?"

"Yes."

"All right, continue on."

"From here on in — although the content of what I say may be somewhat similar — the way it was portrayed becomes much more coherent and logical, at least it's beginning to on March the first. I asked him if he could explain to me how he understood what happened to him and the circumstances of the present charges, and this now is on medication and as he is getting better. 'It all started in December. It was very powerful.' I asked him if he could remember when it was less powerful and he stated, 'Well, I'd been reading the Book of Revelations quite a lot. I read it many times. It started about a year ago.' I asked him why and he stated,

> *'I was kind of religious all the time, at least for the last four years. I was always good to people. I would give them the shirt off my back. I let my roommate wear my clothes. People mean a lot. Friendship counts a lot. I really love my family.'*

"I asked him why he read the Book of Revelation and he stated,

'Because that's the end of the Bible, at the end of time. It was trying to tell me something, like the end of the earth was coming. Chapter 17 says something about Babylon, the great — the Queen of Harlots and abominations of the earth. One day that all just stuck in my mind.'

"He goes on to say that he began to believe in God and one day he would say things like 'I would never see a 29 in crib and then one day I played for it and sure enough I got a 29 in crib' and he thought that was from God. Further on in the interview he begins to talk about:

'[T]hat white woman, be it the Devil, I think, you know, the word, awake. The voices kept saying, over and over, I'm saving the dreams, I'm saving the dreams, you're God, you're God, and I kept saying, I'm not God, I'm Bruce Blackman...Doc, it's all very confusing. I don't know what it's all about. I know what Satan is. It's the death of everything. She first came and said to me, "It's the opposite, or the opposite of" — and then I would say, "Opposite of what?" Life, is that the opposite of death? I don't know Doc.'

"He then spontaneously stated,

'In December, the voices were stronger and stronger. There was a man's voice, dogs barking, a woman's voice and the TV set and the music. I would hear these things in the music. It was as

if it was being programmed into me. It was very powerful December third. I was totally possessed.'

Adilman testified that Bruce told him about the incident in Quesnel when he surprised his sister and put his anti-psychotic medication in her omelet. Blackman told the doctor, "I thought that her kid would be God and would be the answer to my problems. I don't know why." Bruce then went on to talk about having some problems at work with the sanitation crew.

> *"...The guys sort of looked strange at work. One of the guys was even crying. Couldn't figure it out. When he looked at me, he just looked strange. I thought they knew who I was — Satan. It was all over again — she had come to get me, the white woman with eyes of fire, an all white woman, totally white with eyes of fire. I just kept reading the Bible over and over and over."*

"He seemed to be getting distressed at this time in the interview, but I felt it was important to pursue things, and I asked him if he could tell me some of the events that led up to the actual incident. He stated,

> *'When I got to Nelson, I had four hundred dollars. Up there something was really bothering me. I got on the plane and came home. When I came home I only had two hundred dollars. I don't know. I kept taking cabs all over the place. I went home. My Mom, Dad and Rick were ready for dinner. They asked me what I was doing there and how come I came home from Nelson. I told him that I had to come home. They wanted to know where*

the money was. They were really concerned. They wanted to call [the doctor] but I wouldn't let them. The voices kept saying over and over, I got to kill, I got to kill, to save the universe, to save the world. Because of the big bang theory, the big boom. My family is the family of God. When they're dead, they'll go to heaven. My dad is God. The twin brother Raymond is Jesus. The voices kept saying this, they kept saying there's just a short time left to do this, it has to happen before the twenty-fourth or the thirty-first, and then the voices said something about time going backwards. The voices just kept on and on. I had dinner. Things were really bothering me. I couldn't eat. I went downstairs to put on a record. I put the record on, the Who. *There was some song called, "Anywhere, Anyhow" and then I began to interpret what it said about you got to do it, you got to do it. And then I went downstairs and got the .22 gun and shot my parents and Ricky. I then called my other family. They came and I killed them. I killed them to save the world from blowing up.'*

"At the end of that interview he said to me, 'You know, Doc, it's sort of going away now. Things are getting better.' I stated it was probably because of the medication he was receiving. He acknowledged this."

Adilman went on, explaining with sincerity Blackman's progression with drug therapy. On May twenty-fourth, 1983, Bruce was taken off special attention as he was no longer considered a suicide risk, but he continued to receive medication and began attending occupational therapy every day. The Doctor felt that Blackman had made significant progress and that "at the present time," he was no longer exhibiting thought disorder, delusions or hallucinations.

The Doctor continued: "[I have tried] to put some order to this horrendous disorder, and so when I relate these next two interviews I feel that it is important to keep in mind that there are probably memory gaps and even some distortions because we're relying on his memory of what happened eight months ago when he was severely psychotic, and now he has improved.

"I began the interview (of September 28) by asking Mr. Blackman if he could recall for me when he felt that something was wrong with him. He stated, 'It started back in October when I was hunting.' And he relayed for me then that story about hunting, getting the moose. He thought things were going all right in November. He was working, made a point of telling me that his recollection he was always on time for work. He said he didn't think there were any voices in November, and then again,

> *'Everything started coming down. Hearing voices. December 3, 1982. It all started when I watched the TV show "the Magic Christian", Peter Sellers and Ringo Starr. I was getting messages from time, from the past to the future and watched this TV show which I thought he wrote down in the Book of Revelations. After the TV show, at work, I heard voices from my friends saying I was looking for the great white woman. They*

were always pointing out — see that? Isn't she beautiful? I thought they were talking about the great white woman.'

"He then noticed that the salt water at Deep Cove had frozen over and he thought that that was another message from God and he also, at that time thought he was God. He continued:

'Then I got into this business of The Tree of Knowledge – my semen. I wanted everyone to eat from their Tree of Knowledge, but the women didn't have this. They had to drink their blood. Then there was [my sister]. She was pregnant, so she couldn't drink of her blood, so I thought her pregnancy was the great white woman. I had to go up there and see her. I had some medication from [my doctor]. I didn't want to take it. Maybe this is another omen, I thought. The doctor wanted me to give it to the great white woman which was [my sister's] child. So I made an omelet for her and stuck seven tablets in it. She couldn't eat it, she threw it out. The dog ate it. Later that night the dog got paralyzed and they had to take it to the vet and that was just before Christmas, the eighteenth or nineteenth of December.'"

Justice McKenzie asked Adilman if he knew which medication it was that Blackman put in the eggs.

"It was probably the Mellaril, the 25 milligram white tablets that he was supposed to be taking, but he claims he wasn't taking that.

'After I came back at Christmas — it was a nice Christmas, a good Christmas — I was still getting messages from the TV set. I was listening to these voices, thinking that I was God, Zeus. I thought I was Zeus. Even by myself I was hearing voices. The voices that came to my head were Harod, Zeus's wife, the great white woman.'

"He then explained to me again about drinking of the blood and making the concoction in the blender.

'At this time, [my twin brother] was in town. He knew there was something wrong with me. The voices were always there. I started hearing voices about waters being frozen. Our garbage truck was stopped to have it checked for its weight. I thought that was another omen from God.'

"And then,

'When I was reading the Bible — Chapter 10 of the Book of Revelations — I thought that Chapter 10 was me, the Angel of Revelations. John, where I lived, I talked to him and he said, No, you got the wrong idea. I kept saying, No, something good is going to happen because I was the Angel of Revelations. I went to school, January 16, a Sunday, to Selkirk College in Nelson. I took a bus ride up there. On the bus was a girl named Mary. She was really bugged out. She was talking about dying and coming to life and what it was like, coming back to life. I believed every word she said to me. She left the bus. I got to

276

Nelson about 7:30 p.m., went to the dorm and got a bedroom. I went to sleep that night. But before I went to sleep I phoned my sister Bobi and wanted to know if she had her menstrual period yet and she had. So I asked her to drink her blood, and she said that she would. Then I went to sleep. I then woke up Monday to go to school. Instead, I got this idea that I had to kill my family. The whole family, all the children, because in Chapter 10, Book of Revelations, there is the verse six, that the seven thunders utter their voices, but it was sealed up, not to be told so I didn't know the reason why I had to kill my family. I thought the seven thunders were the children of mom and dad, and that there was [sic] only six kids in the family. The seventh one died at birth, which I thought was Jesus Christ, because I thought that time could steal from the future, that's what I thought was Jesus Christ, my little brother Raymond. Jesus Christ died on the cross. Because he died on the cross, that was a message to me, that the whole family should die too, because of the Star of David. Each corner represented one member of my family and I thought the Star of David was the universe, and that the Satanic Star was the universe before January 31...The message to kill the family came from the Book of Revelations because the Book of Revelations is the last book of the New Testament and I thought that was the end of time. I also thought that time possessed me.'"

Dr. Adilman continued: "I then asked him what happened in Nelson and he stated,

'I phoned the cab, picked me up and took me to town — airport — took a plane home — took a cab from the airport to home. I got home. They wondered why. I gave them back the money I had. I said I wasn't going to school. I got ready for bed. I went to the games room, grabbed my [hunting] knife. I went to Rick's room and sat down and talked to Ricky. Went out of the room, left the knife. Ricky found it under the bed. He was scared and told my parents. Dad phoned [the doctor], couldn't reach him. I went to the games room, took a gun and put it under the couch. I concealed the gun, loaded a magazine downstairs. Dad was doing a crossword puzzle in the kitchen. I shot him. Then Ricky in the TV room. Then I went upstairs. Mom was waking up and I shot her. After I shot them all, I phoned Bobi and said I had to see them as something was about to happen. They said, "We'll be there." I said, don't bring John, my brother-in-law. She came over — they all came over. I shot Karon first, then Bobi and John in the garage. He got out and I ran after him. Thought for sure John was the Devil. So I got the gun — I went down and filled my 2.22, shot him. He would not die. I bludgeoned him with a hammer. Also my sister Karon.'

"I then asked him what was going on for him in his head at the time and he stated:

'The Star of David had to be formed because each member of the family is a member of the family of God. Zeus, Harod, Aphrodites, Saturn — I thought all parts of the Star of David. I

*thought the world was going to blow up because the satanic star
was going to come to a close. The big bang theory — I thought
that the children had to die. I thought the universe was going to
die. I thought by killing them, their spirits would go to Heaven
and hold the stars back from blowing up the physical earth.
They would be in Heaven preventing the world from blowing
up.'*

"I asked him more about the killings and he said,

*'The voices told me to do it. They said I was God, Zeus, the one
that had to make the world not blow up. I could save the world
by holding back the stars of the universe, so that they wouldn't
all come together, collide and blow up. By killing the family,
they would all be created into the family of God. I was the
creator. I was creating.'*

"I then asked him if he understood what he was doing and he
stated,

*'No, I didn't. I was compelled to do it by the voices. The white
woman's voice. A great big white woman, God. The Book of
Revelations says the great white whore that sat on the beast,
Chapter 17, that's the woman that told me to do it, that she was
God. It's difficult to remember.'*

"I then asked if what he did was wrong and if he thought that
what he did was wrong and he stated,

'No, I thought it was right, because I had to make the family of God. Each corner of the Star of David was a member of my family. They weren't part of God as long as they were living. I thought the Satanic Star was the star of the universe. It was a beginning and an ending. Where the beginning is, I thought that was the actual star and that Wormwood would destroy the earth. The parents represented the whole star. I thought I was dethroning my Dad, like Zeus who dethroned Titus in Greek mythology.'"

Dr. Adilman asked Sullivan if he should proceed.

Sullivan: "Is that the conclusion of that particular interview?"

"Of the twenty-eighth interview."

"Let's then, Doctor, turn to the final part of your evidence with us today, to the summaries and conclusions that you have reached as a result of the interviews from hearing the evidence for the last couple of days, would you state whatever summary and conclusions you have reached as a result of all the contact, all the material that you have reviewed with respect to this particular case?"

Adilman responded: "Before doing that, Your Honour, I would just like to state that it's very difficult to put any kind of logical order to something that is so illogical, or to put order to such disorder, so in my summary I referred to some things in a way that might offer some clarity to something that is so unclear and confusing.

"In October of 1982, Bruce began to view just about any event as a message or omen to him from God. He was receiving messages from the TV and interpreting them in a bizarre and personal manner. December 3, 1982, is a significant date. On that day, he began to hear voices, particularly that of the great white woman, the whore, who told him that he was God, the Devil and the Antichrist. He misperceived the meaning of all of this, yet considered the voice to be that of God, himself or herself. He became increasingly preoccupied with the concept of the opposites. 'The white woman must be real' — and he had told me this at one time. Since his name was the opposite, namely Blackman, he was Zeus because his name was Bruce. In a later interview he referred and thought he was a reebl because he drank beer and the opposite of beer was reeb, and therefore he was a reebl. He continued to become obsessed with opposites, including the beginning and the end which he interpreted as the end of the world, which then would have to have a new beginning. The white woman was at varying times a male and at other times a female God. The delusions became more and more intense as did the voices. Bruce's thinking processes became the product of psychotic thought and ideation. He became deluded regarding themes of birth and sex, death and destruction. He became convinced that the great white woman or God wanted him to eat from the Tree of Knowledge which he in some strange way concluded was some type of book. The book that one had to eat from the seed of the Tree of Knowledge which was to him semen. One of his siblings had died at birth; that was interpreted as the child of God, namely Jesus Christ.

"In a most bizarre and deluded fashion, he believed that if Jesus died for a purpose, so must the remaining six children and his family. Their death was to prevent the world from ending. As he was God it was his mission to save the world and to save his family from total destruction. He was the Angel of Revelations. In his deluded state he was convinced that his sister, who was pregnant, was the great white woman and her child was Jesus Christ. Bruce's delusions increased as did the voices. He believed that in some way his family represented the six points of the Star of David. The parents represented the whole star. In all of his writings there were numerous pictures, stars and arrows with dots. The Star of David with beginnings and endings. He perceived the Star of David as the new universe and the Satanic Star as the evil or present universe which would collide with the Star of David causing the big bang theory. The result would be the end of the world. In his deluded thinking the only way he could prevent this from happening was by killing the family members so that they would station themselves at the points of the Star of David and prevent the Satanic Star from crashing into the Star of David and thus preventing the world from blowing up. Not only did the number seven determine somehow his mission, so did the numbers indicate the dates at which time this big bang theory would occur. He believed that December twenty-fifth was significant by adding two plus five to equal seven; it represented the day that the world would end since he was the fifth child and his sister Karon the second, it had to be so. He then developed other number sequences, such as twenty-four, thirty-one, and you heard yesterday twelve and the twenty-four and thirty-one are seven days apart which also has significance for when the world would end, and it's interesting to note that Bruce [and his twin brother] were born on October twenty-fourth and Bruce's sister was born on October thirty-first, seven days apart.

"To add more confusion to this bizarre ideation, he conceived that the two sets of twins represent the Four Horsemen of the Apocalypse, again in a most distorted fashion, it appears he concluded that it was essential that all members of the family die and he intended therefore to kill his [surviving brother and sister] since they too had to be at their points on the Star of David.

"[At] the height of his psychosis, Mr. Blackman's thoughts were bizarre and deluded. He was controlled by command hallucinations. From about December third, 1982, he became more bizarre and unpredictable. He believed he had a special mission to save the world from being destroyed. He incorporated seams of astrology, numerology, so called philosophy and religion into a bizarre system of delusional belief. He became convinced that the last book of the Bible – Revelations — was especially addressed to him. At varying times he believed that he was Zeus, the Angel of Revelations or even the Book of Revelations. He believed that he was possessed and was the Devil. At one point he and the remaining siblings were considered to be Antichrists. He was constantly and continuously influenced by the voice of the great white woman. The voices told him the world would end and he must kill his family in order for them to become the family of God. By doing this he could in some bizarre way save them from being destroyed. He followed the commands of the voices and the beliefs and the delusions.

"Based on all the information available to me and the information I have that I have reviewed and the interviews with Mr. Blackman and as well as all of the testimony I have heard in court, it is my opinion that Mr. Bruce Blackman was acutely psychotic at the time he killed the members of his family. His thoughts and actions were a product of his grossly and severely disturbed mental state. He was suffering from command hallucinations and controlled delusions of a most bizarre nature. His thinking patterns were totally out of touch with reality. His actions were governed by the psychotic process."

Sullivan: "And in your opinion Doctor, at the time of the commission of the killings of his six family members, was Mr. Bruce Blackman suffering from a disease of the mind?

"He was suffering — if by a disease of the mind I would conclude that that is a severe mental illness, namely a psychosis called schizophrenia, yes."

"And in your opinion, because of that disease of the mind at the time he killed his family, did that disease of the mind render him incapable of appreciating the nature and quality of the acts that he undertook to kill his family members?"

"Yes, it did."

"And because of that disease of the mind, did that disease of the mind prevent him from knowing that the acts of killing his family were wrong?"

"Yes."

Sullivan concluded his examination. "Thank you, sir."

"Mr. Levenson?" asked Justice McKenzie.

"No questions, thank you, My Lord."

As was his prerogative, the Justice posed some questions for Dr. Adilman. "Doctor, is there in cases like this any detectable organic base for the psychosis?"

"Your Honour, during the course of the time he was in the hospital I had a neurological examination done by a neurologist, electroencephalogram, CT scan…no organic basis at all was found in any of the tests."

"Despite the absence or apparent absence of an organic base, there is no question but that he did suffer in the old fashioned language of the Criminal Code of a disease of the mind, though you cannot assign a place to it, you can describe the condition in terms of the symptoms that are manifested while the person is suffering from it?"

"Yes."

"Can you equate it in any way with a physical illness such as malaria or jaundice, something that comes on in a gradual sort of fashion, goes through an acute phase and then if the patient is fortunate, goes away?"

"In some instances this particular illness does start in an acute fashion and does go away. I think that in this particular instance, Your Honour, the disease was so severe that [it] required medication and probably antipsychotic medication and probably would not have dissipated to the extent that it has without it."

"So far as these external stimulants were concerned, such as the television program and his association in some fashion or other with Jehovah's Witnesses and with their literature and with the incident where the garbage truck was stopped and all that sort of thing, those things, if I understood, would not have anything to do with contributing to his condition, but because of his condition he took a distorted view..."

"Exactly."

"...of those kinds of stimulants?"

"Exactly, yes."

Justice McKenzie addressed the attorneys. "Are there any questions?" There were none.

Dr. Adilman was excused. The court took a much needed break.

TEN MINUTES LATER, Justice McKenzie was back in his court room, as were DeCouto, Sullivan, Levenson and Blackman. The Crown and Defence, however, had not had an opportunity to enjoy their small break from proceedings. They had a pressing matter to discuss. Before the jury was recalled, Levenson addressed the court: "My Lord, my learned friends and I have discussed one brief matter during the break. I [ask] that we be able to address you with regard to this." What Levenson wanted was to inform the jury of the consequences of a verdict under Section 16 of the Criminal Code of Canada, a verdict that would find Blackman not guilty by reason of insanity. "I have the cases here that authority for the fact that it is not improper for counsel to do that [and] I wanted to direct my intentions to Your Lordship and get any guidance Your Lordship has with regard to my intentions."

Justice McKenzie: "Mr. Sullivan?"

Sullivan answered that if case law supported Levenson's intentions, then the Crown had no objection.

Justice McKenzie nodded, then said, "Well, I believe the jury should be told, otherwise they might think that a person upon being found not guilty on account of insanity would be entirely free, and of course that is not the case because of Section 542 (2) of the Criminal Code which reads: 'where the accused is found to have been insane at the time the offence was committed, the court, judge or magistrate before whom the trial is held shall order that he be kept in strict custody in the place and in the manner that the court, judge or magistrate directs, until the pleasure of the Lieutenant Governor of the Province is known.'

"There has been some debate," Justice McKenzie continued, "as to whether or not a jury should be told because there has been debate as to whether a jury should be concerned with the disposition of any case, but I am satisfied that the current state of the law is that a jury should be told this and indeed if counsel had not informed the jury I certainly would have. While we are on that subject, in the event of such a verdict he should be kept in the Forensic Psychiatric Institute, is that right?"

Sullivan nodded. He told the Justice that in the course of examining the next set of witnesses, he'd canvass "what would be the proper designated place."

Justice McKenzie: "Right, thank you. Now, we can proceed…Would you bring in the jury, please?"

The jury returned and took their seats. DeCouto called Dr. Derek Eaves to the stand. DeCouto tendered Eaves as a medical and psychiatric expert, and was not challenged. Nevertheless, DeCouto led Eaves through a Q & A about his credentials which included positions in England, New Zealand, and Canada.

DeCouto: "And what is forensic psychiatry, Doctor?

Eaves: "Well, forensic psychiatry in general means the interface between psychiatry and the law, whether it be civil or criminal law."

"And in respect to Bruce Blackman, you became involved and saw him on several occasions, is that correct?"

"Yes, I did."

288

DeCouto then established that Eaves would be giving testimony based on his interviews with Blackman, as well as the background information he'd received which included the interviews with law enforcement, the medical files from the Forensic Psychiatric Institute, and the clinical notes, especially those of Eaves' colleague, Dr. Adilman. Also to be considered were the medical report of Dr. Hayes who had examined Blackman when he'd been arrested, and the notes from the psychiatrist who'd treated Blackman for the six weeks leading up to the murders.

DeCouto: "Now Doctor, if I could, would you perhaps at this time go briefly into the various interviews that you had with Mr. Bruce Blackman and your observations and conclusions with respect to that?"

Eaves: "Yes. The first interview I had with Mr. Blackman was on January nineteenth, 1983. That interview took one hour and ten minutes in length, between 7:30 p.m. and 8:40 p.m. I had intended to make the interview longer, but in fact I ended it somewhat prematurely on humanitarian grounds because Mr. Blackman was extremely distressed and he showed, during that interview, rather pronounced features of a mental illness. At the conclusion of that interview I came to the diagnosis that he was suffering from a psychotic state, and by this I mean that he was out of contact with reality at that time, and that the likely diagnosis was paranoid schizophrenia.

"He showed during that interview these features: He expressed a belief that he was the Antichrist; that he was possessed by the Devil which gave him instructions to kill his family. He expressed the view

289

that the instructions and the messages came to him in the form of voices. He expressed a feeling that the end of the world was due and that he had to kill his family to save them and to prevent the world blowing up. He expressed a notion that he was possessed by time. When I examined his mental state at that time I felt there was some fragmentation of the form of his thinking, although it wasn't particularly marked. There was, however, an inability to focus his attention on a particular matter, but he would jump from one issue to another spontaneously with certain recurrent themes. And these recurrent themes were delusions or false beliefs that he was the Antichrist, that he was possessed by the Devil, that he was forced to take certain actions and that those actions might ruin various people and he said that just by looking at me that he could also ruin me as well. So he felt that he was having a profound effect on all people around him.

"There was also substantial mood disturbance which hadn't been noticed the previous two days, from my understanding, but there was very marked depression of his mood and some lability[17] of his mood as well. And I also noted that there were auditory hallucinations taking the form of voices which he was experiencing at that time.

"I next examined him on February first, 1983, when I noticed that similar features, the features of his psychosis in fact were even more marked in the second interview than they had been in the first one. The purpose of that interview was really to determine whether, in my

---

[17] Lability refers to something that is constantly undergoing change or something that is likely to undergo change.

opinion, I felt that he was fit to stand trial. He indicated that he had expected the end of the world on January thirty-first, and it hadn't happened and his conclusion was that because it hasn't happened [was because] he'd been tricked by the Devil. He told me that on December third of 1982 he'd been watching *The Magic Christian* with Peter Sellers and Ringo Starr and it marked the beginning of his possession, that it was a very significant event to him. You'll sometimes notice that in schizophrenia that events have a very significant meaning for an individual and it can come with specific events so that it may be marked in steps in terms of their perception of the development of their state. He told me that before that time that he'd become interested in reading the Bible, that he'd felt that songs and television shows had special meaning for him with repeated references to death. He also expressed the view that day that he was suffering from herpes and that was rotting his brain.

"The psychiatric features that I noticed were that I felt he could attend to some reality issues, but that still the psychotic ideation, all the psychotic features had been noted before were very intrusive in his mental state, so that he had very poor concentration when I tried to address specific matters to him. I felt that there was more pronounced thought disorder at that particular time, meaning both the form and the content of his thinking disorder. He described in that interview what he said were meaningless voices, mostly a jumble, although he could hear particular words and one was that he was a psycho killer and what words he could understand made references to God and to possession.

"I next interviewed him on February eighth when he expressed the view that he'd been possessed by hatred, by time and by the Devil. He told me that in the past he'd heard a woman's voice, the voice of an ex-girlfriend, and that he could still hear her crying. He indicated that about one and a half years before he'd begun to read Jehovah's Witness pamphlets, and from that he learned that God would come, that only a few people would enter Heaven, that he, of course, wanted to be one of them. He began to feel that the Devil tried to stop you from entering Heaven. There was, in fact, therefore, a battle between good and evil, and he began in 1982 to hear a voice and the voice said it was Jehovah. And then in early December 1982, he repeated the ideas that he had expressed previously about being influenced by television. He told me that in December that the voice had told him to eat from the Tree of Knowledge, eat thy semen, and he felt possessed by the Devil, he felt possessed by time. He was troubled by the voices to such an extent that he was unable to sleep. He felt then in order to save the world that he had to kill his parents, that the universe would devour itself like a giant sun, that his family were the family of God and that he had to kill them. He felt and he expressed the view at that time that perhaps in fact he hadn't killed them, perhaps he hadn't done it because he wasn't the kind of person that could kill another person, and he commented at that time about the big bang theory and that time would be reversed.

"I next interviewed him on March twenty-ninth, 1983. That was a fairly brief interview, really to assess his fitness to stand trial. It was clear that at that time his mental status started to improve substantially although he was still depressed. His thinking was still slowed down. He didn't describe any current hallucinations at that time and he was, of course, at that time on medication, and he did tell me that the troublesome thoughts that he'd experienced previously were beginning to disappear.

"I didn't see him then until August first, 1983, and at that time he was quite lucid and quite articulate. He was able to give a coherent history of his life and background and I spent some six hours on that occasion going over his history and the development of his delusory system and the events leading up to January seventeenth and January eighteenth, 1983. The purpose of the interview was to take a comprehensive history of him with particular reference to the year prior to January eighteenth of this year, and as I've said, to trace the development of his illness and to assess the degree of disturbance, if I could, on January seventeenth, eighteenth and the days immediately prior to those dates. He told me a lot about his background history, the significant features were these: He told me that he was a twin; that his birth and development otherwise were quite normal, although he did experience some learning difficulties in school and he had some difficulties when younger in relating to other children. He told me that in 1981 and 1982 that Jehovah's Witnesses would call at his home and he began to read the Bible, and there were two elements which he learned from reading the pamphlets; one was that the end of the world was coming, and secondly, that it was important to see God.

"In the summer of 1982, he told me that [he found] Revelations particularly absorbing and he began to feel that the end of the world was

293

due and that he would have something to do with it, and the end of the world would come fairly soon. As I indicated before, he expressed the view that December third was a key date, and he said that from that time on that he felt he was the Angel of the Revelations, that he got messages from television and other communication sources subsequently. He then began to believe that he was God, that he was the Devil, that he was the Angel of the Revelations. He heard the Devil say 'I'm going to eat you up, eat you whole.' He felt that he was God and because of that he had mystical powers. He therefore began to masturbate and to eat his semen because this was the Tree of Knowledge. To eat one's semen meant to understand, and in December, the voices began to be present almost all the time. He began to feel that his whole family were involved in the sense that not only was he God, but that they were all God's family; that he was Zeus, that the men in the family had to eat semen and that the women had to [drink] menstrual blood. He mentioned the incident of making Karon inadvertently [drink] menstrual blood and he mentioned the incident of travelling to Quesnel to see [his surviving sister]. He felt that [her] pregnancy was an omen and that a child of God would be born and it was because of that that he put the medication in her food.

"He told me that he spent Christmas with his family. He felt that God might visit him in a woman's form and marry him. He felt that the marriage would be between a black man and a white woman. The white woman was a reference to Revelations and the black man, of course, was his own surname. In fact God did not come over Christmas. He did tell me that until January he had no thoughts of killing anyone. The voices, nevertheless, got heavier and deeper and were present all the time, and he began to think of suicide. He told me that on January sixteenth, he took the bus to Nelson and on the bus he met a girl called Mary who told him that she'd died twice. That she could transport her body, and she was particularly significant to him at that time because he felt that she had something, some meaning about life and death. In Nelson he proceeded to (his dorm) where he went to sleep and woke up somewhat suddenly with the idea and the notion that he should kill his family in order to save them. They would then become the eternal family of God and would not be dead at all. He recalled that the hallucinatory voices were present from that time on. He travelled home by plane and was preoccupied from that time on that he had to deliver his family before the big bang occurred.

"In coming to an opinion about his mental state at the time of the killings, I considered all the interviews that I had with Mr. Blackman and the material that were mentioned before and I felt there was a great consistency between the accounts that were given in evidence and in fact the accounts that were given to me by Mr. Blackman, that they describe his psychotic ideation externally and the same way that he himself described his own symptoms. I came to the conclusion that he suffered from paranoid schizophrenia and that his illness gradually developed during the summer and fall of 1982, that it reached a peak during December, 1982, and January of 1983. I also came to the opinion that his hold on reality became gradually more tenuous during that period. I did feel that his delusions fluctuated to some extent and I think you can understand that he was experiencing auditory hallucinations from different kinds of sources, that he felt he was hearing the voice of God and the voice of the Devil, and at different times one would take preponderance over the other, so that his delusions in fact reflected the different preponderance, if you like, of the voices which were influencing him so that he felt that he was God, that he was Zeus, that he was Antichrist, that he was Angel of the Revelations. In spite of these fluctuations there was a pattern, although a somewhat fragmented pattern which was developing, and this pattern was something like this: that he felt influenced by external events; he felt things had a special meaning for him; he felt compelled to undertake certain actions and force other people to undertake certain actions as well; he had a mission to save the world; he felt the world was going to be destroyed; he became preoccupied by numbers which eventually related to him and to his entire family; he eventually believed that his family represented the Satanic Star; that he had to become the Star of David; that keeping the points of the star apart would mean saving the world, and in order to do this that he had to kill his family.

"It's my opinion that he clearly had some ability to appreciate the physical nature and quality of his actions and I say this in considering the evidence that [the staff sergeant] gave. He [Blackman] knew that he had a gun on January eighteenth and that if he shot it that he would kill his family. It was not clear that he understood that by killing meant the physical death of his family, for in fact he believed and believed subsequently that he was really saving them and preserving them for eternity. I felt that his thinking was not right, but extremely distorted, although at times there were certain threads of logic which followed from the false premises. Most of the time, however, his thinking became

296

quite illogical and fluctuating. His thinking and behavior became more and more controlled by external forces. It prevented him from considering whether his actions were right or wrong, either in the moral sense or in the sense of being against the law.

"I came to the conclusion that all his actions were governed by his psychotic ideation and were the product of his mental illness. I felt that he was incapable of fully appreciating the physical nature and quality of his actions on January eighteenth, and that because of the serious illness he was suffering from, which was the mental disorder of paranoid schizophrenia, that he was incapable of knowing that his act was wrong.

"I would like to say this: It's my opinion that on the night of January seventeenth and the morning of January eighteenth that he was in a state of florid[18] psychosis. There were periods after the event when there were flashes of lucidity and he could, for example, respond to some of the questions in an appropriate manner, but if you look at that transcript that he very quickly loses track of the questions which were asked of him and his concentration and his ability to deal with the reality-based questions was very poor indeed. Immediately after the incidents there was a spontaneous outpouring of rambling, nonsensical material which was described by [the arresting officer]. This psychotic material would break through his extremely tenuous rationality; in essence, he was really in a kind of a disorganized dream world where he

---

[18] Florid: fully developed: manifesting a complete and typical clinical syndrome.

could hardly tell the difference between reality and unreality. It's only now when you can look backwards and reconstruct things that you can begin to draw the various elements and components of his delusory system together, but I feel there is a danger in doing this, in doing so, in trying to reconstruct his psychosis through the words of a rational man. When I spoke to him on August first, he was, in essence, a rational man. There's the danger that you lose track of the full blown psychotic picture that was in evidence January nineteenth, 1983. The point is this; that psychosis is almost by definition a non understandable state, so there are dangers in attempting to understand the non understandable. In attempting to do that there's a tendency to minimize the degree of the illness that a person suffered from at that time. If you look, as I did, at the drawings which he made on the eighteenth, then you can begin to appreciate the extent and the pervasive nature of his psychotic illness at that time. I have no doubt in my mind that he was acting as he saw it through his psychotic ideation in the best interest of his family and that he felt that what he was doing was right. There are numerous references in the evidence that we've heard to that and I felt that he was driven by an inexorable feeling through his delusory system that he only had one course of action and that was to kill his family and it's because of that in that sense that I have little doubt as a psychiatrist in expressing the opinion that he didn't know that his acts were wrong either in the moral sense or indeed against the law on January eighteenth, 1983."

Sullivan asked, "And Doctor, would you, in conclusion, agree with the opinion of the previous witness that he was, accordingly at that time, suffering from a disease of the mind known as paranoid schizophrenia?'"

Eaves answered: "He was suffering from a serious mental disorder — paranoid schizophrenia — at that time."

"Now, two other questions: the flashes of lucidity he had back in January of '83. That was evidenced in the statement [he made to the staff sergeant]. That is not unusual with a person in that state, is that correct?"

"No," answered Eaves. "Even in the most floridly psychotic person I think as Dr. Adilman said can respond to questions about who they are, what time it is and so forth, but the real point is that because of the pervasive nature of psychotic illnesses as he was in, he couldn't focus for any consistent period of time on those reality-based questions and the intrusive material was always there in a very, very pervasive form so that — if you like — it occupied most of his mental space at that time."

"And lastly, Doctor, with respect to his ability now with the treatment and medication that he had received and being able to recall more in detail and more in sequence and more coherently what happened and transpired in October, November, December of last year and January of this year, that that is not an unusual situation?"

"It's quite usual that they can recall events in much clearer form, but sometimes memory by itself distorts events and you tend to fuse elements together and so forth."

"I have no further questions, My Lord," said DeCouto.

"No questions, thank you, My Lord," said Levenson.

Eaves was dismissed from the witness stand.

DeCouto stood. "My Lord, that is the Crown's case."

Court adjourned in anticipation of the Defence calling one witness and one witness only.

WHEN COURT RESUMED that afternoon, Levenson stood to address the jury. Blackman sat quietly by his side, occasionally looking up at his lawyer, stealing glances at the men and women about to determine his fate, but mostly looking down at his hands folded in his lap.

"Mr. Foreman," he began, "ladies and gentlemen of the jury, you've heard a good deal of evidence here today, very technical evidence. You've also heard me indicate to His Lordship that we are going to try to be as brief as possible under the circumstances. Now, you have been told by His Lordship as well as my learned friend that the course that this trial is taking is an unusual course. It is not the adversarial process in its usual form. The only issue that is going to be left for you to decide is whether the acts of Bruce Blackman were insane acts. Now in that regard I've indicated that the course the trial is taking is unusual. It's unusual for two reasons. It's unusual because most of the elements that are usually required to be proven by the Crown in a case such as this have been admitted. It's unusual also because Crown counsel has taken the position in this particular set of circumstances, this unusual set of circumstances, that the acts in question were in fact insane acts. Mr. Sullivan indicated to you at the outset in his opening comments to you that it was the Crown's position that Bruce Blackman was legally insane pursuant to the provisions of Section 16 of the Criminal Code of Canada and His Lordship has briefly referred you to Section 16 at the outset of this matter.

"Now my reason for calling evidence at this point — you've heard a good deal of evidence — is because regardless of that, the position that the Crown takes, and it is a very fair position under the circumstances, the onus still lies upon the Defence to satisfy you upon the balance of probabilities that Bruce Blackman was in fact insane on January eighteenth of 1983. His Lordship has and I anticipate will outline for you further how the onus of proof works and he has indicated to you that it is on the balance of probabilities rather than beyond a reasonable doubt as it normally would be in a criminal matter. The issue of insanity takes upon it a different standard of proof as he has already outlined to you. Now in that regard I intend to call one witness, the psychiatrist. I expect that he will briefly outline for you what his involvement with Bruce Blackman has been. I expect that he will give you his opinion as to the mental state of Mr. Blackman based upon his own observations as well as his examinations of all of the available materials, including the evidence that has been led by previous witnesses for the Crown. His opinion and diagnosis will be in total agreement with the medical and psychiatric evidence already given by the previous

Crown witnesses in that he will tell you that the acts giving rise to the charges were in fact insane acts. He will further explain to you that the mental condition of Bruce Blackman as you have been observing him over the last three days is modified greatly by almost nine months of treatment and medication, since medication commenced on February eighteenth of 1983; therefore, Bruce Blackman as you observe him today is in a different state as a result of that medication.

"Now in an attempt to allow you to appreciate the physical and mental state of Mr. Blackman prior to the commencement of medication prior to February eighteenth, 1983, you will be shown a videotape of an interview between the psychiatrist, Dr. O'Shaughnessy, who will be giving evidence for me and Mr. Blackman. Now, I expect that doctor will direct your attention to specific aspects of that video tape, perhaps some prior to your watching the tape so that you can direct your attentions to certain aspects of that to see certain manifestations of behavior, and these aspects should graphically represent and support his opinion regarding the state of Bruce Blackman. Now, those observations should also perhaps assist you with regard to considering the evidence that you've already heard from psychiatrists who have given evidence on behalf of the Crown. I ask you to remember that what I have outlined for you here once again is only what my expectations of what the evidence will be and that none of this certainly is evidence at the present time. It does not become evidence until you hear it through the mouth of a witness.

"I call, please, as my first and only witness, Dr. Roy O'Shaughnessy."

Levenson informed the court that he was calling the witness as a medical doctor and psychiatrist qualified to practice medicine within the Province of British Columbia, and an expert in the field of psychiatry. There were no objections from the Crown. Levenson, nevertheless, quickly surveyed the doctor's resume which included degrees and internships in Canada and at Yale University in Connecticut, USA.

"Now," Levenson began his questioning, "you have had opportunity to examine and have numerous meetings with Bruce Alfred Blackman, is that correct?"

"Yes, I have."

"Could you please outline for the court when those visits and interviews took place?"

"My first interview occurred on January twenty-ninth, and in fact on that day I had two interviews separated by approximately an hour and a half. I also interviewed him on February first, February sixth, February ninth, February seventeenth, and October thirty-first of this year."

"As well as having seen Mr. Blackman as previously outlined by you, you have had an opportunity to examine the complete medical file from the Forensic Psychiatric Institute?"

"Yes, I have."

"You have examined police reports, statements taken by the police?"

"Yes, I have."

"As well as autopsy reports and heard the witnesses that have given evidence previous to you in this matter?"

"That's correct."

"With regard to consideration of all of those matters," Levenson continued, "I would like to avoid, if possible, repetition of the same evidence that has been given today, but anything that you can offer as assistance with regard to expanding upon that evidence that has already been led, I would appreciate [it]. [H]ave you, in fact, formed an opinion with regard to his mental state?"

O'Shaughnessy answered: "Yes, I have. My opinion, in fact, has been consistently throughout that Mr. Blackman suffers from a major mental disorder known as schizophrenia of a paranoid type. This is essentially in concurrence with [the other doctors'] diagnoses of him and perhaps just before getting into that I should discuss a bit about the diagnosis of schizophrenia and what is necessary to diagnose schizophrenia."

O'Shaughnessy then described for the jury what had already been presented prior: that schizophrenia is marked by disordered thinking, disordered feelings, disordered perception, disordered content of thought, evidence of delusions, and difficulty in the logical sequencing of thoughts into sentences.

"It's almost as if when you're looking or trying to understand how an individual with schizophrenia perceives their world, probably a simple but perhaps suitable metaphor would be if you took on a pair of very peculiarly colored glasses, say a mixture of any old colour of orange, for example, and wore those glasses consistently, everything you would see would be orange, everything that [others] would see would be in its natural colour. To the schizophrenic individual he would not accept that he was seeing life through orange glasses, but rather that he was the only one seeing life correctly. Everybody else would be wrong. They would be the ones who were crazy. When you understand that metaphor in that way it becomes very easy to understand when the individual of schizophrenia has peculiar ways of seeing their world, that they incorporate into those peculiar ways everything that they have known in the past. For example, (Blackman) had the psychotic ideation that things had relevance to him nowhere else, so he starts to read the Bible. Therefore, the Bible has special relevance to him and no one else. He starts interpreting the Bible through these orange glasses that you or I would not interpret it to be.

"For example; seven, the number seven. In Revelations, he tries to find where that fits in his life. He counts his family members; he finds seven being significant there. The Four Horsemen of the Apocalypse — tries to fit that into his life and recognizes that in his family there are two sets of twins. Clearly in his disorganized way of thinking that has special relevance. You or I would not think so. Mr. Blackman clearly did."

O'Shaughnessy continued to describe what the other doctors had — the voices, the delusions, the hallucinations.

"One final area that is very important in understanding schizophrenia is to understand that there is a disturbance in volition or one's ability to initiate action on one's own. In fact, what often happens is some schizophrenic individuals become quiet, sitting in a corner doing very little. They have no get-up-and-go. At other times — and particularly [in] Mr. Blackman's case — they will feel like their control of their behavior, their volition, does not lie within themselves but rather somewhere else. This is commonly associated with things we call command hallucinations. These are auditory hallucinations that basically give commands to an individual: and [the individual] will feel compelled to follow those commands as if they had no will of their own...

"Now, in the tape [that we will get to shortly], there are a number of things I wish you to watch out for. First of all, unfortunately, the tape has rather poor audio control. It can be heard, but you must listen very carefully. It is approximately [30 minutes], taken at the Forensic Psychiatric Institute on February seventeenth, 1983, which is a day before Mr. Blackman started any kind of antipsychotic medications. Now, the reason that the tape is being shown is that in our understanding of schizophrenia as a disorder there are probably more things we do not know about it than we do. One of the things we do know about it is that its etiology or cause is of a number of determinants. One of the clear determinates seems to be a biological issue going on in the brain itself, like there is some kind of aberration going on in how the different neurons communicate with chemicals called neurotransmitters and that the effect of the tranquilizing drugs we call anti-psychotic are to help correct that imbalance in the brain of neurotransmitters. As a result, [when you see] an individual with schizophrenia who has received medications, [it's] very different [than an] individual who has not, or who has received insufficient medication. In fact, individuals with schizophrenia who are on medication may not be recognized by anyone as having a measurement of illness. They can function in society very well. Many of them have important jobs. They do quite well as a rule. Some do not need recurring hospitalizations, and in Mr. Blackman's case, at the current time he no longer shows any of the aberrations that are typical of schizophrenia that I outlined earlier. In fact, he has no more delusions, no more hallucinations. His will is his own and he shows a more normal affect. What we're [about to see] on this tape is Mr. Blackman before he has been treated with anti-psychotic medications. The first fifteen/twenty minutes of the tape he will talk about the last day and a half, primarily the voices, the strange — *crazy, crazy* — ideas he had about the Bible and how it interfered in his life, and a number of the other kind of delusions, such as him being the Antichrist, the voices of David, etcetera, etcetera, the Star of David. In the last ten minutes or so of the tape, Mr. Blackman through the interview starts talking more specifically about what happened on the night and morning of January eighteenth and his affect changes

307

noticeably. I think you will find that yourself, and perhaps we'll use that as an example to discuss the aspects of schizophrenia on a person's thinking following the tape."

"Doctor," asked Levenson, "you attended the Forensic Psychiatric Institute in Coquitlam, British Columbia, on the evening of February seventeenth of 1983, is that correct?"

"That's correct."

"And at approximately 7:30 p.m., you commenced an interview with Mr. Blackman that is depicted on the video tape in question?"

"That's correct."

"And you had an opportunity in the very recent past to observe that video tape and to satisfy yourself that that is an accurate representation of everything that went on during that particular interview between yourself and Mr. Blackman?"

"Yes, I did."

Sullivan: "I have no objection to the admissibility of this piece of evidence, My Lord."

The videotape was entered as Exhibit 10.

All eyes fixed on the grainy television screen as the VHS tape was played to the court room. The jurors leaned forward in their chairs, while Blackman slumped back in his. While it was extremely difficult to hear the words, the actions and gesticulations of Bruce Blackman on the videotape showed a distraught, distracted and highly disturbed young man. There could be no arguing this evidence. It was, as one juror described it, "shocking".

At the conclusion of the tape, Levenson asked O'Shaughnessy: "Doctor, with respect to the state which is exhibited in that video tape, I'm wondering if you can relate any of your specific findings in this case to aspects of behavior that have been exhibited on that tape?"

"Yes. Perhaps I should start by explaining that this tape was made four weeks after the deaths of Bruce's family. He had been in the hospital that long, although not on medication. He was substantially better than he was on my first examination of him, and the reason for that is that many individuals, in fact most individuals with schizophrenic psychosis, do improve when placed in a structured and safe environment. It gives them that external structure which they lack [on an inner basis]. Most show improvement on that basis; in fact, Bruce Blackman did. There were a couple of findings however that I think are consistent throughout my interviews with him, and [those were] the voices continually harassing him, not letting him sleep, commanding him to do these things that they told him to do and the consistent delusional content. The grandiosity that he was God, he would save the world, and the persecution that he would be eaten up, that he would be killed, et cetera, that the world [would] be destroyed. Those are consistent kinds of findings that I think are vividly portrayed on the tape. Another finding that I think is important to understand and that is the manner in which the hallucinations seem so real that Mr. Blackman would even argue with

309

them. It would not be experienced as simply a thought of his own, but was virtually arguing with his hallucinations and he describes that vividly, I think, on this tape and I think on other sessions we had together.

"Perhaps I should talk and give a greater idea about what led to the actual incident." O'Shaughnessy reviewed the criteria for evaluating mental illness and observing its symptoms. "In addition, we also look at a number of other aspects that are quite apart from [the] mental illness aspect itself. The issue of whether [there were] alternative explanations for this behavior: Was there other motivation or intent? Was there jealousy? Was there anger? Was there disappointment or resentment? Those kinds of issues. [Was] there any history of drug abuse that was significant enough to bring on this kind of situation and on the latter two, both with regard to any other motive for these kinds of crimes, in terms of conflict in the family, fighting, jealousy, there was none that I could detect. There was, however, the importance of the delusional content and the command hallucinations, and the motive for him which is really to save the world, save his family and obey God's commands. He described [in my second interview with him] just prior to the actual killings themselves, he said,

> 'I was in Nelson picking up a millwright course. I didn't attend. The voice said I had to come home and I did. The voices told me what to do and I did them. I tried to resist the voices at times. At times I thought it was the Devil and at times I thought it was

God. I couldn't tell which. Before the crime I thought it was God, but the Devil tricked me.'

"He later went on to say,

'I tried to sleep after dinner, but I couldn't, the voices prevented me from sleeping by possessing me, by telling me I had to kill them. They first told me that in the plane, they said in God we trust, you must trust me. At first I didn't want to, I didn't believe it; at first it didn't seem real. I was combating it at the time. Then it totally possessed me. I wasn't myself. I didn't do it. I thought it was God and he was telling me to save the universe by building the Star of David.'

"He goes on to talk about the Star of David and how that in fact would save the universe which has been [entered into] evidence before."

Levenson asked, "Doctor, in view of your observations in total, your consideration of the evidence before the court and the other pieces of information that I've referred to, are you able to say that as of January eighteenth, 1983, Mr. Blackman was suffering from a disease of the mind to the extent that rendered him incapable of appreciating the nature and quality of his acts?"

"Yes, with qualification if I could give that. The qualification is 'disease of the mind' is not a medical concept in any stretch of the imagination. It is a purely legal concept. As such, medical expertise does not speak directly to that nature; however, it is generally assumed that mental illnesses of the severity of a schizophrenic psychosis, in my understanding, have been accepted by the courts as diseases of the mind. And the rest of that — that question did [it] interfere with his ability to proceed with what he was doing? I think it did, yes."

"All right, and similarly on the date in question are you of the opinion that Mr. Blackman was suffering also in the same basis as you've described from a serious mental illness which prevented him from appreciating — or pardon me, from knowing that the act that he was doing was wrong?"

"Yes, in my opinion he fully believed what he was doing was quite correct."

Levenson: "Thank you, I have no further questions."

Justice McKenzie: "Thank you. Cross examination?"

Sullivan: "No cross examination, My Lord."

Justice McKenzie excused the witness.

Levenson: "That is the evidence I intend to call, My Lord..."

Levenson and DeCouto both addressed the jury, Levenson first, DeCouto following. They reminded the jury that the only question before them was this: Was Bruce Blackman insane at the time he committed the murders?

It didn't take long for the jury to return their verdict: "Not guilty by reason of insanity."

Bruce Alfred Blackman was committed to the Forensic Psychiatric Institute in British Columbia — only minutes from his former home on Spuraway Avenue — where the jury believed he would be held for the rest of his life.

No-one could have predicted what would happen next.

SENTENCE

WHEN BRUCE WAS found not guilty by reason of insanity (NGRI), it meant — more or less — that he would be incarcerated in a mental institution for an indeterminate amount of time. Because of the nature and notoriety of the crime, that probably meant a lifetime of confinement. Bruce himself understood this: He had told the arresting officer, "They'll probably lock me away in a little box for the rest of my life."

But this was prior to 1992, the year a major change in the law was enacted. The law in 1983 — when Bruce was tried — stated that if you were acquitted due to NGRI, you would be detained "in strict custody" at "the pleasure of the Lieutenant Governor," the language vague enough to allow for permanent detention.

But eight years *before* the Blackman tragedy, the law pertaining to mentally ill individuals was already under review. One area of concern was the blanket assumption that *all* mentally ill persons are prone to violence, which is false. Another was the lack of direction regarding the amount of time a NGRI person could be held in custody. The Law Reform Commission of Canada argued that that "[r]estriction of the freedom of a mentally disordered accused or offender should only be imposed when justified."

314

Coincidentally, in 1982, as Bruce was succumbing to schizophrenia, the Department of Justice initiated the Mental Disorder Project as part of a national criminal law review. They found the mental disorder provisions of the Criminal Code of Canada to be "fraught with ambiguities...and often a general lack of clarity, guidance or direction." The topic of basic human rights as contained in the *Canadian Charter of Rights and Freedoms* was also discussed. Was it fair, for example, to confine indefinitely a person found NGRI when the prosecution had not established guilt? And was it fair to automatically detain mentally ill accused persons without some proof that they posed a danger to others?

In 1991, a landmark case known as *R. v Swain* came before the Supreme Court of Canada, arguing that the then-current law regarding detainment of the mentally ill violated the *Canadian Charter of Rights and Freedoms.*

From the British Columbia Review Board's website:

"Mr. Swain, who had been found NGRI, challenged the Criminal Code provisions requiring automatic custody after an NGRI verdict, and release from such custody based on the lieutenant governor's 'pleasure.' He argued that this system was unjust and arbitrary, and breached ss. 7 and 9 of the Canadian Charter of Rights and Freedoms ('the Charter'): "7. Everyone has the right to life, liberty and security of the person, and the right not to be deprived thereof except in accordance with the principles of fundamental justice.

"9. Everyone has the right not to be arbitrarily detained or imprisoned.

"The Supreme Court of Canada agreed with Swain's arguments. The Court recognized that it [was] important to protect the public by preventing dangerous people from being discharged into society, but stated that the *Criminal Code* must do so in a way that respects the *Charter* rights of all persons who commit crimes due to mental disorder. The Court held that the then existing *Criminal Code* scheme breached the *Charter* in two fundamental ways.

"First, the rules were 'arbitrary' because they required judges to automatically place all persons found NGRI into strict custody. This failed to take account of individual circumstances, including those of persons who were no longer dangerous at the time of the verdict. As stated by the Court: '*This detention order is automatic, without any rational standard for determining which individual insanity acquittees should be detained and which should be released.*'

"Second, for detention to be 'indeterminate' — i.e., to depend on the unfettered discretion of the lieutenant governor was not consistent with 'fundamental justice.' As noted by the Court: '*There is no time limit within which the Lieutenant Governor must act. In fact, the wording of the section does not require the Lieutenant Governor to ever make an order.*'

"The Supreme Court of Canada directed the federal Government
to devise a new scheme to address the deficiencies identified
in *Swain*. Parliament responded to the judgment in *Swain* by
enacting Part XX.1 of the *Criminal Code*."

Ultimately, the law as it existed when Bruce Blackman entered
the system was changed. Under Bill C-30, the wording "not guilty by
reason of insanity" was replaced with "not criminally responsible on
account of mental disorder" (NCRMD). Courts were no longer obliged
to order the accused held in strict custody. Instead, courts won the
option of choosing an appropriate disposition or deferring that decision
to a review board. In either case, there were a limited number of
permissible dispositions that included detention in hospital, discharge
subject to conditions, or absolute discharge. However, there was another
layer: The legislation *required* courts and review boards to impose the
least restrictive or onerous disposition necessary, while keeping in mind
the safety of the public, the mental condition of the accused, and the
implications of his or her reintegration into society. Bill C-30 also
mandated a yearly review of any Board disposition other than an
absolute discharge. In other words, the government still had its thumb
upon you *unless* you received an absolute discharge. If that happened,
you disappeared from their radar screen at the same time you lost
whatever government-provided medical structure that had helped you on
your journey from psychosis to wellness.

The creators of Bill C-30 understood that there would always be
some mentally disordered individuals who should never be released

317

because of the danger they posed to society; these "could be involuntarily committed to a secure hospital under the authority of the provincial mental health legislation." This provision naturally relied on the assumption that there would be mental health institutions in existence to provide appropriate care to the dangerous mentally ill. That was before the cost-cutting decision to enact mass closings of mental hospitals across Canada. Bill C-30 contained a "capping" provision that would limit the length of time an unfit or mentally disordered accused could be detained: life; ten years; and two years, depending on the maximum penalty available for the offence charged. Because the capping provisions resulted in enormous bureaucratic and administrative changes for the provinces, the federal government delayed putting them into force, but specified that any existing Lieutenant Governor warrants — such as the Blackman verdict — would continue in force until the capping provisions became law. To the public, this meant that Bruce Blackman would continue to be incarcerated at the Forensic Psychiatric Institute in Coquitlam, B.C., the infamous place known as Riverview.

But not for long.

In the first year after Bill C-30 became law, 31 insanity acquittees in British Columbia were given *absolute* discharges, compared to only two the year before. All 31 of these individuals had been found NGRI prior to Bill C-30. Also in Bill C-30's first year, five individuals found NCRMD were given an immediate conditional discharge to the Vancouver Forensic Services Outpatient Clinic. All five of these individuals had faced serious charges: attempted murder; aggravated

318

assault; and sexual assault. One researcher suggested that the 31 people who were released in 1992 had been languishing unnecessarily in mental institutions as a result of the Lieutenant Governor warrants, like Blackman. Bruce was not one of the 31 given an absolute discharge that year, but he was already enjoying a conditional one.

A 1991 article in the *Vancouver Sun* newspaper ran with this headline: "Killer released; surviving family members fear for their lives." The article quoted one of the survivors as saying, "I lived with [Bruce] (during the height of his delusions) for seven days. I know what he is capable of. You can't put words on it." He also told the reporter that he and some other survivors were scared for their lives now that Bruce had been given a conditional discharge from the Forensic Psychiatric Institute. He said, "[Bruce] said in court that he has not finished the job. That's when he was mentally ill. Now they say he has recovered. But they can't guarantee that he will remain that way."

Dr. Derek Eaves, executive director of Riverview told the reporter that the past eight years in the Institute had not been an easy time for Bruce. (Eaves had testified in court during Bruce's criminal trial.) "Over the years, Mr. Blackman has had the opportunity to examine in microscopic detail the enormity of what he has done and the catastrophic effects on the surviving members of his family. In my view, he is extremely remorseful of what has taken place. There is little he can do to make amends except to conduct himself in a manner that is above reproach. I am sure that's what he will do."

Bruce had been given a Level 1 discharge even before his conditional discharge had been formally approved by the B.C. cabinet. "Anybody who is being considered by cabinet for a Level 1 discharge has likely had escorted passes into the community already," said Eaves. A Level 1 discharge required Bruce to return to Riverview each night, to ensure Bruce was monitored for behavior and medication compliance. Eaves said he considered Bruce to be "essentially recovered at this point."

Illicit drug use was a factor in Bruce's psychotic killing spree, and its absence a factor in his recovery, said Eaves. When asked how the public could be assured that Blackman would not resume taking drugs, Eaves responded that Blackman would be monitored daily, consisting of talks with nurses. Bruce would also continue regular visits with a psychiatrist. The monitoring would be "effective," Eaves said, because "behavioral changes or changes in thinking patterns can be detected by Institute staff."

But one survivor said that wasn't good enough. "What if [Bruce] doesn't return one night?"

The survivor said that he and one other close family member were not informed that Bruce had received a discharge. "You don't know what it has been like for us," he said. "We have moved several times. We have changed phone numbers. You live a life of looking behind you."

In August of 1992, Bruce was elevated from his Level 1 discharge to a Level 2, which allowed him to live outside of Riverview. He lived in a half-way house in Victoria, B.C., on Vancouver Island, a two-hour ferry boat ride from the mainland. He was employed by a company there and was complying with the conditions of his conditional discharge, which were:

1) That he remain under the supervision of the Director of the [Forensic Psychiatric] Institute.
2) That he stay at a place of rehabilitation.
3) That he take prescribed medication and treatment.
4) That he not acquire, possess or use any firearms.
5) That he keep the peace and refrain from the use of alcohol and drugs, and
6) That he present himself when required before the Review Board.

Five months later, in early January of 1993, (10 years after the murders), representatives from the media — some armed with television cameras — entered the half-way house to photograph Bruce and his surroundings. The members of the media burst in unannounced, causing emotional trauma to Bruce and the other residents. Although Bruce had done nothing to encourage this media attention, and despite the fact that he was establishing some "normalcy" to his life, he was immediately sent back to Riverview. The director of the half-way house stated that Bruce's presence there would be too disruptive now that the media knew where he was.

A month later, in February 1993, Bruce was sent back to Victoria, but a petition had been circulated in the area where he had previously lived, opposing his release. The public knew him only as a dangerous, psychotic, mass murderer. This kind of stigma would make his transition from custody to freedom exceptionally difficult.

Stigma — or discrimination — is what plagues many mentally ill persons after they've been shoved through closing asylum doors: The public perception awaiting them can be more daunting than any jury they may have faced. Even if a person is compliant with their medication, even if they fail to ever commit another offense, even if they create a relatively "normal" life for themselves, they — in many ways — still live in fear of what the public can and will do to them. Being mentally ill, and having committed a violent crime while under its influence, brands many of these people with a modern day scarlet letter.

Unfortunately, that is not without reason. For a long time, the professional psychiatric community downplayed the association between mental illness and violent behavior. One such example is a report published in 1983 by psychologist John Monahan and sociologist Henry Steadman wherein they claimed that any association between mental illness and violent behavior could not be proved statistically and further, when the data were corrected for age and other variables, that association dissolved completely. They stated that the "correlates of crime" among the mentally ill appeared to be the same as among any other group.

Almost 10 years later, however, Monahan made a remarkable statement after reviewing and examining new research into the question of whether the mentally ill were more violent than the general population. He said, "The data that have recently become available, fairly read, suggest the one conclusion I did not want to reach: Whether the measure is the prevalence of violence among the disordered or the prevalence of disorder among the violent, whether the sample is people who are selected for treatment as inmates or patients in institutions or people randomly chosen from the open community, and no matter how many social and demographic factors are statistically taken into account, there appears to be a relationship between mental disorder and violent behavior...Denying that mental disorder and violence may be in any way associated is disingenuous and ultimately counterproductive."

But now that it's known — now that the proverbial chickens have come home to roost — what can and should be done?

It is no easy task for a formerly committed individual — especially one who has been charged with murder — to create a "normal" life and provide for him/herself, raise a family, or just stay under the radar. Anyone who has spent years institutionalized lacks the valuable and irreplaceable experience of living in a world where one is responsible for oneself. Life in an institution may or may not have been positive, but release into a world where there are no controls, no paternal overseer, no ready access to help or support could be more frightening than staying "safely" incarcerated. Especially if that person has any issues with medication compliance.

That's why ongoing, available treatment is key, says Dr. E. Fuller Torrey, founder of the Treatment Advocacy Center and author of

The Insanity Offence. Effective treatment that includes medication and various types of therapy, support groups, community services and guidance in healthy living habits can stop the violence, and eventually lessen the stigma.

"We all want to reduce stigma, but until we reduce the high-profile homicides, it will be impossible to do," Torrey says. "They [the high profile homicides] are the main cause of continuing stigma. Individuals with schizophrenia who are *being treated* (emphasis added) are no more dangerous than the general population. However, if they are not being treated, a small percentage are definitely more dangerous than the general population, especially if they are also a substance abuser. So if an individual with schizophrenia who is not being treated and is abusing drugs moves in next door, then yes, people have a legitimate reason to fear that person."

The closing of mental hospitals — deinstitutionalization — effectively transferred responsibility for the mentally ill to the prison system, a system already over-burdened and incapable of providing stable, safe and effective intervention for the mentally ill. The initial impulse to free the non-violent mentally ill from captivity may have been partly a compassionate one, but the reality of it has morphed into something callous and cruel.

Herschel Hardin, a former member of the board of directors of the British Columbia Civil Liberties Association (1965-1974), a champion of liberty and free speech, and the father of a child with schizophrenia had this to say about it in 1993: "The opposition to involuntary committal and treatment betrays a profound misunderstanding of the principle of civil liberties. Medication can free victims from their illness — free them from the Bastille of their psychoses — and restore their dignity, their free will and the meaningful exercise of their liberties."

Dr. Eugene Maloney, a forensic psychiatrist in North Carolina, says that one of the problems in this mental health care debacle is that the decision-making administrators don't always have the medical training necessary to understand the impact of their decisions on the mentally ill. Dr. Maloney has seen how court-ordered out-patient treatment can work. Using long-acting injectable medication, Maloney has witnessed first-hand that medication compliance can transform psychotic and dangerous individuals into productive citizens who can enjoy a relatively "normal" life.

It seems such a simple solution, but Maloney cites the deterioration of mental health care, the corruption of the drug companies, and misguided public perception that mental illness is a reaction to something in the environment. "It's not!" he exclaims. "It's an abnormal functioning of the brain and whatever is going on [voices, hallucinations] is just as real to the patient as my voice is to you right now." He points out, too, that a perfectly good injectable anti-psychotic medication — prolixin decanoate — costs $5.00 per shot. A "new" drug has surfaced, claiming to be better. It costs $1,800 per shot. Who benefits?

Maloney has won prestigious awards for his decades-long fight for the rights of the mentally ill. He helped pass a new commitment law in North Carolina that changed the protocol for intake. "When people were first committed, they had to initially spend three weeks in jail," he said, "and that means everyone from the psychotic killer to your 81-year-old grandmother with Alzheimer's. It was totally unsatisfactory." The new law allowed for immediate commitment to a state mental hospital.

Maloney's mantra, "Psychotic until proven otherwise," is designed to get appropriate treatment to the mentally ill as quickly as possible. Twenty years ago, Maloney headed a review process to evaluate the mental health hospitals in North Carolina. His key finding: "If a black and white TV and a rocking chair could cure schizophrenia, we'd be in good shape."

Improvements were made as a result of the review process, but would end up being for naught as — one by one — the hospitals that offered sanctuary to the mentally ill closed their doors.

AFTERMATH

Aftermath: the period immediately following a usually ruinous event.

ALL TRAGEDIES SHARE one common trait: they are magnets for speculation and hindsight, and the Blackman tragedy is no different. After the fact and with all the evidence neatly skinned, it's painfully evident that the killings could have been prevented or mitigated if the victims had taken certain steps clearly within their scope of action:

1) The Blackman family had the option to have Bruce committed in December of 1982, a month before the murders. They failed to do so. Had Bruce been committed in December, he would have been properly diagnosed. This would have allowed the family to understand the nature of his illness and begin supervised treatment with anti-psychotic medication.

2) When Bruce returned unexpectedly from Nelson the night before the murders, a psychiatrist offered to arrange for him to be medicated in the emergency room at a hospital only a few miles from the Blackman home. Mr. Blackman, Sr. declined, even though Bruce was "ranting and raving" and "talking about the end of the world again." Medication

would have quelled Bruce's symptoms temporarily, and may have altered the course of events.

3) On the morning of the murders, when Roberta called the psychiatrist and asked to have her brother committed, she stated she was going over to her parents' house to see what was wrong. The psychiatrist strongly advised her not to, and to call the police instead. If she had taken the doctor's advice, three lives could have been spared that night.

Why did Bruce's family not understand the severity of his illness? There is no evidence to suggest that they were ever warned that some paranoid schizophrenics sharing Bruce's symptoms have suddenly exploded into episodes of violence so gruesome they can only be called breathtaking. Why did Mr. Blackman, Sr. think that he could "talk Bruce down" on the morning of the murders? Had the topic of violence ever been discussed during Bruce's six weeks of treatment? He had the signs: extreme paranoia; religion and doomsday-themed delusions; delusions of grandeur; auditory, visual and command hallucinations. Each of these ingredients alone was a concern, but together they comprised a recipe for disaster. Bruce had even said to his roommate, "I'm not sure if I'm supposed to die or the people around me." Had the roommate shared this critical piece of information with the Blackman family, would they have taken action?

During the relatively short period of time between the onset of Bruce's mental illness and its climax (46 days), any psychiatrist could have committed Bruce against his will and without the family's approval.

But the treating psychiatrist stated in court that "we like to have the family's approval if at all possible." While the treating psychiatrist signed commitment papers upon his very first observation of Bruce, could he have been more assertive with the family and helped them understand that Bruce needed in-patient assessment and care? Would the family have listened?

The Honorable Timothy Hillman, United States District Judge for the State of Massachusetts says, "Every day in the state and provincial courts of the United States and Canada, countless people like the Blackmans face the harsh realities of the confluence of law and psychiatry. Simply said, there is no easy way to force a loved one who is experiencing a mental health crisis to accept psychiatric treatment short of seeking a court order... Once the patient is in the courthouse, a court clinician will interview the patient and his family to determine the answers to three basic questions: Is he or she mentally ill; is he or she dangerous; and is there no less restrictive alternative than involuntary commitment available? If the answer to all three is yes, the judge will have very little discretion to do anything other than involuntarily civilly commit the patient to a secure mental health facility.

"If the term 'involuntarily civilly commit' and the process of locking up someone who is ill and suffering sounds draconian, there are few options available to the court. These are emergency situations and the conduct which brings the family to court is almost always dangerous and demanding immediate action... [T]he judges who must commit a person to a locked hospital against their will understand the gravity of their order…Thankfully, in a huge majority of these cases, the hospitalization is short, and the patient is often back in the community on a regimen of medicine and treatment in a matter of weeks, or even days."

Such intervention, while extreme, can be the bump in trajectory needed to avert an imminent tragedy.

Six innocent human beings died a brutal death that morning in January, 1983, but they were not the only victims. Bruce Blackman was hunted down and victimized by his "disease of the mind". It taunted, tormented and frightened him so thoroughly that he was rendered powerless against it. Yet, even in his most florid state, Bruce understood he was sick. He had flashes of insight into his condition. He told the arresting officer that he was "insane" and that he "[saw] God all the time." Doctors, psychiatrists and police officers all described how Bruce was "shaking" and that he looked "frightened." Bruce constantly told his family and friends that he was "possessed." The possession scared him so thoroughly that he could neither sleep nor eat. Imagine being so terrified that you can't close your eyes because you believe that the "thing" in your brain will kill you if you do. In his own tortured way, Bruce asked for help over and over, for a way to silence the voices, for deliverance from his possession. He had regular appointments with a psychiatrist and he had been prescribed anti-psychotic medication — both appropriate for his treatment — except that Bruce did not take his medication consistently. Medication non-compliance is, unfortunately, a common problem amongst schizophrenics, especially those who don't understand or believe that they're sick. Could the family have been more diligent in supervising Bruce's medication regimen? Could the psychiatrist have used long-acting injectable medication instead?

Psychiatrist Dr. Eugene Maloney says, "The saddest part of this story is that the murders were preventable. Bruce did nothing to contribute to the development of a malignant psychotic disorder, most likely severe paranoid schizophrenia. Everyone knew he was disturbed, but no one took any effective action. Given the severity of his illness, Bruce should have been hospitalized immediately. When the visiting psychiatrist gave the family a signed commitment paper to use if necessary, it put the burden of hospitalization on the family instead of the medically trained psychiatrist. Everyone either explained away his symptoms or minimized them. I have a rule: If it doesn't make sense, don't explain it away. A psychiatrist should ask the basic questions: 'Are the voices telling you to do anything? Have you ever thought about hurting yourself or anyone else?' When it was obvious that Bruce was not taking his medication regularly, the doctor should have told the family to supervise his medication including counting the pills. Other alternative medications including a powerful liquid medication that is tasteless and odorless, or a powerful long-acting injectable medication could have been offered. The records indicate that Bruce responded well when he was given injectable anti-psychotic medication while he was incarcerated. As severe as his illness was, he was never admitted to a hospital. The take-home message is: If you find a psychiatrist who minimizes your symptoms, find another one."

The Blackman tragedy drew attention from across the nation. Newspapers in every province ran the story accompanied by photographs of a scowling Bruce entering a police car; of the bodies being removed from the house on Spuraway; photographs of witnesses; of the coroner making her statement to the press; old family photos. The story shocked the country, but it was certainly not the only psychotically induced mass murder in Canadian history prior to 1983:

-John Etter Clark, 41, killed seven people in Erskine, Alberta on June 3, 1956, then killed himself. He'd had frequent "nervous breakdowns" and had two years earlier had been hospitalized for one and one-half months because of one.

-Robert Raymond Cook, 21, termed "troubled," killed seven members of his family on June 25, 1959, in Stettler, Alberta. He was executed by hanging on November 14, 1960.

-Victor Ernest Hoffman, 21, a diagnosed paranoid schizophrenic, was released from a mental hospital three weeks prior to murdering nine people at Shell Lake, Saskatchewan. He was found not guilty by reason of insanity (NGRI) in 1968 and died in custody 36 years later.

-Andrew Day, 40, killed his wife and seven children with an axe on December 16, 1929, then slashed his own throat. Police found him wandering the streets in Trois Rivieres, Quebec. He was found mentally unfit to stand trial.

-Tom Hrechkozie, 28, killed seven of his relatives with an axe and knife in Winnipeg, Manitoba on February 3, 1932, saying that ghosts ordered him to do it. He was sentenced to death; his sentence was later commuted to life in prison.

-Matthew Charles Lamb, 18, killed two people and wounded two others in Windsor, Ontario. He was found NGRI and committed to "indefinite care" on January 20, 1967. He was released in 1973, and was killed in action while serving in the military in Rhodesia on November 7, 1976 by an errant shot fired by one of his own men.

-Dale Merle Nelson, 29, murdered eight people in Creston, British Columbia on September 5, 1970. He beat, shot, and stabbed his victims, then performed cannibalistic acts on their bodies. He'd spent two months at the Forensic Psychiatric Institute in Coquitlam, B.C. (Riverview) for depression and a suicide attempt several months before the murders. He was sentenced to life in prison on April 1, 1971. He died while incarcerated.

-Swift Runner, (age unknown), killed and ate six people (his wife and five children) in Fort Saskatchewan, Alberta, in 1879. A Cree Indian, he had become possessed by the "Windigo" psychosis (an aberration characterized by grand delusions and cannibalistic impulses that anthropologists have identified in several Canadian Indian Cultures). He was hanged on December 20, 1879.

-Leonard Hogue, 34, a Vancouver police officer shot his wife and their six children using a borrowed, high caliber revolver, in Coquitlam, B.C. (not far from the Blackman home) on April 19, 1965, then committed suicide. There was speculation that his mental condition had been compromised by a head injury 24 hours prior to the murders.

And on January 17, 1983, the night leading up to the Blackman murders, in Aplington, Iowa, Ethel Mae Franken, 33, shot her husband Darrell, 37, and their three children ages 7 – 13, at their home and then killed herself. Franken had been seeing a psychiatrist for several weeks before the killings and had actually been hospitalized for several days just prior to the murders.

But there was something about the Blackman case that was different, something that captured the country's attention and wouldn't let it go. Perhaps it was Bruce's lack of criminal history; perhaps it was the familiarity of the public with the billboard image of a smiling Irene Blackman reading a copy of *the Province* newspaper. Perhaps it was the "normalness" of the family that made this kind of "out-of-nowhere" violence inconceivable. Whatever spark set the public's interest ablaze, the heat would drive Bruce to seek a bar against the media for his criminal court proceedings and, eventually, for the review board hearings that would determine his custodial fate. Not one of his bids was successful.

IN THE UNITED STATES, during a 100-year period between 1900 – 2000, out of 909 cases of mass murder *more than half occurred within the immediate family*. A *Windsor Star* (Ontario) investigation tracked more than 130 murders and murder-suicides across Canada between

1997 and 2002 in which mental illness played a prominent role. They all occurred in a five-year-period when many provinces were actively closing mental institutions and farming patients out to a community care system woefully underfunded and ill-prepared to manage the onslaught of people needing care.

The *Star* investigation found that mental illness was established as the cause in 108 of those 130 killings. These included murders in which the accused was found not guilty by reason of insanity, and murder-suicides in which mental illness was found to be a determining factor. In those cases, 80 of the 108 victims were related to their killers by blood or marriage (74%). Twenty-three of the victims were known to the killers as friends, neighbours, employees, roommates or fellow residents of a boarding house (21%). Only five cases were considered random. This means that in 95% of the cases, *the killers and the victims knew each other*.

With the closing of mental hospitals across Canada, the United States, and globally, more and more families are forced to provide their mentally ill children and relatives with the care and oversight no longer available through institutionalization. The evidence suggests that the families of the untreated, severely mentally ill may be at a predictable risk for losing their lives.

The evidence is supported in recent cases involving family violence. In October, 2012, Scott Hobson, 32 — a diagnosed schizophrenic — killed his mother by inflicting 80 separate wounds then carving a cross into her chest in Sheffield, England. Hobson had served as a soldier in Kosovo and was also a heavy drinker and user of marijuana. In 2011, Jordan Ramsay — a diagnosed paranoid schizophrenic — bludgeoned his parents in their bedroom while they slept. His father died and his mother barely survived her extensive injuries. Ramsay, 27, was attempting to treat his schizophrenia with vitamins marketed to the mentally ill when he became convinced his parents were aliens and had to be killed. He was found by a Vancouver court to be not criminally responsible due to mental disorder. In 2009, Otty Sanchez — a 33-year old diagnosed schizophrenic — murdered her three-and-a-half-year-old child by dismembering him with a steak knife and samurai swords, then attempted to kill herself. Sanchez told San Antonio police that the Devil ordered her to maim, mutilate, kill and eat parts of her only child. Sadly, the list goes on and many of these spectacularly violent incidents receive little press coverage.

"Unfortunately," says Dr. John Bradford — a leading Canadian expert on criminal insanity — "there is a correlation between severe mental illness and violence. Up until the early nineties, psychiatrists played down the fact there was a relationship because we were worried about the stigma to patients."

Studies have shown that the risk of violence is six to seven times higher among people with major depression or schizophrenia. The risk rises to six to 12 times higher in schizophrenics who drink alcohol and *35 to 40 times higher* for those on cocaine.

However, those from the same group as above may pose no more danger than the general population if they receive appropriate treatment and take their medication. But with the evaporation of psychiatric services, mentally ill individuals very often cannot find help, even if they seek it. They are left to fend for themselves. Many become homeless. The mortality rate of schizophrenics is *four times higher* than the general population, with suicide the leading cause of death. The mentally ill represent the *fastest growing segment* of the prison population. Some estimates project that by the year 2020, more than 60% of people with schizophrenia will have a criminal record. This represents a catastrophic failure by the systems in Canada and the United States to address the need for proactive treatment and support for the mentally ill, who cannot provide it for themselves.

The *Star* investigation uncovered other disturbing trends:

-critical gaps in institutional care, particularly 24-hour emergency psychiatric care. The report cites a lack of psychiatrists and delays in psychiatrists returning urgent calls.

-deficiencies in provincial laws designed to force the dangerously mentally ill to take medication.

-a staggering increase of mental illness in the criminal justice system (the numbers increasing in almost direct proportion to the number of people released from institutions).

-restricted access for many schizophrenics to the most effective — and costly — anti-psychotic drugs.

-inadequate training for most law enforcement officers confronting the mentally ill as "first responders." The mentally ill die at the hands of police officers (in Canada) at the rate of about two per year.

In the United States, things are just as dismal. Between mid-1960 and mid-1980, the nation's psychiatric hospitals were purging their tenants and closing their doors. At the same time, there was a movement organized by several lawyers, and supported by the American Civil Liberties Union (ACLU), that passed a resolution saying that involuntary hospitalization was incompatible with a free society. Those who supported this notion took it further, saying that the mentally ill have a right to be ill, and a right to refuse treatment. Sadly, this tender notion fails to take into account that many severely mentally ill persons do not know they are sick. Would we fail to care for Alzheimer's patients because they refused to eat or take their medicine? Throwing mental patients out on the street and defending that action on the basis of "respecting their freedoms" is nothing short of reckless abandonment.

In his excellent book, *The Insanity Offence*, Dr. E. Fuller Torrey exposes the root of deinstitutionalization's failure. "Most laws governing the treatment of mentally ill individuals assume that such individuals are competent to accept or reject treatment, with the sole exception of obvious dementia. Yet, contemporary research has established that up to half of all individuals with severe psychiatric disorders are not competent to assess their own need for treatment. The consequences of this misunderstanding have led to increasing numbers of mentally ill individuals who are homeless, incarcerated, and victimized, and increasing numbers of individuals who commit homicides and other violent acts. This misunderstanding underlies one of the great social disasters of the late twentieth century."

If it seems as though high-profile mass murders are happening with more frequency, it's because they are. In 2000, the *New York Times* published a survey of 100 "rampage killers" who committed mass killings between 1949 and 1999. The survey excluded gang, robbery and domestic killings and also noted that there was "much evidence of mental illness" in the perpetrators. More than half had histories of serious mental health problems. Forty-eight killers had some kind of formal diagnosis — often schizophrenia — and among these, 24 had been prescribed psychiatric drugs but 14 had stopped taking them. The 100 rampage killers murdered 425 people and injured 510.

-1949-1959: 1 mass killing

-1960-1969: 3 mass killings

-1970-1979: 6 mass killings

-1980-1989: 17 mass killings

-1990-1999: 73 mass killings

In 2012, *Mother Jones* published a survey of 62 identified mass shootings between 1982 and 2012. The survey focused on incidents in which four or more people died (not including the shooter) and were not gang-related or part of an armed robbery. It further limited the study to only those in which guns were used as the weapon. The survey reported that a majority of the shooters were mentally ill (schizophrenia and suicidal depression) and had actually displayed signs of it before setting out to kill. Of the 62 shooters, 36 also killed themselves and seven died at the hands of police. The number of mass shootings per decade per the *Mother Jones* report:

-1982-1992: 14 shootings

-1993-2002: 19 shootings

-2003-2012: 29 shootings (including 7 in 2012 alone).

These two surveys published between 1999 and 2012 both suggest that mass killings are increasing in incidence, and that individuals with severe, *untreated* mental illness are responsible for at least half of such killings.

Before Bruce Blackman "delivered" his family to Heaven in 1983, the irony is that in 1982, as he was spiraling into schizophrenia, there *was* help available. He *could* have been committed to a psychiatric hospital if his psychiatrist had insisted. He *could* have been medicated against his will. He and his family could have received a generous measure of assistance. Today, sadly, it is a very different story. The mother of a violent 18-year-old schizophrenic was quoted in the 2002 *Windsor Star* article. She said, "If only we could get proper help for her, things might be different. But the system sucks and if you're mentally ill, God help you." The parents barricade their daughter's door each night and take turns standing guard because she has told them she will murder them if given the chance. They believe her.

IN 1993, GOVERNMENT officials helped Bruce Blackman change his name in anticipation of his release. A new name symbolized a new start, but more practically it was designed to help him avoid unwanted scrutiny and attention as he set about trying to establish himself in a potentially hostile world outside the asylum.

The Review Board charged with determining his custodial fate had to balance concern for the public's safety, his mental condition, and the implications of his reintegration into society. For years, Bruce had been buoyed by numerous layers of support; unquestionably, these carried him on his journey from psychosis to stability.

In 1995, Bruce appeared before the Review Board for the last time. If he was granted total freedom, his institutional support systems would disappear. Given the concerns of the survivors, what convinced the Review Board that he was ready to be set free? When I requested a copy of the transcript outlining the Review Board's conclusion, and how they justified their decision, I was told that the record had been "destroyed."

In June of 1995, Bruce Alfred Blackman — under a new name — was given an absolute discharge and quietly released into the community.

Except to very few people, his whereabouts are unknown.

EPILOGUE

Fourteen years later

STAFF SERGEANT CLARKE had spent the last weeks leading up to retirement stripping his office of personal mementos. He'd never considered himself the sentimental type, but he was surprised at the things he'd accumulated over the years, tangible memories of events or moments that clearly meant something to him at the time: a plaque from the Rotary club honoring the program he'd created for troubled youth; two commendations for bravery; all of Darren's hockey team photos; key chains from Cancun, Disneyworld, and a couple of cigar boxes left over from a memorable, all-male trip to Cuba.

Today was his last day and he'd nearly called in sick. Walking through the doors of the detachment office one last time took every ounce of resolve he had. The past thirty-four years had taken their toll: He'd seen too much of the worst in people. He wanted out before misanthropy cast a shadow over the last light of his humanity.

"I brought you this," said Gladys, walking in to his office, holding something the size of a triple-layer cake, wrapped.

"You put wrapping paper on a cake?" asked Clarke.

"Very funny. Just open it."

Clarke took it from her. It weighed at least five pounds, maybe more. He ripped open the Christmas-themed paper and saw immediately that it was a scrapbook, ten inches thick.

"I've been working on this for awhile," Gladys said.

On the cover, she'd cut out a magazine picture of a grizzly bear standing up on its hind legs as if to attack. In its front paw she'd pasted a picture of a giant bottle of White-Out.

Clarke frowned. "I don't get it."

Gladys put herboth hands on her hips. "Remember that bad business awhile ago? You know, the boy who killed his family?"

Clarke remembered of course — how could he ever forget — but the "grizzly" reference took him a moment. There had been so many spectacular misspellings in the fourteen years since the Blackman tragedy it was hard for Clarke to recall specifics.

"Well, Gladys, I thank you for this," Clarke said. "I'm sure it took you a lot of time."

"Anyway, aren't you going to look at it?" she asked. Clarke could hear disappointment bubbling in the question.

He opened the book. In it was a 34-year record of every case he and Gladys had worked on together: newspaper clippings; magazine articles; copies of letters from outraged citizens. And attached to every single case was the original, misspelled memo that Clarke had slashed apart with his red pen. It was as much a documentary of their relationship as it was a chronicle of the criminal caseload they'd shared. There was something indescribably intimate about it. He was unprepared for the tears that came to his eyes.

"Gladys," he stammered, "I don't know what to say."

"Say congratulations."

"Hmmm?" Clarke frowned.

"I'm retiring, too."

"Gladys!" Clarke said, a little too loudly. "Good for you," he said, recovering. Clarke knew how little money Gladys had earned in their three decades together. "You know, if you stay a little longer, your retirement benefits will be higher."

"Dumont," she said, the first time she had ever used his given name, "I am well aware that you have protected me all these years. You may think I'm dumb, but I'm smart enough to know that the staff sergeant who replaces you will either fire me or make things so uncomfortable that I'll be forced to quit. This way, if he knows my retirement is just around the corner, he'll tolerate me and my…creative… typing for awhile."

344

Clarke nodded.

"I want you to know how much I will miss you," she continued. "You showed all of us how to behave whenever things were really bad. I'm just sorry I couldn't have done a better job for you."

"Well, we'll both have funny stories to tell, won't we?"

"Yes, we will." Clarke and Gladys looked at each other.

"Marjorie," said Clarke, and Gladys smiled. She couldn't remember the last time anyone had called her by her real name. "I wish you all the best."

"Anyway," she said, and left.

FIRST ON CLARKE'S list of "Things To Do Once I'm Free" was a trip to the neighbouring province of Alberta to visit his son Darren who'd started his own guiding outfit. Clarke didn't really care to hunt — he'd had enough of guns — but it would be a way for them to spend some quality time now that Clarke was free to do it. And he'd wanted to explore the Canadian Rockies as part of his long-neglected bucket list.

As he packed his old four-door Chrysler full of boots, rain gear, bug spray, blankets, and coolers with food for the journey, Clarke couldn't help but feel that this trip would be symbolic. Once he began to drive toward the Rocky Mountain range, toward his son, and his freedom, he would be laying down distance between his old life and the new one. While it was true that there were awful images festooning his mind — things he'd never be able to forget — he hoped that with time they'd recede further and further into the foggy, unreliable landscape of memory.

Clarke had managed to quit smoking again after a brief affair with nicotine in 1983. In place of cigarettes he had taken to smoking good cigars and he lit one now before backing out of the driveway. With the window open, he navigated through the clots of Coquitlam traffic to the Trans-Canada Highway which would take him all the way across southern British Columbia and into Alberta. But traffic wouldn't thin for awhile. He'd have to be on the road for a couple of hours before commuter traffic gave way to logging trucks. Stalled at one impasse, he watched with amusement as drivers honked and flashed each other one-fingered hand signals. This would be the first time in decades he'd be able to drive without a police radio announcing some kind of bad news. *Something worth savouring,* he thought.

The first night on the road, Clarke stayed in a hunting cabin just outside of the small town of Sicamous. Part of the daily rate — $19 — included use of an all-terrain vehicle to get to the one-room shack. He was to pick up the keys at a gas station, which he found easily. The people had knocked off early and left the ATV and cabin keys in an envelope taped to the door. Clarke smiled at their naiveté.

Inside the envelope was a rudimentary map. Scrawled on the outside was a reminder that there were "no amenities" in the cabin. The ATV was mud-crusted, its fenders cracked and the seat ripped. To its front basket, Clarke attached a small cooler with some food, water, and a little bag with toothbrush, flashlight, matches and cigars. He inserted the key and cranked it, skeptical, but it started immediately and enveloped Clarke in a blue halo of exhaust smoke. He looked at the hand-drawn map then followed the rustic path, bumping over rocks and ruts, until he found the cabin. Half of the moss-covered roof sagged as though it might cave in at any moment. When Clarke unlocked the little padlock to open the door he was hit with a wave of smells: mold, decay and mouse urine. Something scurried overhead in the rafters. The place was about as old and dumpy as it could get.

"Perfect," he thought.

With no electricity to light the cabin, when evening fell it dropped a curtain of darkness so complete he could not even see his hand in front of his face. In the absence of humming refrigerators and overhead power lines, the silence was exquisite. Clarke could hear everything outside of the cabin as clearly as if he were standing on the other side of the door: crickets, frogs, animals foraging. He heard something snuffling around out there, something bigger than a deer.

For a moment, he became a cop again. Was a person here to do him harm?

Clarke lay on his back on the surprisingly firm cot and thought about the book Gladys had made for him. All those cases over so many years, all that angst adding up, tipping the emotional scales bit by bit. Clarke had interviewed hundreds of people for victim impact statements, yet he was deeply aware that every crime's echo vibrated through more than just the immediate victims. He'd seen some of his own men so emotionally wrecked by cases that they eventually left the force. He'd seen jurors who had permanent nightmares after being forced to look at crime scene photos. Occasionally officers would "turn bad" in reaction to the darkness they'd seen. Even Clarke himself never became immune. Gladys' book was the physical manifestation of what Clarke had been carrying around for nearly forty years, and what he knew he would carry with him forever — the memory of every person who had ever died a wrongful or tragic death under his watch. Clarke considered himself lucky to get out before this ugly business of law enforcement had stripped away the last layers of his veneer. Sometimes he thought it was a miracle that he hadn't lost himself, or his mind. Gladys' book weighed five pounds on the scale, but the true weight of its contents could never be measured.

CLARKE WOKE 10 hours later while it was still dark. The dampness in the cabin had seeped into his joints and the hardness of the cot had done nothing good for his back. He sat on the edge of the cot waiting for the various muscle spasms and stabs of pain to finish dancing around the contours of his body. Outside, a little breeze rustled the leaves and pushed branches against the cabin. The birds were not yet busy. It was such a pure silence, Clarke thought, and he paused a few more moments to enjoy it before making his creaky way outside.

At the door, he sucked in one last breath of the stale air. His frugal night had been exactly what he'd needed: a transition lacking interference — no radio, no newspaper, no artificial sound, and no tragedy. Just him, in the dark, with a promise of light ahead. He replaced the little padlock on the clasp, straddled the ATV, then turned it on, shattering the beautiful silence with rude blasts and sputters. By the time Clarke made it back to his car, dawn had arrived. He'd had to maneuver much slower in the dark, the light from the ATV's wan yellow headlamp barely illuminating the path ahead.

Clarke dropped the keys in the locked deposit box at the gas station and headed to the nearest restaurant — a mom-and-pop truck stop — for a big breakfast of eggs, pancakes, bacon, sausage, bran muffin and extra large coffee. Other than pit stops, he didn't want to have to pause again until he arrived at Darren's.

The Trans-Canada Highway had taken Clarke on a snaky and sometimes hair-raising drive through the steep Fraser River canyon. Below him, the "Mighty Fraser" — a wide, rapid-choked river perpetually gray with silt — made its powerful way down to the Pacific Ocean. Where it flowed through the place where he lived and had worked in Coquitlam, the River was less than 20 miles from where it emptied into the Strait of Georgia. During that final 20-mile journey it surged past Riverview — the mental hospital in Coquitlam — then the B.C. Penitentiary, a castle-like maximum security prison set high on a hill overlooking the river — and finally the New Westminster court house where Clarke had spent more hours than he cared to remember.

How ironic that these dismal places had some of the best views in the province. The Fraser River was so big and so potent it was thought to be impervious to anything man could throw at it, but run-off from logging operations, pollution from agricultural fertilizer, the clear-cutting of its forests, and the discharge of untreated sewage into its veins had all but drained the river's blood. The once-plentiful salmon population had been threatened to the point where the fisheries department sounded the alarm. Man was exceptionally good at ignoring consequences, thought Clarke. It was murder of a different kind.

By the time he reached Darren's home in Golden, close to the Alberta border, Clarke was ready for his driving trip to be over. His back still ached from sleeping on the cot, and his ass was practically numb. But he forgot all that when he saw his only son striding down the driveway, smiling, arms outstretched. "*Dad!*" Darren shouted, wrapping his arms around Clarke and thumping him on the back. "I can't believe you're finally here. You're going to love it."

"My back already hates it but I'm sure it'll get better."

"It will. Are you hungry?"

They sat down inside Todd's small house and ate potato chips and lunch meat from plastic sandwich bags.

"Listen, Darren. Don't tell any of the other customers what I did for a living, OK?"

"But Dad, you have such great stories."

"I know, but people get weird around cops. They feel like they can't tell their stories about driving drunk, or shoplifting, or the time they talked their way out of a ticket. It's better that they don't know. They'll have more fun."

"What should I tell them?"

"Tell them I'm a handwriting analyst."

"OK."

"We can get some mileage out of that."

Darren raised his eyebrows.

"The other thing, Darren, and I'm telling you this because I want you to know." Clarke paused. "I'm ready to leave 40 years of bad memories behind." Clarke paused again, for a long time. "I got out before it ate me up. But I'm trying to forget most of what I've seen." He folded his hands on the table.

Darren nodded, smart enough to know that this might be the only time his stoic father would ever confide in him this way. He listened.

"I want to spend time with you," Clarke continued. "Son, I want to get to know you." They both looked down. Clarke's responsibility to his job had robbed him of his responsibility to his family. "One thing I know for sure is time is short and it's not guaranteed." He looked past Darren, out the small window behind his son's shoulder.

"OK, Dad," Darren answered. When he was sure his father had finished, he said, "Come meet the rest of the crew. They're out in the garage packing up."

"A crew," said Clarke. "You've got people working for you. Not an easy thing these days, Darren, especially out here." Clarke put his hand on Darren's shoulder. They walked.

"You'll like the horse wrangler. He's a real character — like right out of *Gunsmoke* or something. The cook and go-fer is a new guy this season. I'm not sure how he's going to work out, but he's trying."

"Work ethic?"

"No problem there. He works hard, always looking for something to do. Good with the customers and he cooks a decent breakfast. He doesn't talk much about himself. I call him the hockey player."

"Why is that?"

"Well," Darren smiled, "I can tell he's kissed a hockey stick more than once. Broken nose, broken jaw. Sometimes he has trouble finishing a sentence. He also loves his beer."

"You've just described half the population of Canada."

Darren laughed. "Yes, and they all find their way here."

"Where'd you get these guys?" Clarke asked.

"They came out of nowhere right when I was looking for help. The wrangler worked for another operation that folded, and the new guy showed up, said he'd work one trip for free just to prove himself."

"Well," said Clarke. "You've always had good luck that way, but be careful. You need people you can count on out there." Clarke nodded in the general direction of the mountains. "Don't settle."

They walked out back to the garage where two men were busy loading supplies into a white trailer festooned with mud spatter. It wasn't hard to spot the wrangler: a black, felt cowboy hat atop his head; heavy, smooth leather chaps; spurs with rowels that jingled when he walked; red paisley bandanna tied around his neck; a white moustache tinted brown from chewing tobacco. He was tossing tack[19] into the trailer.

Clarke waited until the man had set a saddle down inside the trailer. "Festus, right?" Clarke smiled.

"*Wail*," the wrangler drawled, and Clarke had to stifle a laugh, "They do call me Festus," the man answered, and Clarke was surprised when the wrangler's voice sounded just like it. "It ain't my name but I'll answer to it."

"I'm Dewey," Clarke said, extending his hand, "Darren's father."

---

[19] Tack refers to horse equipment: saddles, bridles, etc.

"We've been hearing some stories 'bout you," Festus said, *"Hopefully they ain't true!"* Festus went off on a laughing riff that sounded almost maniacal, then turned his back on Darren and Clarke to grab another saddle off the wall. Darren looked at Clarke and mouthed the word, "See?" Clarke smiled and shook his head.

"Now I want you to meet John," said Darren, nodding toward the back of a chubby man in a red-checked lumberjack shirt and navy blue down vest. His salt-and-pepper hair was twisted into a long braid down the center of his back. There were two rifles cradled in the crook of his left arm and as he was grabbing for a box of ammunition, Darren called out. "John," he said, "Come meet my Dad."

John set the box of ammunition down and paused, as if gathering himself. He wiped his hand on his jeans as he approached.

Clarke froze.

Time and tide had intervened, and even with the trauma to his face there was no mistaking the man with the rifles.

It was Bruce Alfred Blackman.

"Hi," he said, grabbing Clarke's unresponsive hand, "I'm John. Welcome to the hunt."

SCHIZOPHRENIA FAST FACTS

From schizophrenia.com, johnshopkinsmedical.org, Treatment Advocacy Center

WHO
Schizophrenia occurs in all societies regardless of class, color, religion or culture.

WHAT
Schizophrenia is a mental illness that usually strikes in late adolescence or early adulthood, but can develop any time in life. Signs and symptoms vary among individuals, but all people with the disorder show one or more of the following symptoms: delusions (false beliefs); hallucinations (hearing voices, or seeing, smelling, tasting and feeling things that are not there); disorganized speech (incomplete and/or nonsensical statements); and "negative symptoms" (lack of motivation or interest, abandonment of personal hygiene, decreased emotional expression, etc.) Schizophrenia cannot be cured, but it can be successfully treated with anti-psychotic medication and psychiatric therapy.

WHERE
The Prevalence Rate for schizophrenia is approximately 1.1% of the population over the age of 18. At any one time, as many as 51 million people worldwide live with schizophrenia including 6-12 million in China; 4.3-8.7 million in India; 2.2 million in the USA; 285,000 in Australia; more than 280,000 in Canada; and over 250,000 diagnosed cases in Britain.

Of the millions of people who have schizophrenia in America,
> -6% are homeless or live in shelters
> -6% live in jails or prisons
> -5-6% live in hospitals
> -10% live in nursing homes
> -25% live with a family member
> -28% are living independently
> -20% live in supervised housing (group homes, etc.)

WHEN
Schizophrenia typically begins in early adulthood between the ages of 15 and 25. Males tend to develop schizophrenia earlier than females, between ages 16 and 25 for men compared to 18 and 25 years of age for women. The average age of onset is 18 in men and 25 in women.

WHY
Current theory is that schizophrenia is the result of a genetic predisposition combined with environmental exposures and/or stresses during pregnancy or childhood that contributes to the disorder. One study cites that heavy consumers of cannabis at age 18 are more than 600% more likely to be diagnosed with schizophrenia over the next 15 years than those who did not take it. Although studies differ, it does appear that

substance abuse at a vulnerable age (before 18) and for those pre-disposed to developing the disease can contribute to the onset of symptoms.

RESOURCES

National Alliance on Mental Illness. www.NAMI.org

Treatment Advocacy Center. www.treatmentadvocacycenter.org

National Institute of Mental Health. nimh.nih.gov

Bring Change 2 Mind (how to lessen stigma).
www.bringchange2mind.org

Mental Health.gov. www.mentalhealth.gov

Centers for Disease Control and Prevention.
www.cdc.gov/mentalhealth/

Mental Health Canada. www.mentalhealthcanada.com

Canadian Mental Health Association. www.cmha.ca/mental-health/

Mental Health.ca. www.ementalhealth.ca

Canadian Coalition of Alternative Mental Health Resources. ccamhr.ca

GEOGRAPHICAL LOCATION OF THE BLACKMAN MASSACRE IN THE PROVINCE OF BRITISH COLUMBIA, CANADA

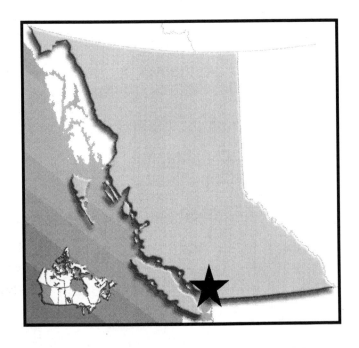

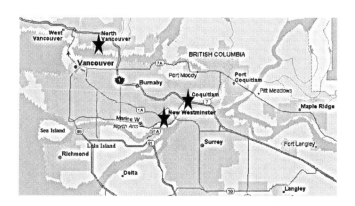

Map detail. Shown are the locations of North Vancouver (high school and apartment), Coquitlam (scene of the crime), and New Westminster (site of the murder trial). Not shown is the location of Riverview Mental Hospital where Bruce Blackman was committed. It is located approximately at the number 7, below the town of Coquitlam, only minutes from the former family home.

The Blackman family home on the morning of January 18, 1983. In the driveway, parked in front of the Toyota truck, is the camper van the Blackmans used for their hunting trips. A neighbour referred to it as "their pride and joy".

Photo © L. Haupt (used with permission)

Argyle Secondary School in North Vancouver where Bruce
attended high school.

Photo © Janice Holly Booth

Deep Cove in North Vancouver. When the salt water here froze, Bruce thought it was a sign from God.

Photo © Janice Holly Booth

"Her face known to thousands." Irene Blackman was the poster girl for *the Province* newspaper, where she worked. When asked why Irene was chosen to represent the newspaper – as opposed to a professional model – one editor said, "She looked nice". *Photo © The Province. (Used with permission)*

The Law Courts in New Westminster, BC, site of Bruce's Supreme Court murder trial.

Photo © Janice Holly Booth

The Forensic Psychiatric Institute where Bruce was committed was better known as "Riverview" because it overlooked the Fraser River. The West Lawn Building (pictured above) is one of its most iconic. The building was shuttered in 1983 as the asylum began its systematic closing. Riverview was permanently closed in 2012.

Photo © Janice Holly Booth

Riverview Hospital was added to the Canadian Register of Historic Places in 2009, but many of its buildings are in extreme disrepair, as seen here in this detail of the porch balusters at the West Lawn building entrance. In spite of – or perhaps because of – its creepiness, Riverview Hospital continues to be the most-filmed, off-studio location site in Canada for motion picture and television productions, including many episodes of the *X-files*.

Photo © Janice Holly Booth

"God has no place here"

A sentiment shared by many is represented by graffiti scrawled on one of the columns of the West Lawn Building. *Photo © Janice Holly Booth*

One of the "cottages" on the grounds of Riverview. Patients preparing for release would live in these structures in order to develop independent living skills. Bruce would likely have lived in one of these. *Photo © Janice Holly Booth*

Supervised by RCMP officers (right), a body is removed from the Blackman home. There was a shortage of morgue vehicles that day. Removal of the bodies would take three times as long.

Photo © Colin Price/THE PROVINCE (Used with permission)

The country came to know Bruce Blackman through this photograph taken as he was leaving the courthouse in Port Coquitlam on January 19, 1983, the day after the massacre.

© THE CANADIAN PRESS/Nick Didlick (used with permission)

ABOUT THE AUTHOR

Born in British Columbia, Janice Holly Booth spent more than two decades as a non-profit CEO before becoming a full-time writer and speaker. Her first book, *Only Pack What You Can Carry*, is about personal growth through solo adventure travel and was published by National Geographic in 2011. Janice currently resides near Charlotte, North Carolina.

www.janicehollybooth.com

Photo © igstudio.biz

87383428R00230

Made in the USA
Lexington, KY
23 April 2018